Reimagining Professional De
in Schools

This fascinating and vital book seeks to challenge the effectiveness of current practices in professional development by urging educators to rethink professional learning for teachers and teaching assistants. It importantly brings together ideas about teacher professionalism and how to build creative and trusting cultures in which high expectations are not compromised.

Throughout, teachers describe significant professional learning and growth, often through dynamic partnerships with others, that allows them to inspire imaginative possibilities; different and creative ways to ignite hope and opportunity for children. Four key themes guide the reader through the collection of chapters: professional capital, learning communities, teachers as researchers and subject-specific professional development. They explore:

- The types of professional development approaches that support teachers to make meaningful changes within their practices.
- The conditions and school cultures that are needed for teachers to meaningfully prosper from professional development.
- The impact that unintended consequences of system accountability drivers and funding have on teachers' experiences of professional development.
- The ways in which the development of curriculum and pedagogy can be integrated with models of professional development, particularly in the creative arts.

Packed with innovative ideas and practical suggestions and co-written by researchers and practitioners, this book highlights the importance of using research evidence to develop teachers' practice within the realities of their own classrooms and schools. This will be a key read for teachers, school leaders, teaching assistants and student teachers.

Eleanore Hargreaves is Professor of Learning and Pedagogy at the UCL Institute of Education, London. Her key research area is investigating the experiences of children in classrooms and how schooling can become more learning-friendly to support them.

Luke Rolls is Assistant Head Teacher at the University of Cambridge Primary School. His main areas of interest are in developing primary curriculum, pedagogy and assessment through high-quality professional development as an entitlement for all teachers.

Unlocking Research

Series editors: James Biddulph and Julia Flutter

Unlocking Research offers support and ideas for students and practising teachers, enriching their knowledge of research and its application in primary school contexts. Packed with imaginative ideas and practical suggestions, the series aims to empower teachers, teaching assistants and school leaders to take research-informed and principled approaches to making necessary changes in schools so that teaching and learning ignites the social imagination for twenty-first-century educators and learners.

Reimagining Professional Development in Schools
Edited by Eleanore Hargreaves and Luke Rolls

Inspiring Primary Curriculum Design
Edited by James Biddulph and Julia Flutter

For more information about this series, please visit:
www.routledge.com/Unlocking-Research/book-series/URS

For professional development resources linking to chapters in this book, please visit:
http://unlockingresearch.org/reimagining-professional-development-in-primary-schools/

Reimagining Professional Development in Schools

Edited by Eleanore Hargreaves
and Luke Rolls

Routledge
Taylor & Francis Group

LONDON AND NEW YORK

First published 2021
by Routledge
2 Park Square, Milton Park, Abingdon, Oxon OX14 4RN

and by Routledge
52 Vanderbilt Avenue, New York, NY 10017

Routledge is an imprint of the Taylor & Francis Group, an informa business

British Library Cataloguing-in-Publication Data
A catalogue record for this book is available from the British Library

Library of Congress Cataloging-in-Publication Data
A catalog record has been requested for this book

ISBN: 978-0-367-26450-5 (hbk)
ISBN: 978-0-367-26451-2 (pbk)
ISBN: 978-0-429-29333-7 (ebk)

Typeset in Bembo and Helvetica
by Newgen Publishing UK

MIX
Paper from
responsible sources
FSC
www.fsc.org FSC™ C013985

Printed in the United Kingdom
by Henry Ling Limited

Contents

Professional teacher communities as creative, inspiring sites of learning

Luke Rolls and Eleanore Hargreaves

In the early hours of a Sunday morning in September 2019, Sarah Thomas set off to swim the English Channel wearing only her costume, goggles and cap. She returned to land 54 hours later having crossed between Dover and Calais four times, covering a distance of 130 miles and breaking the previous record by a complete crossing. During her swim, Sarah was stung in the face by a jellyfish, vomited repeatedly from a stomach infection, battled against the currents and suffered ongoing pain from salt water aggravating her throat. A year before, Sarah had recovered from successfully overcoming breast cancer via 20 rounds of chemotherapy, surgery to remove tumours and 25 sessions of radiation therapy. She trained for swimming the channel while holding down a full-time job. The reservoirs of human endurance and dedication are quite staggering. What might the conditions be for such achievements?

After completing her second crossing and hitting an all-time low, her words demonstrate the power that community gives in times of great demand (Calvert, 2019):

> When we did the turn in Dover I tried to eat some baby food and I threw that up ... I was really demoralised and was close to quitting. I thought, 'Two laps is plenty, who cares?' But my crew re-motivated me. They didn't let me dwell on any negatives. If I said, 'I feel sick', they said, 'You'll be all right, it's not a big deal, just keep swimming.' I threw up all over my friend Karl, and he was like, 'It's OK, just let it out, you'll feel better once you're done.' I am a strong, independent, intelligent, capable woman. I have an iron will and dogged determination. I've always prided myself on being tough and being able to take care of myself. If I've learned anything from marathon swimming and cancer, I've learned I will always need people who love me to keep me moving forward when I can't quite get there on my own.

How does this story of courage relate to the purpose of this book? Albeit a different form of extreme, her journey is perhaps not so dissimilar to those that teachers and teaching assistants take in crossing the wavy seas of teaching and learning. People who work in these roles have the challenging feat of inspiring a multifaceted group of individual children. They embark on professional journeys that, as well as being joyful and of great reward, often include stamina, patience and personal sacrifice. Their true stories are usually invisible, untold and unmeasured. Like swimmers, they do not have much control of the climate – of their institution or political context – and yet like Sarah, with certain conditions manage to achieve superhuman accomplishments, finding productive ways through for children.

There are several indicators within the profession to suggest that collectively we have not found the right conditions for teachers to do this important work. Teachers in the UK are leaving at an unprecedented rate, many having decided to move to other career paths within the first few years of training (see Chapter 2). Many professionals who entered teaching as a career of service to help children flourish seem to find the current working conditions unfit for purpose. What is extinguishing their enthusiasm from such an important and potentially rewarding career?

With a relatively young teacher workforce by international standards (OECD, 2018), poor levels of teacher retention is highly problematic for implementing educational reform, significantly undermining efforts to build knowledge, expertise and networks in the system. While some research has previously queried why teachers' rate of improvements appear to flatline after a few years, findings by Kraft and Papay (2014) show that in 'supportive' schools, the trajectories of teachers can be ones of sustained professional growth. These schools appear to balance external pressures and whole-school priorities with opportunities for teachers to construct and assimilate new learning within their practice.

There is consensus among researchers and policy makers that teachers have a significant and lasting impact on children's lives (Hattie, 2008). And yet much less attention is focused on how we should support structuring their own professional learning. If we know that teachers have a formative impact on children, it would follow that our investment in their development should be central to any drive for improving the education system. It is puzzling then why teacher learning opportunities for the profession as a whole appear to be so lacking in coherence and investment. These coexist within a system characterised by hyper-accountability and 'standards-based policy reform', where the experience of being a professional can become diminished by perceived external pressures. We find teachers in the UK as having lower levels of job satisfaction and lower ratings of the value of the professional development they receive in comparison to many other countries (Sims, 2017). By not attending to the central role of teacher learning, the sustainability of teaching becomes weakened. When teachers have to effectively swim alone and sometimes in very challenging circumstances, understandably for some, the personal cost–benefit of the journey becomes less appealing.

Through drawing on examples where teachers and researchers have written in partnership, this book works to imagine things differently – what could our profession look like? How could professional learning influence possibility thinking for our children and the schools where they go to learn? And when teachers are already achieving so much in spite of the considerable system and contextual challenges they face, what might be possible if we improved the structures and thinking that underpin their daily lives?

Of course, professional development is not the only issue relevant to teacher retention and recruitment; it is important that teachers' professional learning is considered within the wider educational and social, political context. This book seeks to ask questions about how teachers can be supportively challenged to thrive in their roles through problematising professional learning as a mediating factor. We explore:

- The types of professional development approaches that support teachers to make meaningful changes within their practices.
- The conditions and school cultures that are needed for teachers to meaningfully prosper from professional development.
- The impact that unintended consequences of system accountability drivers and funding have on teachers' experiences of professional development.
- The ways in which the development of curriculum and pedagogy can be integrated with models of professional development.

Within the chapters in this book, teachers describe significant professional learning and growth, often through partnerships with others; growth that allows them to inspire and ignite hope and opportunity for children. A simple yet sophisticated explanation for theorising what might be under the surface of such meaningful professional learning is the self-determination model of Ryan and Deci (2000). They demonstrate through research studies across the globe that creative learning – as part of a person's well-being – will only happen when that person feels competent, agentic and related. Illustrated in examples through this book, teachers need to believe that they are doing well rather than feeling that they are being constantly reprimanded. They need to feel empowered, that they can exercise agency by making and having direction over decisions themselves. And they need to feel related to their colleagues through learning communities and other face-to-face interactions. Without these attributes, self-determination theory suggests that, beyond being compliant, profound experiences of teacher learning tend not to flourish.

Self-determination theory and its emphasis on grasping challenge does not mean impoverished expectations around the life-changing work we expect and ask of teachers. Quite the opposite; as Myatt (2016) points out, as humans, we are in fact drawn to challenge. In the case of the swimmer Sarah Thomas, she was supported to achieve her goal through coaching by others to continue, despite feeling overwhelmed and her goal was situated within her belonging to a supportive and expert group of people who believed in her aspirations. Through such affirming of practitioners' competence, agency and relatedness, teachers, like other professionals can experience the required 'psychological safety' (Edmonson, 2002) to start engaging creatively with the complexity of synthesising theory, research and practice about learning.

Contexts for professional learning: barriers and opportunities

The narratives in this book demonstrate the impact that various accountability measures seem to have on teachers' sense of agency and teaching practices. Many accounts bring out how such invisible forces of influence appear to significantly shape the enacted experiences of teachers and children in the classroom. For example, Winstanley and Moule (Chapter 10) note how shifts in the assessment criteria for writing have fashioned writing away from authentic experiences based on audience, purpose, enjoyment and creativity, to a technical pursuit of working to a checklist. Cremin and Durning (Chapter 9) list similar issues where 'reading for pleasure' can be marginalised in schools and where teachers are experiencing restricted scope to develop children's *will* of reading beyond attending to their *skill*. In several chapters, we see the important role that school leaders play in shielding teachers from external pressures through creating supportive communities of practice; ones where teachers can share their successes and struggles and provide mutual support (Cordingley & Hughes, Chapter 3; Kerschner, Dowdall, Hennessy, Owen, & Calcagni, Chapter 8; Rolls & Seleznyov, Chapter 5). At the level of the classroom, we see teachers and researchers who are committed to understanding their professional competence in terms of children's needs in the classroom (Hargreaves & Scott, Chapter 7). In collectively problematising and enquiring into their practice, they share unique insight into the lives of their learners and their own professional practice.

Our framework shown in Figure 1.1 builds on Oates's (2013) work on 'control factors' in order help us to consider the levels of context in which professional development takes place.

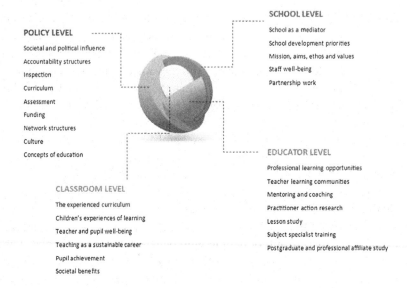

POLICY LEVEL

Societal and political influence

Accountability structures

Inspection

Curriculum

Assessment

Funding

Network structures

Culture

Concepts of education

SCHOOL LEVEL

School as a mediator

School development priorities

Mission, aims, ethos and values

Staff well-being

Partnership work

EDUCATOR LEVEL

Professional learning opportunities

Teacher learning communities

Mentoring and coaching

Practitioner action research

Lesson study

Subject specialist training

Postgraduate and professional affiliate study

CLASSROOM LEVEL

The experienced curriculum

Children's experiences of learning

Teacher and pupil well-being

Teaching as a sustainable career

Pupil achievement

Societal benefits

Figure 1.1 Layers of context interacting with professional development in schools

Source: Image courtesy of www.slideshare.com.

The level of policy sets out powerful structures that influence schools and teachers, including funding, curriculum, assessment, accountability and school networks. At the school level, leaders have to mediate these pressures with the needs and ethos of their individual context, their development priorities and the well-being of their staff. They can benefit from working with other schools or professionals in these endeavours although these network structures in the UK appear to now be disparate and varied. Teachers in turn find themselves positioned within these tensions, likely experiencing varying amounts and quality of professional development opportunities alongside the demands of their role.

Governments in recent years have given a renewed emphasis on school 'autonomy' allowing some increased level of choice. For schools, however, having agency is a far more complex notion than being given simplified 'choice'. Having weak curricula guidance for example may give schools freedom of sorts, but in reality creates huge inefficiencies and asks of schools to recreate work that requires domain-specific knowledge and expertise. Case examples in this book speak of a more meaningful experience of agency where there is support for structured collaboration between teachers, subject specialists and educational researchers. Such partnerships on a larger scale require more whole-system thinking about how curriculum, pedagogy, assessment and professional development can be more coherently developed together.

A number of barriers have been identified for why more time is not spent by teachers in the UK on professional development, including cost, work responsibilities and the quality of provision available (House of Commons, 2018). A Department for Education (DfE) report (Sims, 2017) appears to show recognition that in reality, operational school or accountability-related matters often impede teachers' entitlement to high-quality professional development. Some teachers choose to seek professional development opportunities outside their institution through postgraduate study or by spending their free time outside of school networking with other educators.

When the minds of policy makers turn to system reform, the practices of other education systems are often looked to for answers. Undoubtedly, much can be learned from looking to other 'high-performing' jurisdictions, but without understanding their nuances, such 'borrowing' seems to have a tendency to overlook the policy, cultural and institutional contexts of those countries. We suggest that rather than appropriating whole accountability systems or isolated areas of provision, it might be more pertinent to borrow and adopt the *professional learning structures* that have created areas of strength. In Japan, for example, we see well-established and embedded practices around mentoring for early career teachers. In countries such as Finland, teachers are funded to master's degree level, and supported to specialise further within their chosen field of education. In Shanghai, maths teachers are given considerably reduced timetables to study children's learning alongside their teaching commitments. And in cases around the world, such as burgeoning teacher learning communities in Egypt (Hargreaves, Elhawary,

& Mahgoub, 2018), we see bright spots where teachers experience their role in education as a professionalising one imbued with purpose.

Outline themes of the book

There are four key themes to guide the reader through the collection of chapters: professional capital, learning communities, teachers as researchers and subject-specific professional development. The reader will also note other themes pertinent to their own context and interest. Each chapter offers detail and principles on which professional development and learning has been nurtured.

Developing teacher professional capital

Several chapters in the book explore the distinct routes through which teachers become inspired and inspiring professionals, offering optimism as well as recognition of the current barriers to change. In Chapter 2, Alison Peacock delineates how the Chartered College of Teaching can support the competence, agency and relatedness of teachers. In Chapter 4, Twistleton and Truby focus on learning as professional inquiry and narrate an example in which expertise in practising dialogic pedagogy was developed through one teacher's account. These chapters emphasise the need to develop and affirm teacher capital as a starting point as well as the opportunity of accreditation for teachers' learning.

Supportive and collaborative teacher learning communities

In Chapter 5, Rolls and Seleznyov explore what we can learn from teachers in Japan who use lesson study to understand better children's learning through processes of collaborative planning, observation and dialogue. In Chapter 6, Lofthouse, Lofthouse and Whiteside consider how a mentoring and coaching community can best affirm and support a teacher's ongoing professional learning. Chapter 12 by Biddulph and Carris focuses specifically on how teachers' sense of their own agency can enrich community, leading to the creative learning of school communities. Finally, Glazzard, Stokoe and Stones attend to the central issue of teacher well-being in Chapter 14. These chapters all speak to how teachers' sense of their relatedness to support others enhances their professional learning.

Teachers as researchers

In Chapter 3, Cordingley and Hughes revisit the usefulness of different models of professional learning, drawing directly on recent educational research findings in the field. In Chapter 7, Hargreaves and Scott conceptualise research evidence as children's voices, which enlighten teachers' approaches to learning and help them explore the teacher's own voice in internal dialogue about her/his own learning.

In Chapter 8, Kerschner and colleagues consider the teacher as researcher within her/his own practice and as part of the school community. All three chapters highlight the importance of teachers experiencing agency in directing their own research inquiries.

Subject-specific professional development

In Chapter 9, Cremin and Durning discuss how teachers can be supported to help children arrive at a love of reading for pleasure. In Chapter 10, Winstanley and Moule focus on the accompanying challenge of developing teachers and children as writers. In Chapter 11, Lord and colleagues explore how collaborative problem-solving in mathematics can become an enriching part of teachers' repertoire and in the process develop subject-specific professional knowledge for teaching. In Chapter 13, Rao and Wheeler describe and analyse how through embodied cognition, teachers can learn to 'feel alive' through the learning and teaching of music. These chapters demonstrate how in order to enculturate learners into subject-specific disciplines, teachers themselves have to develop an identity that grows in relation to the subject. Teachers need to be supported to enjoy reading or writing themselves, to 'feel' the power of music or relish the challenge of a maths problem.

Finally, the Afterword, by Series Editor James Biddulph, provokes readers to reconsider the role of teachers as competent, agentic and collaborative beings whose professional status depends on teachers using and developing specific theories, research and practices. Practices that reinforce the rigour and authenticity of the profession and challenge those external voices whose values do not accord with teachers' own.

What we hope the book and indeed the series of Unlocking Research books will achieve is the development of communities of practice, teachers, teaching assistants, school leaders and governors. That educators are provided with the right conditions to engage deeply with questions of how learning and teaching might be imagined in primary classrooms. The book does not give foolproof answers to solve the dilemmas related to professional development. Instead, it hopes to exemplify cases of what can happen when communities of practitioners work together to better understand how children learn and what teachers can do to support this.

As Sarah Thomas affirms at the beginning of our chapter, professionals need one another in both form and spirit. However, they also need the structures, time and investment around them to root this collaboration in expert, research-informed and principled approaches. As distinct from professional development that is 'done' to teachers considered as deliverers, we envisage in this book professional learning to be a joint enterprise that goes beyond 'sharing practice'.

Reforming professional development for teachers in the UK needs to be part of wider system reform. Without looking at the quality of professional learning that teachers experience, we will not be able to improve the quality of our education system. And when we look at the issues surrounding teacher learning, we see a complex web of interdependent factors that need to much better coalesce around their professional challenges and the needs of children. In this book, we affirm the unlimited potential for teachers to mirror and support the life-changing journey of growth they bring about in their students. It is perhaps when teachers are better empowered to swim this crossing, despite its challenges, that we can start to imagine the hopeful possibilities of where future generations might take us.

References

Calvert, H. (2019, 24 September). 13 reasons we can be inspired by Sarah Thomas' record-breaking Channel swim. Retrieved from www.redbull.com/gb-en/sarah-thomas-channel-swim-inspiration.

Edmondson, A. C. (2002). *Managing the risk of learning: Psychological safety in work teams.* Cambridge, MA: Division of Research, Harvard Business School.

Hargreaves, E., Elhawary, D., & Mahgoub, M. (2018). The teacher who helps children learn best: Affect and authority in the traditional primary classroom. *Pedagogy, Culture & Society, 26*(1), 1–17.

Hattie, J. (2008). *Visible learning: A synthesis of over 800 meta-analyses relating to achievement.* London: Routledge.

House of Commons (2018). *Committee of Public Accounts retaining and developing the teaching workforce: Seventeenth report of session 2017–19 (HC 460).* London: House of Commons.

Kraft, M. A., & Papay, J. P. (2014). Can professional environments in schools promote teacher development? Explaining heterogeneity in returns to teaching experience. *Educational Evaluation and Policy Analysis, 36*(4), 476–500.

Myatt, M. (2016). *High challenge, low threat: Finding the balance.* Woodbridge, UK: John Catt Educational.

Oates, T. (2013). *Education, assessment and developing a comprehensive qualifications framework.* Cambridge, UK: University of Cambridge.

Organisation for Economic Cooperation and Development (OECD) (2018). *TALIS 2018 results (volume I): Teachers and school leaders as lifelong learners.* Paris: OECD.

Ryan, R. M., & Deci, E. L. (2000). Self-determination theory and the facilitation of intrinsic motivation, social development, and well-being. *American Psychologist, 55*(1), 68.

Sims, S. (2017). *TALIS 2013: Working conditions, teacher job satisfaction and retention.* London: DfE.

2

The importance of the Chartered College of Teaching: a professional body for the future identity and status of our teachers

Alison Peacock

Introduction

In this chapter, I present the argument for developing the culture of our *teaching* profession towards proudly becoming a *learning* profession. I explain the rationale for building voluntary membership of the Chartered College of Teaching, a professional body with royal charter that seeks to celebrate, support and connect teachers to provide world-class teaching that benefits pupils and society. I discuss the importance of raising the status of the teaching profession as a global community and present notions of collegiality and collaboration as a means to build the quality and expertise of education. Within this, I consider the importance of professional pride and identity in the context of career development and collective standards that replace punitive external accountability. Fundamentally, I call for professional status that builds a thirst for evidence-informed pedagogy through greater engagement with educational research and enquiry.

Initial teacher education

For too long, there has been a tacit assumption that initial teacher education is sufficient to enable new teachers to be fully equipped for the demands of the classroom. The proposed Early Career Framework (DfE, 2019) gives welcome recognition to the importance of building expertise over time and in the context of lived classroom experience. No longer, one hopes, will the notion exist that teachers having completed their training will know exactly what to teach, how to assess learning, how to manage support staff, how to create and maintain a well-ordered learning environment, how to liaise with families and confidently ensure that sufficient support and challenges will be offered for every child. The role of a teacher is incredibly demanding and complex. Embracing this complexity and supporting teachers in their quest for ways to provide optimal learning is long overdue. In some parts of the world, the role of the teacher has much higher status than that currently experienced by colleagues in England. The art of refining pedagogical knowledge over time, in harness with other colleagues, is recognised as an important facet of professionalism. Somehow in England, we have assumed that teaching is more intuitive than scientific. Pupils, parents and fellow teachers assume you either have the makings of a great teacher or you don't. Teachers who thrive within schools appear unassailable. They manage classroom behaviour seemingly without effort while achieving high standards of achievement and attainment as if by magic. When I began teaching I recall feeling that I had no choice other than to look like I knew what I was doing and sound like I knew what I was talking about. It wouldn't do, I realised, to ask my colleagues too many questions or to reveal that there were aspects of the curriculum that I had scant knowledge of. After all, my staff colleagues were all incredibly busy with skills invisible to the novice eye, and I was fresh from university supposedly ready to enable others to learn. The reality was that I found my first year of teaching incredibly hard and almost resigned. There were no opportunities for professional development other than the experience of learning through mistakes and constantly trying to survive. Although I recall many highlights from my first year of teaching, these are more than balanced out by feelings of 'winging it' and acting as if I knew what I was doing. How much better then, if I had been offered structured support within the first few years of my professional life, before I was ready to help others.

Early Career Framework

The attrition rate of teachers (25 per cent leave within the first three years) has meant that the Department for Education (DfE) has begun to look seriously at how to alleviate some of the pressures experienced in the first few years. The DfE has recently consulted upon a new Early Career Framework (DfE, 2019) that will support the first two years of teaching. Our team at the Chartered College of

Teaching has been involved with the design and recommendations for this new framework. The framework builds on the eight existing Teachers' Standards (DfE, 2012) and are published with further detail in the new Early Career Framework. The standards detail:

- high expectations;
- how pupils learn;
- subject and curriculum;
- classroom practice;
- adaptive teaching;
- assessment;
- managing behaviour;
- professional behaviours:
    - importance of professional development;
    - strengthening pedagogical and subject knowledge;
    - seeking challenge and feedback;
    - engaging critically with research;
    - reflective practice.

The Chartered College seeks to support students and teachers in their early career as they transition through this new framework and provide resources and articles in each of the core areas of teacher standards. Mentors and coaches will also need support materials and they seek to provide these online, so that they are readily available.

Challenges facing the teaching profession in England

There are increasing challenges in both recruitment of new teachers and also in retaining teachers in schools. The annual government investment in teacher training in England alone exceeds £700 million annually (National Audit Office, 2016). Set against an attrition rate of over a quarter of teachers within the first three years of teaching and almost a third of teachers within the first five years (Worth, Lynch, Hillary, Rennie, & Andrade, 2018) at a time of diminishing budgets, this is clearly unsustainable. The number of British teachers working internationally is approaching a quarter of a million (COBIS, 2019). There is now an undeniable recruitment and retention issue within the teaching profession as evidenced by a recent National Foundation for Educational Research (NFER) report (Worth & van den Brande, 2019). Core findings include:

- The secondary school system is facing a substantial teacher supply challenge over the next decade that requires urgent action.
- Retention rates of early-career teachers have dropped significantly between 2012 and 2018.

- There are acute challenges in recruitment and retention of teachers in long-standing shortage subjects such as physics, maths, modern foreign languages and chemistry.
- Teachers work longer hours in a typical working week than similar people in other professional occupations.
- There is more unmet demand for part-time working among full-time teachers than there is for similar professionals.

Over successive years the role of the teacher has become ever more demanding. Wider society, parents, employers and politicians look to the education system to prepare our young people for the future but our teachers, instead of feeling buoyed up by the expectations of their expertise, too often feel blamed and overworked. The recruitment and retention strategy published by the DfE (2019) has been largely welcomed but the fact remains that we need to raise the status of our teaching profession through greater recognition of the skill needed to be a teacher and to show this appreciation through appropriate career development and remuneration.

The recent political approach of austerity has led to schools facing impossible budgetary decisions while also being expected to achieve more with less.

The movement away from local authority control towards charitable trusts of academies has led to increasing national fragmentation across vast regions of England. The demise of the National College for School Leadership additionally led to a sense of isolation for some school leaders and a decreasing presence of a guiding ethic and collective purpose.

Greater awareness and prevalence of emotional and mental health issues has begun to affect not only children and young people, but also parents and teachers themselves. A sense of an overwhelming demand upon individuals places the school very often at the heart of the community as the place where norms will be upheld and understood, even enforced. All of this means that to teach is also to lead and to provide an example for wider society. This places huge responsibility on teachers, especially the youngest and least experienced of our colleagues.

Probably the single greatest challenge to teachers and school leaders currently is the pressure of external accountability in the form of the inspectorate and performance data. Additionally, performance-related pay has often been interpreted by school leaders as a requirement for teachers to provide numerical assessment data as evidence of their impact and efficacy.

Why do we need a professional body?

In May 2012, the House of Commons Education Committee recommended the establishment of a member-driven college of teaching to create a professional organisation similar to the royal colleges already established for medicine (House of Commons, 2012). A subsequent report by the Prince's Teaching Institute (PTI, 2014, p. 4) lent further support to the case for establishing this professional body:

> This is an idea whose time has come. A new college of teaching has the potential to become the deeply respected voice on professional matters that teaching needs, and to develop the teaching profession in this country as the finest in the world. In doing so, we believe that it will make a significant contribution to the lives and life chances of children and young people in this and future generations and so to the success of our country.

A professional body has a different but complementary role to that of professional associations or teacher unions. The challenge for such a body, the Chartered College of Teaching, is to bring the notion of a 'self-improving' education system to life via a voluntary, independent, membership organisation that seeks to set the highest professional standards as a mark of quality and effective performance. Teacher unions are an established part of the education landscape providing support with issues related to industrial relations and to a wide range of important workforce and policy issues. The role of the professional body, however, is not to engage in employment issues but to provide guidance and resources to the profession as a whole about the role of the teacher as a professional educator.

Collegiality

It is too tempting to seek easy answers within education. The role of the Chartered College of Teaching, however, is in part to enable educational professionals to engage with complexity in their quest for solutions. The competitive culture of league tables and inspection grading has in some cases led to a very challenging environment across the English education that seems to incentivise blame and shaming. In an important move to disrupt negativity, the Chartered College aims to facilitate a broad and rich discourse in education grounded in both theoretical and professional knowledge. It seeks to provide a respectful forum for debate and reflective discourse that takes necessary account of context. Through building collective teacher agency in a culture of collegiality the Chartered College believes that it can raise the status of our profession.

Fellowship status (FCCT) has been established with this particular aim in mind. Over time, the Chartered College would anticipate that teachers with chartered status would naturally seek to attain the recognition of fellowship but is aware that change would need to take place quickly as the demands upon our education system are immediate. At the time of writing, the Chartered College has already assessed successful applications from 500 fellows. Fellows of the Chartered College comprise of educationalists with a minimum of ten years' teaching experience who can demonstrate evidence of their impact both within their own educational setting and beyond. This group will begin to form the backbone of a collegial approach to developing collective expertise and sharing professional knowledge informed by theory. The Chartered College aspires to curating this insight via its termly journal *Impact* and through a series of discussion papers that will explore both the debate and the range of research evidence available.

Chartered status

The Chartered College of Teaching was granted a supplemental Royal Charter in 2017, enabling the professional body to offer chartered status to teachers and school leaders. Colleagues who have been teaching for a minimum of ten years are also eligible to be nominated and apply to become a fellow (FCCT). A pilot accreditation and assessment framework was developed during 2016–2018 with an extensive pilot cohort of 150 teachers drawn from all phases of education. A first 'test and learn' phase is now underway with a second cohort of teachers with a view to scaling up this status both in England and internationally. The aspiration of the Chartered College is to develop a standard for teachers and also for leaders and teacher educators that builds recognition globally for expert education professionals.

The Chartered Teacher programme provides mentoring from experienced colleagues drawn from members and fellows. The notion of collegiality that the Chartered College represents delineates responsibilities, ethics, values and practices that signal willing compliance to upholding shared professional standards of the highest order. The programme is underpinned by assessment against three core professional principles. These principles were developed at the Chartered College following research into international comparative standards and through consultation with a wide range of stakeholders:

Professional knowledge:

1. Has and maintains deep knowledge of subject area or area of specialism.
2. Has a critical understanding of subject or specialism-specific pedagogy.
3. Has deep knowledge of the most effective pedagogical approaches and how children and young people develop and learn.
4. Has understandings of how to design, implement and evaluate a range of assessment types.
5. Has knowledge of education trends, debates and policy.

Professional practice:

6. Maintains a productive classroom environment with a culture of learning.
7. Plans excellent lessons and lesson sequences.
8. Delivers excellent lessons and lesson sequences.
9. Ensures that all children and young people learn and make progress.
10. Works effectively with others to provide appropriate academic and pastoral support.

Professional behaviours:

11. Critically evaluates and reflects on their own practice.
12. Is committed to engaging in relevant, career-long professional learning.
13. Exhibits collegiality by supporting, and learning from, others.
14. Demonstrates high standards of professionalism.
15. Engages critically with research and evidence.

The role of the Chartered College will be to enable accredited providers to offer training that will ultimately lead to successful accreditation against the professional principles. This is a status rather than a qualification and as such there will be an expectation that participants will update their knowledge and be able to evidence their contribution to professional learning and development of others throughout their career.

Feedback from participants of the first cohort of chartered teachers presents a powerful rationale for professional learning that directly makes a difference within classrooms. Not only are participants excited about the reading they have done and the opportunities created to share their emerging ideas, they are also in many cases able to chart, via their reflective diary, the actions they have taken that have begun to make a difference both in their own classrooms and in those of colleagues. The strength of professional learning that requires teachers to evidence the impact of their work in the classroom feels transformative. This book is an example of the kind of text that will support colleagues in the future as they seek to engage in practitioner research.

Career opportunities within the teaching profession

It is important to consider ways in which we can better manage talent among teachers. Human resources expert Mandy Coalter (2018) writes persuasively about the importance of planning for talent growth within our teams. There are some promising examples of this within groups of schools forming multi-academy trusts (MATs) but there is much more that could be done at a system level. In the past, there has been too great a reliance on the vocational promise of a career in teaching. Goodwill has been expected because of the frequent motivation to make a difference, offer opportunities for others, enhance social mobility, contribute to society and enhance the collective good. However, as accountability pressures have increased along with excessive workload, low morale in some cases has become a consequence of a performativity culture. It is not enough to say that teachers transform lives if a consequence of this is burnout or ill health. Now that the government has offered greater autonomy and diversity of career routes through disruption of the previous local authority leadership, opportunities arise to offer career opportunities driven by a self-improving school-led system.

The Chartered College of Teaching believes there are three core career pathways requiring expert pedagogical knowledge, expertise in curriculum design and understanding of assessment:

Chartered teacher (CTeach):
- Classroom practice/subject and or phase expert.

Chartered teacher (CTeach lead):
- Leader of learning/curriculum design/collective expertise and removal of barriers to learning instead of 'monitoring'.

Chartered teacher educator (CTeach educator):
- Teacher educator/coach/mentor.

The work of global grassroots networks such as WomenEd and BAMEed have an important role to play in highlighting the vital necessity of flexible working models, recognition of gender and ethnic bias and the importance of offering inclusive leadership opportunities that illustrate the change we need to see.

Ethical leadership

In head teacher Carolyn Roberts's powerful book, *Ethical Leadership for a Better Education System* (2019), she argues for a language of ethics that supports our collective thinking and debate. In particular, the Nolan principles for public life (Committee on Standards in Public Life, 1995) call for:

- selflessness;
- integrity;
- objectivity;
- accountability;
- openness;
- honesty;
- leadership.

In addition, the commission added the following virtues:

- *Trust*: leaders are trustworthy and reliable.
- *Wisdom*: leaders use experience, knowledge and insight.
- *Kindness*: leaders demonstrate respect, generosity of spirit, understanding and good temper.
- *Justice*: leaders are fair and work for the good of all children.

- *Service*: leaders are conscientious and dutiful.
- *Courage*: leaders work courageously in the best interests of children and young people.
- *Optimism*: leaders are positive and encouraging.

An ethics forum has been established under the auspices of the Chartered College of Teaching as one of the professional services offered to members. The forum is there to support leaders as they make decisions in a climate where hyper-accountability may cause some to feel their judgement becomes clouded. It meets termly and aims to promote, uphold, develop and support ethical leadership. The forum seeks to offer a practical way of enabling and sustaining ethical debate. The current DfE Teachers' Standards (DfE, 2012, p. 14) state that teachers are required to 'uphold public trust in the profession and maintain high standards of ethics and behaviour'. This assumes, however, a shared understanding of ethical principles. The aim of the ethics forum is to facilitate and develop shared understanding among leaders and therefore among the entire education workforce. The Committee on Standards in Public Life has given endorsement to the ethical leadership framework. An 'Ethical Leadership in Education Pathfinder Project' supported by the National Governance Association has recruited schools from across England. It is envisaged that this group of school leaders will contribute to an emerging body of case-study material and discourse that will encourage others to lead courageously.

Pausing a career in teaching

Language is very powerful. The notion of 'pausing' one's career in teaching is a notion that the Chartered College of Teaching wishes to embrace. There may be many personal circumstances or career decisions that cause an individual teacher to move away from the profession. Once an individual has trained to teach and has worked as a teacher within a school, the Chartered College aims to build collective pride in that expertise. If an accountant diversifies her career and becomes a business leader, she does not deny her professional roots. A recent secretary of state for education in England was proud to keep in touch with her professional status via membership of her accountancy professional body as this formed part of her career identity. The Chartered College seeks to embrace this culture across the profession with those who are teaching, but crucially also with those who are retired or are currently pursuing another career path. To train to teach is to be a teacher for life. To keep up to date with research and practice in education is to be in a position to influence and support the work of the teaching profession and ultimately to continue to contribute as part of public service.

Teaching as a global career

Given that almost a quarter of a million teachers trained in the UK are now teaching in international schools, with numbers of British international schools expected to increase to 4,200 by 2013 (COBIS, 2019), there is an opportunity to embrace the international dimension of what it might mean to become a teacher. There are half a million teachers working in English schools, currently almost half this number again are teaching overseas having trained in England. Interestingly, when surveyed, 44 per cent of teachers working globally were keen to return to teach in the UK in the future (COBIS, 2019). The Chartered College of Teaching is keen to support the professional development of colleagues teaching overseas via the teacher learning benefits of membership and through recognition gained by studying for chartered teacher status internationally. The post-nominals MCCT, CTeach, have the capacity to offer cachet across the world as to achieve chartered status is to provide rigorous evidence of pedagogical skill.

Evidence-informed pedagogy

When the *Cambridge Primary Review* published its final report in 2010, Professor Robin Alexander (2010, p. 496) called for teachers to engage with evidence: 'Teachers should be able to give a coherent justification for their practices citing (i) evidence (ii) pedagogical principle and (iii) educational aim, rather than offering the unsafe defence of compliance with what others expect. Anything else is educationally unsound.' Essentially, this is a call for teacher agency inspired thorough knowledge about learning and teaching. Alongside greater agency we also need humility. Too often it would appear that those seeking to influence education are in pursuit of the quick fix. Greater teacher knowledge builds lesser tendency towards false certainties or one-sided solutions. A more informed intellectualised profession is both more confident but also more effective.

Leadership of learning

The Chartered College of Teaching has formed a leadership advisory group that comprises representatives from the National Association of Head Teachers (NAHT, 2018), the Teaching Schools Council, the Association of School and College Leaders, the National Governance Association, Ambition Institute and the Institute of School Business Leaders. This group, with representation from fellows of the Chartered College and observers from the DfE, meets regularly to debate how to support educational leaders across the country. Their work is further enhanced by a leadership research group that comprises academics working with the Chartered College to advise on evidence-informed approaches to leadership of learning from early years through to post–16 provision. Indeed some of the authors of this book are engaged in this work with the Chartered College.

Leadership of learning that is informed by research and evidence is very different to leadership driven by fear of accountability measures. The Chartered College hopes to design and pilot chartered leadership status in the future. This status would provide a means for school leaders to build their knowledge about research and evidence-informed practice within their own context, as an alternative school improvement tool to the traditional learning walks, book scrutiny and lesson monitoring activity. This form of professional knowledge would enable school leaders to think differently about how best to manage the challenges and opportunities within their setting. The Chartered College is seeking to develop this status in the near future and will aim to include as many current Office for Standards in Education, Children's Services and Skills (Ofsted) inspectors as possible within the first few cohorts. Additionally, it is seeking to develop chartered teacher educator status for those working within school-centred initial teacher training (SCITT) providers and teaching schools. Further chapters within this book will provide a valuable resource as this work takes shape.

Self-regulation of the teaching profession

The stress induced by the threat of inspection is undeniable. Ultimately, the sign of true success of a profession-led system will be when the majority of schools are held to account via peer review, instead of by an external inspection body. Of course, there will always be a need for a regulatory body that ensures schools safeguard the needs of young people, but that 'last resort' role could be managed by Her Majesty's Inspectorate of Schools (HMI) as part of the overall self-improving teaching profession. The Chartered College of Teaching is pleased to contribute to evaluating the potential of peer review of schools as it moves forward to achieve a truly self-regulated school system.

Respecting a plurality of voices

One of our core aims as a teaching profession should be to recognise and celebrate diversity of teaching approaches while acknowledging that there is far more that binds us together than drives us apart in our experience as teachers. There will always be a range of views about how best to organise schools, how to approach teaching according to context, whether to be led by enquiry or direct instruction, but our collective professional knowledge combined with understanding of the theoretical should lead us to build an ever-expanding corpus of knowledge that should be shared among us.

The energy that builds around 'can do' as opposed to blame and deficit is something that the Chartered College of Teaching seeks to harness and is a feature of this book.

Building communities of practice

A truly collegiate profession recognises the imperative to grow colleagues' understanding and knowledge throughout their career. Building knowledge about research theory that resonates with practitioners requires a culture shift in our approach to professional learning. We need to collectively move from a passive approach to development to a much more proactive role for each individual teacher as a professional. Currently, there is an expectation within schools that the staff or department meetings provided are occasionally 'topped up' with an opportunity to attend some external continuing professional development (CPD). In recent years however, those teachers choosing to engage with social media have accessed opportunities to attend free or low-cost conferences and gatherings such as ResearchEd at weekends or during holidays. These events have been generated by teachers wishing to learn from other colleagues in pursuit of stories of practice that are directly relevant to classrooms.

This trend was evident back in 2016 when a series of 13 conferences held in universities across the country took place to support colleagues' thinking about assessment 'beyond levels'. These events started on Twitter and swept the country using the hash-tag #LearningFirst. The first #LearningFirst event was held at Sheffield Hallam Institute of Education in May 2016, attracting over 500 teachers all excited to gather together to share and learn about approaches to assessment without national curriculum levels. The event was coordinated by Julie Lilly (retired head teacher) and Sean Cavan (Sheffield Hallam University), sponsored by Frog Education and offered completely free of charge to attendees. Speakers with national roles attended and gave their time without fees. Workshop sessions were organised by teachers for their peers. Humour, rather than fear, was the order of the day. This initiative set the stage for the emerging Chartered College of Teaching as a professional body with the convening power and vision to bring colleagues together to support rather than blame, to celebrate teachers' knowledge and connect the profession with evidence and research.

The Chartered College seeks to support the flourishing of local networks of colleagues wishing to build their knowledge about developments in areas such as cognitive science and psychology as well as sharing classroom practice inspired by academic study. Many networks have sprung up across the country working in association with the Chartered College to spread ideas and innovation. The Chartered College aims to establish a directory of speakers drawn from the teaching profession who can offer their immediate experience and expertise enhanced in many cases by recent study of a further degree in education or through study on the Chartered Teacher programme. Where existing organisations offer professional learning for teachers, the Chartered College seeks to work in partnership and promote what is on offer. It is keen to work with subject associations, teacher and leadership unions and organisations such as the Schools', Students' and Teachers' Network (SSAT), the Youth Sports Trust and many others. Where possible the Chartered College also encourages initiatives that give recognition to colleagues. Working in partnership and benefitting from collaboration makes all of us stronger and more knowledgeable on behalf of our children and young people.

How can we help policy makers?

The Chartered College of Teaching offers an opportunity for the government of the day to engage with the teaching profession in a non-adversarial manner. Through its fellows' round tables, membership surveys, engagement with its leadership development group and associate research committee, it provides opportunities for respectful debate.

The Chartered College believes that the future of the teaching profession is one of practice and policy informed by a combination of professional knowledge and wisdom, combined with the theory of research evidence. We have everything to gain and precious little to lose through working together in a community of kindness and hope.

Summary

In this chapter I have outlined ways in which the Chartered College of Teaching as our professional body can help teachers' professional identity:

- Initial teacher education is only the start of a teaching career.
- Recruitment, retention, austerity, hyper-accountability and mental health needs mean that the teaching profession is facing greater stress than ever before.
- The Chartered College as a professional body can play a role in raising the status of teachers in society through greater collegiality and for some, achieving chartered status and/or fellowship.
- Ethical standards must be a lived set of experiences. Ethical leadership and pioneer schools are beginning to contribute to the language of ethical choices.
- Career pathways throughout teaching, flexibility of working practices and teaching as a global career are all considered as a means to maintain the positive identity of teachers throughout their working lives.
- Self-regulation through peer review instead of Ofsted inspections is envisaged as the new way forward for a self-improving system.
- Evidence-informed communities of practice that emphasise the plurality of voices will ensure that our professional voice is heard.

- A robust self-improving system that is coordinated and supported by a central professional body brings hope through cohesion.
- Contributions to this book provide an excellent starting point for giving greater recognition to teachers and enhancing their professional identity.

References

Alexander, R. J. A. (2010). *Children, their world, their education: Final report and recommendations of the Cambridge Primary Review.* London: Routledge.

Coalter, M. (2018). *Talent architects: How to make your school a great place to work.* Woodbridge, UK: John Catt Educational.

Committee on Standards in Public Life (1995). *Nolan principles.* Retrieved from www.gov.uk/government/publications/the-7-principles-of-public-life/the-7-principles-of-public-life--2.

Council of British International Schools (CBIS) (2019). Retrieved from www.cobis.org.uk/research.

Department for Education (DfE) (2012). *Teachers' standards.* London: DfE

Department for Education (DfE) (2019). *Early career framework.* London: DfE

House of Commons Education Committee (2012). *Great teachers: Attracting, training and retaining the best.* London: HMSO.

National Association of Head Teachers (NAHT) (2018). *Improving school accountability.* Retrieved from www.naht.org.uk.

National Audit Office (2016). *Training new teachers.* London: National Audit Office.

Prince's Teaching Institute (PTI) (2014). *A new member-driven college of teaching: A blueprint.* London: PTI.

Roberts, C. (2019). *Ethical leadership for a better education system.* London: David Fulton.

Worth, J., Lynch, S., Hillary, J., Rennie, C., & Andrade, J. (2018). *Teacher workforce dynamics in England.* Slough, UK: NFER.

Worth, J., & van den Brande, J. (2019). *Teacher labour market in England: Annual report 2019.* Slough, UK: NFER.

3

Leading professional development that works for pupils and teachers

Philippa Cordingley and Eithne Hughes

Introduction

How can we best guide teachers and leaders to learn? What influences our ideas about what professional development should be and how do we evaluate the impact that such activities have on pupils? Our conceptions about the purposes, forms and outcomes of teacher professional development reflect fundamental beliefs about how teachers and leaders grow and how this might be best facilitated. This chapter explores what research can tell us about these questions, what principles might guide us, the role of 'knowledgeable others' and how evidence-informed approaches can inform and empower practitioners to make positive changes to their provision. We term professional development as continuing professional development and learning (CPDL) to emphasise the reflexive processes involved when practitioners construct meaningful experiences of professional growth. We conclude by offering some ways forward for schools and practitioners wishing to implement the types of CPDL that can make a difference to both pupils and teachers.

Until very recently, evaluation of continuous professional development (CPD) programmes have been almost entirely occupied with the practice of the teachers rather than the responses of pupils. It appears that both researchers and funders have begun to recognise the limitations of such an approach. Since its founding, the Centre for the Use of Research and Evidence in Education (CUREE) has worked to create systematic reviews of the research around CPD (Bell, Cordingley, Isham, & Davis, 2010; Cordingley, Bell, Evans, & Firth, 2005). Alongside this UK focus, the New Zealand government's Best Evidence Synthesis (BES) programme has similarly offered large systematic reviews encompassing meta-analyses of the most up to date and relevant research studies. CUREE's publication *Developing*

Great Teaching (Cordingley et al., 2015) was written as one such accessible over-view for practitioners about evidence for CPDL and four important, arguably new, insights into the affordances and limitations of the current field of research:

1. The importance of attending at least as much to the contributions and experiences of the teachers participating in CPD activities and in their follow-up classroom exchanges with pupils as to the contributions of CPD facilitators; surfacing clearly the importance of the L in CPDL.
2. The important contribution of the large-scale government investment in mar-shalling research in this complex field.
3. The need to make stronger connections between CPD programmes and the CPD components of other interventions and school leadership.
4. The lack of research about leadership of CPDL, notwithstanding the findings from the Robinson Leadership BES (Robinson, Hohepa, & Lloyd, 2009), which highlighted the crucial nature of school leaders' contributions to mod-elling and promoting professional learning to pupils' success.

Supporting CPD, together with the contributions teachers make and the benefits they draw from it are, however, challenging enterprises to research. Together they represent the integrated process of CPDL.

Researching CPDL is challenging because:

(a) CPDL makes significant practical, cognitive and emotional demands on those involved, while being, at root, focused on the pupils whose learning teachers wish to enrich.
(b) CPDL includes a wide range of activities, so the variables are many, interactions are dynamic and frequently take effect through internal, intellectual and intensely personal processing.

What do we really know about effective CPDL?

The *Developing Great Teaching* systematic review of research (Cordingley et al., 2015) highlights the importance for teachers to have opportunities to engage in iterative, evidence-rich and sustained cycles of experimenting with new ideas (Schön, 1987). The notion of organising professional learning around aspirations for pupils challenges teachers to specifically identify how their pupils' learning processes and outcomes will look different as a result of their reflective enquiry. This contrasts with well-established practices of CPD programmes that work on the basis of analysing the needs of specific groups of pupils.

Research syntheses point us towards helping teachers to develop a very spe-cific picture of the way in which their pupils' learning processes and outcomes will be enhanced if their own learning is successful. They are then able to use this to test and refine plans for supporting their own professional learning. Through our work at CUREE, we have settled on two particular principles that appear important to incorporate into CPDL protocols. These include the following:

- Providing new ideas/information in the context of teachers' self-identified, *individual starting points* and building on these in differentiated ways. In effect, these highlight the importance of the teachers' ability to accurately reflect and evaluate that starting point.
- *Contextualising* new approaches and pedagogical knowledge and skills for different subjects and for different subgroups of pupils.

The reflection that follows reflects the type of informed CPDL leadership that Emma Bishop (personal communication, 29 July 2019), a maths teacher at Brynellian school in Wales, provides for her team:

> My experience of effective CPDL is born from a leadership team who advocate evidence-informed and reflective practice. They were willing to trust staff to take risks and experiment with ideas and approaches, supported by research in the field, but ultimately driven by professional judgement of what I believed my pupils, in my particular setting, would respond to and benefit from. With access to specialist expertise from CUREE, I was afforded the tools to engage colleagues in classroom-based enquiries. These tools include templates for micro-studies and evaluative processes, with an emphasis on the cyclic, iterative nature of research's role in CPDL.
>
> One such powerful tool for practitioner research, the Route Map (CUREE, 2017), was developed as an interactive document that allows for a network of stakeholders in education to refer to a base of accessible thematic literature and subsequently contribute their research trajectories and accounts.
>
> I specify stakeholders rather than practitioners, as, in addition to tangible outcomes for my CPDL, my notion of what constitutes educational research has also been challenged. This has led me to rich, thought-provoking discussions about the role of ethics in educational research between colleagues and altered my perspective of the need to develop a 'culture' of evidence-informed and reflective practice in schools that can be both rooted and adapt with the times.

As well as identifying their starting points, practitioner research asks of teachers to start to develop 'theories of action' around an aspect of their provision and collect data to gauge its impact. In doing so, teachers appear to be best supported when they engage in dialogue that:

- helps them 'surface' and thus reflect on and review their assumptions and beliefs about the content of what they teach and about their learners;

- provokes and disrupts developed patterns through trying new approaches that help teachers to see, analyse and reflect on practice with the benefit of a fresh pair of eyes;
- uses shared risk-taking, and the reciprocal vulnerability it generates, to accelerate the trust building needed if teachers are to genuinely disrupt the status quo;
- focuses on exploring evidence about how learners are responding to the changes teachers are making so that the teachers themselves can make evidence-informed refinements.

The role of the 'knowledgeable other' and specialist expertise

While teachers bring with them considerable expertise and benefit from within-school collaboration, the presence of an outside 'knowledgeable other' can help generate new ways of thinking into their practice. Through specialist expertise, advisors can add powerful ingredients into teachers' repertoires in creative ways: demonstrating and exemplifying practices, drawing out the underpinnings of relevant research, encouraging reflection and supporting them to understand pupil data and effective evaluation practices. Alongside mentoring and specialist coaching, collaborative enquiry and lesson study (see Rolls & Seleznyov, Chapter 5) are well-established approaches that, *when supported by specialists*, align with teacher and school development.

At CUREE, we have found that the role of 'knowledgeable other' was most often assumed by consultants away from the day-to-day context of teaching. Their independence and neutrality appear to support their ability to challenge ortho-doxies, mobilise knowledge and examples of practice from other settings, bringing alive for teachers relevant areas of research.

Leading professional development and practitioner learning

CPDL can be misconceived as the activity that arises from staff meetings or workshops. We use the analogy of electrical pylons to illustrate how school meeting routines such as these can become confounded with the process of professional learning that they aim to produce. While the electrical pylons can be seen as the connecting structures that provide a time in the week for teachers to take stock and plan improvements to their practice, it is the electricity hidden within that is at the core of the professional learning. We can easily underestimate the conditions needed for the electricity to flow and the strength of the carrying structures. The core purpose for professional learning structures such as meetings is to reach deep into and elevate pupils' and teachers' routine experiences of school. Teachers' expectations of the relevance and impact of such meetings is borne of their experiences. These are all dependent on a school climate that builds trust through providing rich opportunities for professional learning, is open to evidence from within and outside their setting and builds up a momentum around CPDL activity.

Emma Bishop (personal communication, 29 July 2009), who has also carried out research into effective CPDL, speaks about the leadership of CPDL as something dependent on school cultural norms:

> We cannot be proficient in our use of research, without attending to and optimising the school climate. To do so, we need to nurture professional competencies of teachers and so engage everyone within it. This, as I have learnt on my own CPDL journey, relies on successful coaching and mentoring that scaffolds and inspires by focusing on pupil outcomes.

If researching the impact of teachers is difficult, disentangling the variables involved in school leadership research proves to be even more challenging. However, Viviane Robinson's synthesis of research evidence about school leaders' contributions to pupil success provides a significant contribution (Robinson et al., 2009). Robinson's analysis explored direct and indirect links between leadership and student outcomes by focusing on studies of interventions in teacher professional learning that had a positive impact on student learning, and then identifying the role played by leadership in creating the conditions that enabled those outcomes. In total, the researchers identified eight dimensions of leadership practices and activities linked to student outcomes. The dimensions of leaders' contributions for which an effect size could be established in this synthesis are:

- promotion of and participation in teacher learning and development (ES 0.84);
- planning, coordinating and evaluating teaching and the curriculum (ES 0.42);
- establishing goals and expectations (ES 0.35);
- strategic resourcing (ES 0.34); and
- ensuring an orderly and supportive environment (ES 0.27).

The three dimensions not assigned an effect size because of differences in the type of evidence available, included:

- creating educationally powerful connections;
- engaging in constructive problem talk;
- selecting, developing and using tools to build coherence, to enable teachers to negotiate complexity and to manage the cognitive, emotional and practical demands of new policies and approaches (such as protocols for evaluating the relevance, applicability and usability and the CPDL requirements made by potential new curriculum materials).

Robinson et al. (2009) also have important things to say about the role of tools in developing powerful routinisation of professional learning so the benefits of CPD can be embedded. They identify these as mechanisms that help schools to build *capacity to embody evidence and ideas* in ways that shape/scaffold actions for *coherence in* the actions of multiple stakeholders. Such tools support school leaders to help teachers use their CPD to improve their practice in relation to a specific task. Robinson et al. suggest three important characteristics of tools that are effective for supporting the leadership of professional learning:

- They should be based on sound theories of how the learning they are designed to support can best be accomplished.
- They should define and illustrate what good practice looks like.
- They should be selected and designed for ease of use so they can genuinely be used to transfer to learning, rather than being experienced as a learning object or impediment. For this to happen she explains that leaders need to take account of the practical, cognitive and affective demands the CPD support makes of the teacher.

In the context of a discussion of evidence about effective CPDL, we would argue that school leaders themselves should model and reflect back to their teams their own professional learning and development. 'Practising what we preach' communicates a level of commitment that can be positively infectious and represents a key leadership behaviour towards inspiring others. Effective professional learning environments are those in which it is easy for teachers and middle leaders to embed follow-up to CPD programmes within enquiry-oriented and sustained professional learning routines.

As the Organisation for Economic Cooperation and Development (OECD) paper 'Schools as Learning Organisations' concludes, 'leadership ultimately provides direction for learning, takes responsibility for putting learning at the centre and keeping it there' (Kools & Stoll, 2016, p. 58), using it strategically (Marsick & Watkins, 1999) and translating vision into strategy (Kools & Stoll, 2016) so that the organisation's actions are consistent with its vision, goals and values. We define this as 'learning leadership' (Kools & Stoll, 2016).

Professional development for leaders

Self-evidently, such leadership demands practical, intellectual and emotional work. We do not yet have a strong enough research basis to know exactly what constitutes effective facilitation of leaders' professional learning. We do, however, have a descriptive review that compares the evidence about the professional learning of teachers and school leaders (Cordingley, Bell, Holdich, & Crisp, 2012). This review posed the question 'What models of professional learning delivery for *leaders* are more likely to improve student outcomes'?

The review showed how school leaders, just like their colleague teachers, needed sustained sequences of iterative experimenting with new ideas as they developed new approaches and policies. They also needed opportunities to test these through the lens of their aspirations for all their learners (pupils and staff). The importance of developing practice and an underpinning rationale side by side is particularly important for leaders who have to convince so many different stakeholders that their approach will work in multiple contexts. But school leaders also have some additional and distinctive needs from their teacher colleagues. This review suggests the following:

- Leaders need *opportunities to work across school boundaries* if they are to be able to make the strange familiar and the familiar strange in sufficient depth to explore the consequences of drawing new practices and approaches into school life and professional learning.
- Like teachers they need support in *managing complexity*, but this needs to work at a whole-school level and accommodate an even wider variety of starting points than teachers encounter in classrooms. Such tools and frameworks should define and illustrate progress and excellence at whole-school level in ways that enable coherent use by a number of different people. Tools and frameworks of this kind are important in facilitating confident delegation, so it is no accident that school leaders value benchmarks and kite marks that attempt to codify high-quality approaches from multiple angles.
- Finally, and perhaps most importantly, the review highlights the importance and delicacy of recruiting leaders who are in high-stakes accountability roles into a stance that is *genuinely open to learning*. Accountability pressures pull school leaders towards presenting as optimistic a picture as possible. The occupation of the apex of the generally hierarchical understanding of academic progress means school leaders need courage and confidence to be explicit about those things they do not yet know or understand. In hierarchical systems, for leaders, even more than for teachers, presenting oneself as an expert is considerably more comfortable than highlighting one's areas for development. It is not surprising that this evidence points to the need to take great care in inducting school leaders into professional learning roles. Similarly, the review emphasises the elapsed time and trust building required for this.

There are two interesting and important links between these points about recruiting leaders into a learning role and the evidence from Robinson et al. (2009) described above. First, established leaders who start to make explicit the process and benefits of professional learning and its outcomes position lifelong learning as integral to expert as well as novice practice; too often leadership learning support is associated with new or struggling leaders or teachers. Second, it suggests highlighting the contribution that the research behind development of new policies makes to leaders' professional learning and how it will make a powerful and direct contribution to the learning of colleagues. This, in turn, is likely to help leaders understand

and position self-disclosure about their own learning as an act of professional generosity rather than a revelation of need or weakness.

> Take, for example, a school leader, working with CUREE to understand and enhance school improvement following a very early and contentious conversion to an academy. The school principal was struggling to build colleagues' confidence in sharing performance review goals with those who were planning the CPD offer. Having recognised that he needed to rebuild trust in leadership, he decided to learn in public to carry out performance review discussions in ways that generated rather than undermined staff trust, as a way of building confidence in involving a wider group of teachers to analyse and interpret the implications of performance review targets for CPDL planning. He videoed his performance review discussions and assigned ownership of the recording to the teacher involved but asked them to coach him in public on how he could have improved that discussion, using the recording to illustrate unhelpful contributions (or to make it available for other volunteers to use in that way) during weekly CPD twilight sessions. Within a very few weeks this public display of courageous professional leadership learning had created a sea change in professional trust (and a long queue to use the school's video cameras to support professional learning).

School-wide development

In addition to focusing on evidence about how school leaders help to lead CPDL through their own professional learning, it is important to look at the evidence about how they create systems to support this and teachers' learning on a sustainable basis, in order to consider what we think the research suggests is an effective professional learning environment for leaders and teachers that mirrors and models an effective learning environment for pupils. While Robinson has identified the key building blocks in the abstract, where can we turn for more concrete illustration of those core activities being deployed in real-world contexts? As with research into CPD, it is in studies in which CPD played a major role rather than in studies of school leadership or CPD per se that we have found our richest examples. In a study for Teach First CUREE colleagues were asked to identify the key characteristics of schools that were exceptional in transforming life chances for pupils in schools serving very vulnerable communities and to compare these with the characteristics of schools who were making strong but not exceptional contributions (Bell & Cordingley, 2014). Strong schools were, of course, doing many of the things that exceptional schools were doing, but it appeared that they were either doing these less intensely or less consistently.

Exceptional schools approached systematising of CPDL in quite distinctive ways, which included the following:

- *Professionalising the facilitation of CPD support.* For example, all coaches and mentors were trained and accredited and their early practice was evaluated to ensure that the support they offered made a difference to teachers as well as to pupils.
- *Investing heavily in induction for all colleagues new to the school or working for the first time in a new role.* This included colleagues arriving in senior posts. The goal was to lay a strong foundation of a shared approach to teaching and learning and a shared language for investigating and developing it. In the early days the emphasis may have been on CPD offered to new colleagues but this rapidly transitioned into arrangements that positioned them as proactive professional learners taking responsibility for their own and each other's learning through collaborative enquiry, structured lesson study or co-coaching.
- *Organising CPD and CPDL* around (a) a well-researched, whole-school model of pedagogy; and (b) the core principle of identifying and removing barriers to learning for each and every learner (teachers and leaders as well as pupils).

School and CPD leaders need to treat their 'staff as their class', to plan for and support colleagues' learning with the same care and depth that they hope their colleagues will plan for and support their pupils' learning.

A follow-up study plotted the way schools in similar circumstances approached CPDL at earlier points in their school improvement journey (Cordingley, 2016). Schools at very early stages of development were emphasising the importance of consistency but very often failing to provide a CPDL infrastructure that enabled colleagues to understand why the practices they were being asked to adopt consistently were being adopted or the support needed to genuinely put them to work.

The way forward: a practitioner's perspective

When the authors of this chapter started to explore together the practical implications of this evidence for teachers and school leaders, a number of very concrete issues emerged. The authors suggest the following principles in light of these:

1. At teacher level, CPDL needs to be understood more holistically; teachers need to be able to explore new and developing understanding, skills and practices in the context of their pupils' needs and of day-to-day practice. Teachers seeking

to create a coherent professional learning pathway need to be on the lookout for opportunities to do the following:

- Translate broad CPD and performance review goals into specific aspirations for subgroups of pupils. This will help them to explore ways of applying new ideas and approaches in depth, iteratively and through refining their approach incrementally, over time. They will be able to do this in the light of deep, qualitative as well as quantitative evidence about how pupils are responding.
- Develop professional learning skills and routines that enable them to wrap CPDL activities around the day job. For example, they might develop enquiries, lesson study, structured, collaborative video-based peer observation and/or coaching.
- Explore summaries of high-quality research studies and the results of teachers' micro enquiries during ongoing departmental and phase meetings.
- Approach CPDL from multiple levels:
  - From 'within', though an exploration of pupils' perspectives on where learning is stuck.
  - From beyond, by drawing on wider research and theory to challenge and review orthodoxies to identify evidence-based possibilities for 'unsticking' learning.
  - From CPD leaders, through support that is designed to be appropriate, relevant and contextualised within a no-blame school culture that encourages risk-taking.
  - From colleagues, through lateral partnerships that enable collegiate testing, challenging and debating the outcomes of participation.
  - Towards the profession more broadly, though a willingness to contribute to scaling up so that the learning goes beyond the parameters of the teachers' own classroom.

2. At a leadership level, whether CPD facilitation and support takes place beyond or within school, the professional learning journey needs to be framed by the rhythms, systems, accountability structures and values that constitute the whole-school professional learning environment. This, in turn is framed by school leaders' own approaches towards their own and colleagues' professional learning, so:
  - Leaders need to read widely and understand what is known and so be trusted that their ideas are rooted in the research literature about professional learning in their context. Funding constraints alone mean that the latest fad can neither be afforded nor encouraged as part of this learning cycle. Leaders need to sift and sort research evidence to create a coherent and meaningful curriculum for CPD support and CPDL. There can be no room for exploring approaches with little or no evidence to support their likely efficacy, such as offering generic CPDL without enabling teachers to contextualise their learning for particular subject contexts or groups of students (Cordingley et al., 2015).

- Leaders need to exert influence sensitively with respect to CPDL. It is difficult for teachers to truly grow and develop if their leaders do not demonstrate that they too are capable of learning from their own professional learning, that of the staff and indeed from the children in their own school. If teachers are to be able to connect their own personal and professional learning priorities with the school's CPDL offer, teachers need to understand clear rationales for the use of their precious time.

- Leaders need to visibly model a formal commitment to the development of all key stakeholders in their school, including the governing body. This means continually balancing the development of trust, the fostering of innovation and the recognition of the importance of risk-taking, so that teachers can develop agency in developing professional knowledge through effective professional learning. The process of professional learning as being something dynamic needs to be kept alive.

- Leaders need to be courageous and bold, understanding and accepting that effective CPDL is not a quick fix but a long journey of improvement that will take many twists and turns. This strategic and long-term development horizon needs to be articulated and embraced so that we avoid an input–process–output approach to practice. A no-blame culture is vital here, coupled with action by leaders to shield their 'class' of staff from external short-term pressures by focusing on the fundamentals of growing the learning of teachers to support student learning. They need, in effect to ensure that no one, including themselves, inadvertently pulls up the plant prematurely, to check that it is really laying down a strong root system.

In conclusion, for CPDL for teachers to succeed for pupils, leaders need to ensure that the principles that underpin a coherent CPDL curriculum are geared towards creating a coherent curriculum for pupils and are understood by all players. This includes developing understanding of how CPDL links to the school's vision and strategic direction in a way that feeds moral purpose and courage. This, in turn, makes it possible for all members of the school community to galvanise CPDL as a means of building a whole bigger than the sum of its parts. It is when this shared understanding is in place that schools become organisations that live out high expectations of learning at every level.

References

Bell, M., & Cordingley, P. (2014). *Characteristics of high performing schools*. Coventry, UK: CUREE.

Bell, M., Cordingley, P., Isham, C., & Davis, R. (2010). *Report of professional practitioner use of research review: Practitioner engagement in and/or with research*. Coventry, UK: CUREE, GTCE, LSIS & NTRP. Retrieved from www.curee-paccts.com/node/2303.

Cordingley, P. (2016). *Putting the petal to the metal: Gaining momentum in accelerating pupil progress.* Coventry, UK: CUREE. Retrieved from www.curee.co.uk/node/3273.

Cordingley, P., Bell, M., Evans, D., & Firth, A. (2005). The impact of collaborative CPD on classroom teaching and learning: What do teacher impact data tell us about collaborative CPD? Retrieved from http://eppi.ioe.ac.uk/cms/Default.aspx?tabid=395&language=en-US.

Cordingley, P., Bell, M., Holdich, K., & Crisp, B. (2012). *Understanding what enables high-quality professional learning.* London: Pearson.

Cordingley, P., Higgins, S., Greany, T., Buckler, N., Coles-Jordan, D., Crisp, B., ... Coe, R. (2015). *Developing great teaching: Lessons from the international reviews into effective professional development.* London: Teacher Development Trust.

CUREE (2017). GwE route map. Retrieved from www.curee.co.uk/node/5022.

Kools, M., & Stoll, L. (2016). *What makes a school a learning organisation?* OECD Education Working Papers, No. 137. Paris: OECD Publishing.

Marsick, V. J., & Watkins, K. E. (1999). Looking again at learning in the learning organization: A tool that can turn into a weapon! *Learning Organization, 6*(5), 207–211.

Robinson, V. M. J., Hohepa, M., & Lloyd, C. (2009). *School leadership and student outcomes: Identifying what works and why, best evidence synthesis.* Wellington, NZ: Ministry of Education.

Schön, D. (1987). *Educating the reflective practitioner: Towards a new design for teaching and learning in the professions.* San Francisco, CA: Jossey-Bass.

4

How outside organisations work with schools in developing professional learning

Sam Twiselton and Andrew Truby

In this chapter, we begin by looking at what we mean by the term 'expert teacher' and then explore how schools can create the optimal culture and conditions for supporting professional development in partnership with outside organisations. To exemplify some of the key challenges in practice, the chapter includes a case study about a Department for Education (DfE) Strategic School Improvement Fund project in South Yorkshire, which considers evidence-informed school improvement at scale.

What makes someone an expert and why does it matter?

What do we mean by 'expert teacher'? It is not a straightforward question. As Sternberg and Horvath (1995, p. 9) state, 'there exists no well-defined standard that all experts meet and no non-experts meet'. They claim instead that experts bear a 'family resemblance' to one another. Teaching expertise can be usefully viewed as similarity-based, in which similarity is defined as increasingly shared features and decreasingly non-shared features. So expert teachers may be different in some ways but are sufficiently similar to be classified as such.

Sternberg and Horvath (1995) argue that a 'prototype model' of expertise provides a convenient way of representing the central tendency of all the exemplars within the category. They propose three main features: *knowledge, efficiency and insight*.

In relation to *knowledge*, it is not so much the amount of knowledge that matters but how it is organised in the memory. In general, experts are sensitive to the deep structures of the problems they solve – they are able to group problems together according to underlying principles and relate them to propositional structures and schemata. In contrast, novices tend to be more sensitive to surface features.

The second key feature of expertise is *efficiency*. Experts can do more in less time. They not only perform better than novices but they seem to do so with less effort. What is initially effortful and resource-consuming becomes effortless and automatic with practice. This aspect of expertise links to knowledge. If the expert has access to a store of meaningful patterns, corresponding to classroom situations, recognising and utilising them in problem-solving situations requires less effort. Experts typically spend a greater proportion of time trying to understand the problem, whereas novices spend more time in trying out different solutions.

The third feature of teaching expertise is *insight*. This aspect of expertise links closely with efficiency in that experts reach solutions through seeing into a problem deeply and understanding its nature. This allows the expert practitioner to distinguish information that is relevant in order to make the most efficient use of the time available and draw on the most pertinent areas of knowledge.

To summarise, the prototype expert is knowledgeable in a way that is accessible and organised and whose knowledge covers a range of domains including subject, pedagogy and context. They are able to perform many activities rapidly with little cognitive effort allowing them to invest more effort in the most impactful problem-solving. In doing this, they are able to encode information to arrive at insightful solutions.

Tochon and Munby (1993) studied novice and expert teachers' classroom practice and noticed significant differences in the way they worked. They describe expert teachers as mainly centring on the intensity of particular moments, in which they pull together a range of knowledge to inform professional action. This places emphasis on the ability to perceive the demands of a situation as it arises and draw on several sources to make the most effective response. In contrast, novice teachers take an essentially linear approach to their decision-making with a strong emphasis on planned use of time. They direct their actions mainly through preordained planning and are much less likely to respond contingently or even to be open to the need to do so.

How can teachers develop expertise? What helps and hinders this process? One of the authors' own studies is of some help here. Twiselton (2004) investigated the types of knowledge and understanding that student teachers develop as they acquire knowledge and become more expert over the course of their initial teacher education (ITE). Twiselton found that (partly dependent on how far through the ITE programme they were) student teachers could be placed into one of three main categories (or points on a continuum): *task manager, curriculum deliverer* or *concept/skill builder*. The task managers (who were likely to be near the beginning of ITE) viewed their role in the classroom in terms of task completion, order and business – without explicit reference to children's learning. The curriculum deliverers saw themselves as there to support learning, but only as dictated by an external source – a scheme, curriculum or lesson plan – and they struggled to give a rationale for why what was being taught mattered in any other terms. In contrast, the concept/skill builders (likely to be at or near the end of ITE) were aware of the wider and deeper areas of understanding and skill needed by pupils that underpinned their learning objectives. Of the three types, the concept/skill builders were much more likely to be able effectively, consistently and responsively to support learning at every stage of the learning experience. The most outstanding quality that separated the concept/skill builders from the other two categories was their ability to see the 'bigger picture' and give a rationale for what they were attempting to do in terms of key principles and concepts.

To a large extent, these categories reflect the different stages of development student teachers go through as they grapple with more knowledge and experience and get to grips with different aspects of their practice. It is perfectly natural to need to focus on tasks and management initially (after all these are often prerequisites to learning), to go through a period when learning is dictated by a detailed but constrained set of predetermined plans and eventually to have enough knowledge and experience to be more focused on a richer, more responsive from of practice.

While there was undoubtedly a strong developmental element to the factors that determined which category a student teacher belonged to and how long they stayed in it, length of experience was by no means the only factor. Student teachers' progress towards being able to think and behave in a way that was nearer the notion of 'expert' described above was supported and accelerated if they were working in a culture that required them to reflect on and articulate their thinking about their practice and ideally to have a basis for comparison and critique with other methods through engaging with the evidence base that underpins them.

Teachers who were 'delivering the curriculum' without fully understanding what underlay it appeared to have a grasp of the content but not of how the content is connected within the subject or the ways of knowing that are intrinsic to the subject. The study's findings suggest that in order to develop deep and broad expertise, teachers need time and space to be able to distance themselves from the practicalities of the school setting, which can be overwhelming in the immediacy of their demands. Connections need to be made with subject domains beyond the curriculum and the world beyond the classroom. Time and effort needs to be given to developing beliefs and values about the subject domains that will help give validity to the importance of these connections. The culture of the school needs to facilitate this kind of thinking and making links with outside organisations may be a beneficial way.

How can schools/groups of schools create a climate and culture for developing expertise?

From the outside of the education system looking in, it would be reasonable to assume that school cultures would be among the most positive given the positive energy from the children, the opportunities to collaborate with colleagues and of course the 13-week holidays. The reality is vastly different and school workplaces can be extremely negative places and statistics confirm that teacher retention is an increasingly serious concern. The three-year retention rate in England's state primary schools fell from 80 per cent in 2011 to 73 per cent in 2017 (Worth, 2018). However, it is interesting that some schools appear to be more successful at retaining teachers than others. Why is this so? Culture and climate are heavily dependent on effective leadership and over the past 20 years, studies have suggested that increasing employee engagement can lead to improved performance and, in order to be engaged, employees must develop a sense of trust in the organisation's leadership (HR Research Institute, 2018), including their choice of outside organisations to partner with.

The recent focus on teacher workload from DfE (2018) and the Office for Standards in Education, Children's Services and Skills (Ofsted) is encouraging leadership teams to evaluate the time spent on particular activities and how much impact this is having on learning. Despite the explicit attempted myth-busting from senior Her Majesty's Inspectors (HMI) (Ofsted, 2018), many schools still believe that they need to focus on time-consuming activities, which are not supported as effective by evidence. For example, it is common for head teachers in schools that 'require improvement' to state that they are aware that their practices around marking and feedback are excessive and unwarrented in terms of impact; however they need to continue to do this until they achieve a 'good' Ofsted grade. Through the work of organisations such as the Education Endowment Foundation (EEF), which is well known for its Toolkit which compares interventions by both impact and cost, there are signs in the system that school leaders are beginning to use evidence to inform strategic decisions, with the latest figures showing that 59 per cent of senior leaders are using the EEF Toolkit (EEF, 2018). Finding the right school improvement strategy or curriculum approach is one part of the challenge. However, careful consideration is needed – selecting the plan is easier than implementing it.

The role of culture in schools has clearly always been an important factor and has become vital during more challenging economic times, where leaders have been required to show greater resilience, to think more carefully about how to do more with less and to make tough decisions regarding school budgets. While finance plays a part in this, when we look at high-performing jurisdictions, the key lesson does not appear to be purely about the percentage of GDP going into education but about how the system grows and develops great teachers. Sharing good practice alone simply does not work (Hargreaves, 2012) and teachers will not improve without a deliberative intervention (Lortie, 1975); school leaders therefore need to be more intentional about improving classroom practice. The days of one-off staff meetings where disengaged teachers listen to a diluted version of a course that a colleague has attended are hopefully a thing of the past as the system offers a much more developed understanding of professional learning. The

DfE continuing professional development (CPD) standards (DfE, 2016) provide a strong basis for planning and designing professional learning and ensuring that the most important features are included.

When teachers are asked about how to create learning for their children that is irresistible, which inspires the children and leads to their total engagement, most would be confident in describing the conditions for this. How many leaders could genuinely claim that the professional learning offered at their school is equivalent? To develop a really positive professional culture and an inspiring place to work is not solely down to senior leaders. In fact, it requires the commitment and energy of every single member of the organisation to make this a success. Given that the actively disengaged can have a greater impact on the organisation than those who are engaged, it is important that any behaviour that is not having a positive impact on the professional culture is challenged, including passivity, because positive cultures require 100 per cent buy-in from the team. The hardest group to engage are those who are actively disengaged so this may not be the best place to start. It is often easier and more rewarding in the short term to focus on converting the 'not engaged' team members into 'actively engaged' by working out what is likely to inspire them. For example, this may be an experienced teacher who had previously been considered to be highly competent but is now not performing at the same level they used to. It is unlikely that this teacher's competence is decreased and so rather than focusing primarily on the performance, leaders need to understand what factors are behind the behaviours and how might a teacher's motivation be increased. When a teacher rediscovers their passion for the job, this can be extremely infectious to others in a team.

It may seem rather ironic to ask how many schools could genuinely call themselves learning organisations given that this is of course their core business. However, experience tells us that the conditions for learning that are in place for the younger learners are not necessarily in place for the professional learners. The DfE CPD standards, developed with the Teacher Development Trust, refer to professional development as a partnership between leaders, teachers and external providers, based around five key principles:

DfE CPD standards

1. Professional development should have a focus on improving and evaluating pupil outcomes.
2. Professional development should be underpinned by robust evidence and expertise.
3. Professional development should include collaboration and expert challenge.

> 4. Professional development programmes should be sustained over time.
>
> And all this is underpinned by, and requires that:
>
> 5. development must be prioritised by school leadership.
>
> *(DfE, 2016)*

In order for teacher development to be successful, it needs to be prioritised and this may require stopping or doing less of something else. For example, in the case of introducing a mastery approach to mathematics at St Thomas of Canterbury School in 2016, cultural change and subject knowledge development were identified as requiring significant attention. In order to identify the right priorities, leaders needed to consider the profile of pupils currently in the school alongside historical data, taking a holistic approach and investing time in exploring the issue before moving too quickly to implementation. Through the exploration phase, leaders can better understand the areas of the development for the school and then go about choosing an evidence-informed approach to address these. Leaders need to work closely with external expert providers to design sustained programmes that draw a strong commitment from the participants, opportunities for practice, structured collaboration, reflection and evaluation. In order to challenge current beliefs and change existing practice, professional development programmes need to be structured over a sustained period of time.

In some very successful schools, a clearly defined career framework with specific development programmes are specified at each stage. Teacher development needs to be intentional and proactive. There is a need for clear mechanisms to monitor the general outcomes of the programme and to support teachers who are struggling. In the same way that schools would put in place intervention for pupils as early as possible, the most successful schools appear to mobilise effective support to their teachers swiftly, empowering them to take ownership of their development at the earliest possible stage. Unfortunately, there is still a negative perception of so-called 'support plans' within many schools, when in fact, support plans have the potential to be used positively as a way of forming a personalised CPD programme. From our experience as system leaders in South Yorkshire, schools who have created supportive organisational cultures are more likely to have created an environment that enables positive, constructive and professionally enabling approaches. Such help may come from outside expertise, as illustrated in the next section.

Outside expertise: the role of HEI and other external organisations

The UK was the fifth largest national economy in 2018 by nominal GDP, but places 58th in the world rankings for the percentage of GDP that is spent on education (World Bank, 2016). If we take PISA mathematics, for example, England has a similar proportion of high-achieving pupils in mathematics to the average across members of the Organisation for Economic Cooperation and Development (OECD) (DfE, 2017a); however, the gap between the highest- and lowest-achieving pupils in mathematics is bigger than in most other countries (Jerrim, Grey, & Perera, 2018). Such inequity of outcomes however appears to relate not just to children but also to the way teachers are viewed. In China, the term 'teacher' is used as a compliment because of the high professional and social status of the role, equivalent in the UK to a general practitioner doctor, or for some highly acclaimed teachers, even a surgeon or senior medical consultant. This often strikes UK teachers as quite a constrast to the way they feel they are viewed and presented publicly in the media. While there are no simple answers to this challenge, there is a glimmer of hope with the Early Career Framework (DfE, 2019), designed to support teachers in the important first years of their journeys as educators.

The Early Career Framework sets out an accreditation system for teachers and an entitlement to appropriate mentoring, professional development and time. In order to raise the profile of the profession, building recognised accreditation and qualifications could strengthen partnerships between the school-led system and outside organisations such as higher educational institutions. There is scope to expand on the promise of the Early Career Framework to something that recognises and accredits CPD at each stage of a teacher's career. Many teachers begin to gain master's-level credits during their initial teacher training, but do not take this any further either because they are simply surviving their first few years in the classroom or the school does not ascribe value to it as a form of CPD. With the DfE's commitment to the Early Career Framework, there is a genuine opportunity to reshape these patterns so that more teachers can have the time, support and opportunity to engage meaningfully with professional learning and reflection. Another important development has been the establishment of the Chartered College of Teaching, which holds the Royal Charter for the teaching profession (see Chapter 2 of this book). The Chartered College's third cohort of teachers studying for the award of Chartered Teacher Status were inducted in April 2020.

One of the challenges that the education sector currently faces is that it has evolved very quickly in recent years and this has resulted in a sense of disjointed policy or a lack of alignment. What might be happening in one part of the country, or in a particular multi-academy trust (MAT), is not the case for all teachers. Nationally, offers of professional development are inconsistent. This is of core significance because teacher development holds the key to system improvement. And with such improvement, there would also come a reduction in the pressures exerted on schools to revert to short-term thinking and 'quick fixes'. Expert teachers become not only change makers within their class but also highly skilled mentors who are able to draw on a range of evidence around effective teaching from inside and outside the organisation, and do so with a high level of scholarship. Achieving such a self-sustaining system would represent a transformative step for primary education.

Where we get the balance right and work together with common goals, the relationship between universities and schools can be extremely powerful. A great example of this is a curriculum conference that has emerged from a partnership between Sheffield Institute of Education and Learning Unlimited Teaching School Alliance. The Education Inspection Framework has highlighted a need for schools to focus more on curriculum design and this partnership has brought together senior academics and schools with expertise in this area. The common goal: to support schools to design a curriculum that has the best possible chance of power-fully addressing social disadvantage. There have been cases in the past where school leaders may have fallen into the trap of making decisions about particular approaches or resources based on personal preferences or anecdotal reporting; however, we are now collectively moving towards a sector that is using evidence more skilfully in making decisions about the things that really matter. The EEF Toolkit has made it easier for school leaders to navigate research summaries from a range of studies and it is becoming increasingly common for school leaders to use a logic model as part of their theory of change. History has taught us that a little bit of knowledge can be a dangerous thing and a prime example of this was the reporting on the impact of teaching assistants, misinterpreted by both politicians and the media at the time because they stopped at the headline data and did not engage meaningfully with the research. This is where school leaders need to be supported to unpick the Toolkit and see it as a starting point. There are a number of interventions that, on the sur-face, appear to be a magic bullet with claims of eight months' additional progress. However, the technical data may show quite mixed results with some of the studies having little or no impact. It is positive that leaders are drawing on this level of evidence when making decisions about school improvement but it is important to strike the right balance between making research accessible for busy leaders, along-side creating a culture of digging deeper and asking more questions during the exploratory stage before moving to implementation.

We now turn to look at a case study of a project we have been involved with. This example highlights some of the potential benefits for schools in working in partnership with outside organisations.

Case study: Strategic School Improvement Fund (SSIF)

The DfE Strategic School Improvement Fund (DfE, 2017b) is a partnership between Learning Unlimited TSA, Mathematics Mastery and Sheffield Hallam University and is based on the principle of carrying out school improvement at scale by working with a group of schools where there is a similar issue and implementing an evidence-led approach. The rationale is that through collab-oration, this model becomes more efficient and sustainable. Co-author Andrew Truby reflects on the process of engaging with the project:

> As an experienced national leader of education, this process has challenged
> my previous understanding of school improvement and has encouraged me to

take a more critically evaluative approach. For example, by really considering the specific school-based issue being grappled with, I have given more time to understand the current reality of the school. It can be easy to fall into the trap of assuming that we know 'what works' in school improvement; however, there may in fact be very limited evidence to support it. The process of designing a research-informed project to address a specific school improvement issue across a range of schools has led me explore in more depth the types of and strength of the evidence on which decisions are being based. To this end, having the support and partnership of educational researchers has been invaluable.

One solution

The SSIF project took a four-dimensional approach to transforming English and mathematics education (see Figure 4.1) and was aimed at improving outcomes in mathematics and reading across 23 primary schools through the implementation of Ark's Mathematics Mastery programme and our own Mastery English programme. In addition to working directly with class teachers, the project focused explicitly on developing senior and middle leaders. The project built on the established relationship between the Learning Unlimited Teaching School Alliance and Mathematics Mastery with an aim to improve maths teaching through the provision of curriculum materials and high-quality professional development. Other key partners were the Centre for Research and Knowledge Exchange at the Sheffield Institute of Education, who supported the evaluation of the project both on an ongoing basis as well as part of a longitudinal evaluation.

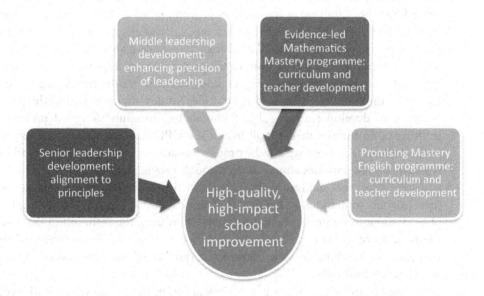

Figure 4.1 School improvement leadership strategy

The SSIF project was designed using the logic model provided by the DfE and drew on significant professional experience. The issues identified across the group of schools were reasonably clear to identify from performance data, discussions with school leaders and local intelligence. This was our first experience of using the logic model and it provided a clear structure to identify the issue, consider the long-term outcomes and work back from there; an approach advocated by Guskey (2016):

Critical stages or levels of information

Level 1: participants' reactions.
Level 2: participants' learning.
Level 3: organisational support and change.
Level 4: participants' use of new knowledge and skills.
Level 5: student learning outcomes

Guskey (2016) suggests that it can be helpful to start with the desired learning outcomes at student level when designing professional learning, as this focuses the pathway on where we want to end up.

The logic model was used to outline the theory of change, later refined in discussion with Dr Bronwen Maxwell at Sheffield Hallam University, who provided invaluable support and challenge throughout the project. The theory of change underpinning this project was based on the active ingredients required for a struggling school (judged as 'requires improvement' or an equivalent) to improve. In order to impact on the quality of teaching, it was essential that the school had the leadership capacity in both the senior and middle leadership to fully embrace the change that would be required to adopt the mastery approach. Through analysis and discussion, teachers' subject knowledge in mathematics and technical aspects of English were identified as key areas for development within the project. In order to develop teacher subject knowledge, carefully designed professional learning opportunities that met all five of the CPD standards were designed. One of the key considerations within the project was around reducing teacher workload, which both programmes aimed to do through providing teachers with structured guidance, flipcharts and resources. This also led to a challenge because less confident teachers sometimes interpreted 'faithful adoption' as rigidly following lesson plans without using professional judgement. However, the team found that overall the benefits of following a well-structured curriculum model outweighed these risks, because teaching could improve more quickly where there was clarity about what success looks like.

Related to this challenge, a key consideration in the design of the SSIF project was to define 'active ingredients – the essential principles and practices within a programme that relate to the underlying mechanism of change' and to consider 'where to be tight and where to be loose' (Sharples, 2018) with the schools involved in the project. Within the Mastery English programme, there were aspects where schools may be able to be flexible and still have positive impact on outcomes, whereas other components such as physically having copies of certain books were fundamental to the approach and could not be neglected. One of the lessons learned during the project was that the planning and implementation stages of school improvement are not related in a simple way. While it is important to clearly identify the active ingredients and show fidelity to these (Sharples, 2018), there is also something inherently human in effective school improvement because leadership is responsive, adaptive and very often intuitive: we need to adapt to the needs and behaviours as they arise.

The final stage of the evaluation was not yet completed at the time of writing, however, early indications show that there has been a marked increase in the average standardised scores in both mathematics and reading. The ongoing monitoring has highlighted improvement in classroom practice, teacher confidence and, most importantly, the pupils are responding exceptionally well to the approach. For example, pupils are now answering in full sentences, using precise mathematical language and report that they are enjoying reading.

This project has been invaluable in terms of learning and reflecting on school improvement at scale. The lessons learned so far can be summarised into three main areas: readiness, commitment and culture.

1. Readiness

A school needs to be in a position to be able to engage with this type of project. Where schools have not been as successful or have required significant support by the project team, this has usually been due to either the school having a range of other priorities outside of the SSIF project or that the quality of provision is very weak and therefore more fundamental work is needed before implementation. A readiness audit would be a useful addition to the process. Readiness is referred to in section 4 of the EEF implementation guidance document, with motivation and capacity as two main indicators of implementation readiness. Capactiy issues are relevant and range from difficulty in terms of financial, recruitment or absence issues, to those relating to culture and ethos.

2. Commitment

Although participation in the project was voluntary, the emphasis may have been perceived as being centred on what the SSIF team would provide to the schools rather than what the schools would need to commit to. In some cases, there was a misunderstanding about the level of commitment required. In the best cases, leaders were fully behind the project and this collaborative effort led to significant improvement in the schools (noted in two recent inspection reports). Where leaders had not fully supported the project, this tended to slow down the process with teachers in these cases reporting feeling unsure about a school's direction. What additional interventions do schools need and what mechanisms should serve to activate these? Could a self-referral system improve things?

3. Culture

Developing a positive professional culture was a key focus of the senior leadership sessions and head teachers who made positive changes within their schools. The SLE visits highlighted situations where the situational context of the school was not conducive to improvement. For example, where a head teacher was focused on a deficit budget, supply costs to release teachers or the small size of the school rather than the school improvement priorities, the potential for significant change was considerably undermined. Such cases tended to result in a dependency culture where school leaders appeared to feel that they did have the capacity to cope with driving improvements themselves and leaned heavily on the SSIF team to support them in an unsustainable way. Where the culture was more positive, challenges were quickly overcome and the positive mindset of school leaders inspired the team to be motivated towards success. The schools where the culture was perceived as more positive engaged more with the sessions, met deadlines more quickly, were more confident about articulating their understanding and oversaw the reported improvement in the classroom.

Conclusions

In conclusion, the main lessons learned from these project has been to ensure fidelity to each stage of the implementation processes involved in a school partnership strategy. School leaders considering a school improvement issue within their own school may wish to consider the following questions:

- Are we focusing on the symptoms or the cause? What is the real issue?
- If we are basing our analysis on data for students who have now left, what does it is look like for current pupils? To what extent is this an issue for the school now?
- What does the evidence tell us about potential options?
- When we look deeper at the literature, how strong is the research basis for a chosen course of action?
- Keep revisiting the 'why?' What is the purpose of this intervention?
- How could we design the optimal implementation plan for our setting?
- How could we engage the team at a hearts and minds level?
- Which external expertise should we include?
- What are the active ingredients? Where do we need to be really tight and where can we be loose?

- What are we going to stop doing so that we can start doing this?
- How will we know whether we are successful? Have we got a clear process evaluation?
- Is there an opportunity to involve a researcher to develop a case study so that our learning can contribute to the existing literature in this field?

References

Department for Education (DfE) (2016). *Standard for teachers' professional development.* Retrieved from www.gov.uk/government/publications/standard-for-teachers-professional-development.

Department for Education (DfE) (2017a). *Achievement of 15-year-olds in England: PISA 2015 national report December 2016.* Retrieved from http://publicinformationonline.com/download/141422.

Department for Education (DfE) (2017b). *Strategic school improvement fund.* Retrieved from www.gov.uk/guidance/strategic-school-improvement-fund.

Department for Education (DfE) (2018). *Workload reduction toolkit.* Retrieved from www.gov.uk/government/collections/workload-reduction-toolkit.

Department for Education (DfE) (2019). *Supporting early career teachers.* Retrieved from www.gov.uk/government/publications/supporting-early-career-teachers.

Education Endowment Fund (EEF) (2018). *Evidence summaries: Teaching and learning toolkit.* Retrieved from https://educationendowmentfoundation.org.uk/evidence-summaries/teaching-learning-toolkit.

Guskey, T. (2016). Data: Gauge impact with 5 levels of data. *Journal of Staff Development, 37*(1), 32.

Hargreaves, D. (2012). *A self-improving school system towards maturity.* Cambridge, UK: National College. Retrieved from https://dera.ioe.ac.uk/15804/1/a-self-improving-school-system-towards-maturity.pdf.

HR Institute (2018). The state of employee engagement in 2018: Leverage leadership and culture to maximize engagement. Retrieved from www.hr.com/en/resources/free_research_white_papers/the-state-of-employee-engagement-in-2018-mar2018_jeqfvgoq.html.

Jerrim, J., Greany, T., & Perera, N. (2018). *Educational disadvantage: How does England compare?* London: Education Policy Institute.

Lortie, D. (1975). *Schoolteacher: A sociological study.* London: University of Chicago Press.

Office for Standards in Education, Children's Services and Skills (Ofsted) (2018). *Ofsted inspections: Myth busting.* Retrieved from www.gov.uk/government/publications/school-inspection-handbook-from-september-2015/ofsted-inspections-mythbusting.

Sharples, J. (2018). *A school's guide to implementation.* Retrieved from https://educationendowmentfoundation.org.uk/tools/guidance-reports/a-schools-guide-to-implementation.

Sternberg, R. J., & Horvath, J. A. (1995). A prototype view of expert teaching. *Educational Researcher, 24*(6), 9–17.

Tochon, F., & Munby, H. (1993). Novice and expert teachers' time epistemology: A wave function from didactics to pedagogy. *Teaching and Teacher Education, 9*(2), 205–218.

Twiselton, S. (2004). The role of teacher identities in learning to teach primary literacy. *Educational Review, 56*(2), 157–164.

World Bank (2016). Government expenditure on education, total (% of GDP). Retrieved from https://data.worldbank.org/indicator/SE.XPD.TOTL.GD.ZS.

Worth, J. (2018). Latest teacher retention statistics paint a bleak picture for teacher supply in England. Retrieved from www.nfer.ac.uk/news-events/nfer-blogs/latest-teacher-retention-statistics-paint-a-bleak-picture-for-teacher-supply-in-england.

5

Easily lost in translation: introducing Japanese lesson study in a UK school

Luke Rolls and Sarah Seleznyov

Introduction

Lesson study is a collaborative approach to professional development that originated in Japan. Translated from the Japanese words *jugyou* (instruction or lesson) and *kenkyu* (research or study), it is a process in which teachers collaboratively plan a lesson, observe it being taught and then discuss what they have learnt about teaching and learning. In lesson study, the 'intermediary inventive mind' is that of the collective group; the wisdom of a teacher community that develops through the close study of children's responses to carefully designed learning experiences.

Recent increased interest in international league tables and policy borrowing from high-performing nations has led to an increase in 'travelling reforms' (Steiner-Khamsi & Waldow, 2012). These reforms are borrowed from other nations to address perceived problems in performance. In the UK, Japan, Singapore and China in particular have been popular sources of policy borrowing. However, an increasing number of authors have begun to challenge the feasibility of global borrowing, highlighting issues of culture, politics and over-reliance on student data as a success indicator. Sahlberg (2011, p. 6) (who is not against global borrowing per se) describes how a 'network of interrelated factors – educational, political and cultural – ... function differently in different situations': he believes it is presumptuous to attribute the success of a national educational system to one aspect of its practices.

Despite these notes of caution, since Stigler and Hiebert (1999) first wrote about lesson study, it has become a popular travelling reform and its global spread is increasing. Lesson study has emerged internationally through a bottom-up approach: numerous schools have adopted the approach in the absence of funding, direction or research findings because they perceive it to be valuable. It has been explored in countries across Europe, Asia, Africa, North and South America and several international hybrid models drawing on its practices have emerged, for example Hong Kong's 'Learning Study'. Barber and Mourshed's (2007) report on 'the world's best performing school systems' brought lesson study to the UK's consciousness and its recent popularity links to a recent national focus on promoting more effective and evidence-based models of teacher professional development.

However, if lesson study is to be adopted as a professional development approach by UK schools, it will be important not to assume that direct 'translation' of practice will be unproblematic. While recognising the appeal and power of lesson study for countries beyond Japan, Isoda (2007, p. xxiii) warns that 'moving outside of its own historical and cultural context may entail the loss of some of the powerful influences that shape and give direction to lesson study in Japan'. Similarly, Chokshi and Fernandez (2004, p. 524) state that 'lesson study is easy to learn, but difficult to master'. They fear that US educators 'focus on structural aspects of the process … or … mimic its superficial features, while ignoring the underlying rationale'. Isoda (2007) recognises that lesson study may undergo 'creative transformation' as it is adapted to a different culture. Murata (2011, p. 10) goes further, stating that 'modifications are expected and essential in order to adopt and use [lesson study] effectively'. However, she also highlights the danger of losing what is powerful if too many modifications are carried out.

Critical components of Japanese lesson study

In order to explore issues of 'translation' it is important to understand both lesson study's surface features and underlying rationale. Its critical components are frequently contested in the English language literature and few Japanese studies are available in translation. In fact, Japanese educators have begun to realise that there is a need for a more explicit articulation of lesson study (Fujii, 2014). Seleznyov's (2018) wide-ranging literature review puts a particular focus on Japanese-speaking authors since they describe lesson study at its source and it identifies its critical components:

1. Identify focus

Teachers compare long-term goals for student learning to current learning characteristics in order to identify a school-wide research theme, which may be pursued for two or three years. Having a shared research focus supports close collaboration among teachers. In Japan the focus is often one that works across multiple subject areas, for example developing independence or curiosity.

2. Planning

Teachers work in collaborative groups to carry out *kyozai kenkyu* (study of material relevant to the research theme). This leads to the production of a collaboratively written plan for a research lesson. The detailed plan, written over several meetings, attempts to anticipate student responses, misconceptions and successes for the lesson.

3. Research lesson

The research lesson is taught by a teacher from the planning group. Other members of the group act as silent observers, collecting evidence of student learning. The focus is on observing student learning, not judging teaching.

4. Post-lesson discussion

The group meet to formally discuss evidence gathered, following a set of conversation protocols that ensure the focus remains firmly on what teachers have learned. Learning in relation to the research theme is identified to inform subsequent cycles of research.

5. Repeated cycles of research

Subsequent research lessons are planned and taught that draw on the findings from the post-lesson discussion. These are new lessons and not revisions nor reteachings of previous research lessons. In fact, Japanese authors state that since each research lesson is designed with a particular class in mind at a particular point in their learning, to teach it to a different class is unethical (Fujii, 2016). Lesson study should focus not on creating a 'perfect lesson' but on gradual, incremental changes to teachers' practice that will enable improved learning for all students.

6. Outside expertise

There is input from a *koshi* or 'expert other' into the planning process and the research lesson. The *koshi* comes from outside the school and is either from an academic or practice background, for example a local area adviser, a university professor or a highly experienced teacher.

7. Mobilising knowledge

Networking occurs across schools or through the publication of group findings.

Why lesson study?

It is clear from the critical components listed above that lesson study is not a simple adaptation of current UK approaches to professional development. So why might schools consider adopting it? In opposition to the recent Department for Education's (DfE) focus on the quality of entrants into teaching, many in the education world are keen to focus on developing the practice of current teachers, noting that teacher in-school variability is far greater than inter-school variability and that teacher quality is perhaps the greatest predictor of pupil outcomes. In Japan, lesson study is seen as a process that enables all teachers to improve their practice throughout their career. How does lesson study achieve this?

Lesson study's approach to enabling teacher improvement aligns with recent calls for UK teachers to be more engaged in and with research. Hallgarten, Bamfield, and McCarthy (2014, p. 66) distinguish between passive research-led practice, whereby teachers follow guidance that policy makers claim is rooted in research, and active research-informed practice, whereby teachers are 'empowered to find, use and apply the research that is available'. Lesson study has all the features of an effective school-based research process. It begins with an analysis of data, involves identifying a question to pursue, uses classroom practice as a concrete experience by which to analyse the success of changes to practice, requires teachers to gather evidence to inform reflection, is repeated in cycles that refine and enhance learning and involves a final analysis and reporting of findings.

This lesson study research process is a structured and iterative process of collaboration involving mutual learning, aligning with a significant focus in professional development literature on the importance of collaborative teacher learning. Lesson study mimics powerful professional development models like professional learning communities (Stoll & Louis, 2007) and communities of practice (Lave & Wenger, 1991) with its focus on establishing shared research themes, collaborative lesson planning and 'collective knowledge creation' through the post-lesson discussion, 'open-house' research lessons and publication of findings. The goal of lesson study is to produce collective intelligence through high-quality talk between teachers, transforming tacit knowledge into explicit and creating new social knowledge. Powerful collaborative conversations around shared practice build trust, encourage non-judgemental challenge and increase the likelihood of teachers changing their practices.

Finally, effective professional development needs sustained time and a long duration: 'professional development must be seen as a process, not an event' (Guskey, 2002, p. 388). Time enables teachers to surface theories of learning and ensures greater depth of learning. A lesson study research theme will last for at least two years and involve considerable teacher time.

It seems therefore that lesson study offers the potential for transforming teacher practices: in line with research evidence on effective teacher professional development it engages teachers in and with research through structured collaboration and operates over a sustained time frame. What is important to consider therefore, is whether it can be translated effectively into the UK education system and schools.

Can lesson study be translated into a UK context?

Several researchers have written about the challenges of adopting lesson study in non-Japanese contexts but there is very sparse literature on the nature of implementation in the UK. However, the international literature raises several major concerns that are of relevance to translation into UK schools. Several international authors note timetable and workload issues as an impediment. In the UK, Godfrey, Seleznyov, Anders, Wollaston, and Barrera-Pedemonte (2019) found that when sufficient time was not allocated to lesson study, such that teachers had to commit their own time to the process, the engagement of teachers and their stated learning was considerably less. Wake, Foster, and Swann (2013) also noted that UK teachers were reluctant to devote the required time to production of a detailed lesson plan. In Japan, time is built into teachers' weekly schedule to accommodate lesson study and they are also willing to devote considerable amounts of their own time to its processes.

Why are UK schools and teachers reluctant to commit time to professional development processes like lesson study? The issue of teacher workload and its impact on recruitment and retention is now acknowledged by the DfE, but little attention has been paid to its impact on professional development. Changes to teacher practice take considerable time, and will only happen over a lengthy period of time: this belief has shaped lesson study's critical components. As an indirect outcome of accountability, workload is now acknowledged to have led to teachers in the UK spending their time on things that lead neither to changes in practice nor to improved learning, for example extensive written feedback, detailed lesson planning and data entry. This appears to leave them with little energy to commit to professional development beyond the statutory requirements of the school. Several researchers have noted that local accountability pressures mean teachers are unwilling to engage in lesson study or are heavily focused on curriculum coverage to the detriment of learning about pedagogy.

The hyper-accountability system in the UK also influences schools by putting an increasingly rigid focus on short-term measurable impact. Lewis, Perry, and Murata (2006, p. 6) compare the US response to lesson study, with researchers 'proposing randomized controlled trials and horse-race style comparisons' to Japan, where 'lesson study has been used for a century without summative evaluation'. In the UK, there is similar pressure on schools to prove impact through short-term pupil outcomes and to demonstrate value for money, with even the Educational Endowment Foundation conducting the majority of its impact evaluations over one, or a maximum of two years. Lesson study is seen as enabling a ten-year journey towards expertise, and a Japanese school's research theme may last for several years.

Accountability in the UK has also led to a significant fear of lesson observation. Despite the fact that evidence of the impact of systematic lesson observation on student outcomes is 'generally limited' (Coe, Aloisi, Higgins, & Major, 2015) and that judging teachers through observation has been shown to be unreliable, formal judgemental lesson observation has become an engrained aspect of the accountability system in UK schools. Lesson observation has been 'done to' rather than 'done with' teachers, reducing ownership and autonomy, both key features of effective professional development, and leading teachers to see it as a threatening unsupportive process. Lesson study, on the other hand, promotes a learning approach to lesson observation; teachers take ownership of their learning and take risks in experimenting with new approaches collaboratively with their peers. Wake et al. (2013) noted that UK teachers tended to avoid conflict in post-lesson discussions by being polite (rather than constructively critical) in what one could perceive as an attempt to make the lesson observation aspect of lesson study less threatening. How can UK teachers be persuaded to rethink their fear of lesson observation as a judgemental process?

The national culture shapes the education system, which in turn shapes the professional development approach of schools. One cannot automatically assume that lesson study will be easily implemented in UK schools (see Figure 5.1).

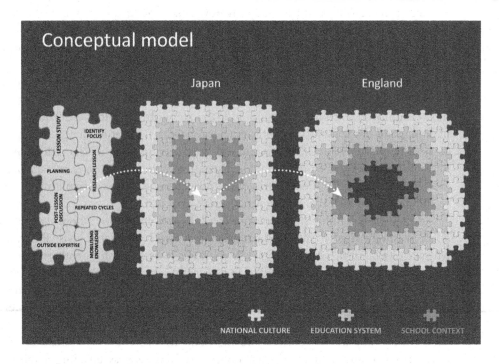

Figure 5.1 Comparison model of lesson study in Japan and the UK

A story of implementation

The following is an account of the journey of implementation of lesson study by Luke Rolls at the University of Cambridge Primary School.

Building a culture of trust

Before visiting Japan, I had experimented with lesson study over two cycles of enquiry, but realise in retrospect that I had only really taken the very first steps towards understanding the challenges of implementation in a UK primary school context. In Tokyo, I was fortunate to meet with a Ministry of Education advisor and university lecturer who specialised in researching and facilitating research lessons. He began by explaining that the first priority of lesson study is to create a trusting community of practice. He had worked in both Japan and abroad in Kazakhstan and could easily point to instances in which lesson study had been a demoralising experience for the teachers involved. For example, where teachers had not had the opportunity to make use of an expert adviser or collaborative planning group or when it came to the post-lesson discussion, many areas of weakness of the lesson were harshly evaluated by senior teachers in front of colleagues, leaving the lead teacher with a sense of failure. What became clear was that rather than there being a singular form of professional development known as 'lesson study' internationally, in practice it took many forms and it was the *how* of its implementation that held the key to its potential.

I returned to my own school with a moderated understanding of the principles of Japanese lesson study and faced the challenge of bringing a form of professional development that depended on a form of open professional learning culture that was almost the polar opposite to the high-stakes nature of formal observations and performance management strategies in the UK. On my side was the fact that I was working in a new school that had made a concerted effort to create a collaborative ethos among staff and a strong professional learning culture (Watkins, 2001). Nevertheless, teachers were arriving to work at the school from difficult school contexts and they often referred to feeling scarred by the accountability-driven management strategies they had become accustomed to. So much so that several were considering leaving the profession before joining the school.

During an induction session at the beginning of the school year with our growing number of teachers, I introduced the aims, purpose and processes of lesson study. I explained that lesson study was a collaborative endeavor focused on children's learning (not the teacher) and that there was a definite distinction to be made clear between lesson study and other forms of observation (see Table 5.1).

Table 5.1 Characteristics of lesson study

Lesson study is ...	Lesson study is not ...
Developmental for teachers	Judgmental of teachers
An opportunity to closely observe pupils' learning in a classroom environment	Judging the teacher against the Office for Standards in Education, Children's Services and Skills (Ofsted) criteria
About a jointly planned and jointly 'owned' lesson	About teacher delivery of a lesson they 'own'
Research-based and focused on evidence, including what has been seen and heard in a given lesson	About what we imagine is happening
Challenging yet supportive	Critical and unsupportive
Problem-solving together	Identifying issues for someone else to resolve
A collaborative analysis of what leads to successful learning	Demonstrating one person's formula for successful teaching
Context-specific and concrete	Generic and theoretical
A series of discussions and observations	A one-off observation
An honest and open process of collaborative planning and reflection	Planning behind closed doors and teaching in isolation
About teacher learning in relation to the research theme	About creating a 'perfect' lesson

While teachers could see its benefits, several commented afterwards that the idea of teaching in front of all their colleagues did not sit comfortably. Teachers needed to experience and gain trust in the processes of lesson study. To flip this dynamic, we decided that the head teacher and the senior leaders would teach the first research lessons of the year to model the intended process of collaborative teacher learning and research. This led to the rather unusual circumstances of newly qualified teachers feeding back to senior leaders on the quality of learning that took place in their classrooms at the beginning of the year. And so, in this move away from performativity, teachers were situated as learning researchers, enquiring together into the gap between what is intended in teaching and what children experience. Research lessons needed to communicate through implementation that they could be an affirming and professionalising experience for both the lead teacher, the planning team and other observers in the group. Indeed, after lessons, teachers invariably thanked each other with a real sense of appreciation for the rich opportunity of observing children's responses to learning so closely. The process of lesson study made clear to all that learning was an impossibly complex area of study, but one that benefitted from collaborative enquiry. At the beginning of the third year during a lesson study induction session, an experienced teacher commented: 'Joining the school, I was quite nervous about teaching in front of all my colleagues but it wasn't like that at all. It's a really positive experience and you learn a lot from it.' As my Japanese advisor had suggested, trust and shared professionalism were the foundations for teachers to take the leap of faith needed to invite others into their classroom. As the school has grown, we now recruit new members to the team by specifically looking for professional competencies of collaboration and self-reflexivity as key determinants of employability.

The successes of lesson study

The development of lesson study began alongside the research and development of our own curriculum model. The three pedagogical 'golden threads' of habits of mind, oracy and dialogue and playful enquiry had strong research bases but needed to be articulated and contextualised to make academic findings translate into the classroom. In striving for wider curriculum aims of creating confident, intercultural citizens, we prioritised oracy and dialogue in our school development plan for its wide-ranging potential for personal, social, cognitive and emotional development. The main strategic partners were the the Cambridge Educational Dialogue Research group (CEDiR), whose research into effective classroom dialogue informed the planning of research lessons. At the end of the first year, the lesson study findings around shared practices in oracy and dialogue were brought together and formalised into the school's teaching and learning handbook. These shared pedagogies became school-wide practices that formed a common language of discussion and planning. In the second year, the lesson study cycle continued to enquire into the role of dialogue to support classroom learning and produced further shared thinking into practices in collaborative learning. While the school had always been fortunate to attract talented teachers, something began to shift; leaders and visitors started to comment that after having spent time in classrooms, they were seeing similarities in the ways children were speaking and interacting in the classroom. Norms were embedding around children giving reasons for their ideas, building on the ideas of others and querying those they did not understand; the very areas that had been focused on in the first cycles of lesson study enquiry.

For the second two-year cycle, the leadership team sought to better understand the conditions in which play might support the development of learning autonomy in children. The Play in Education Development and Learning (PEDAL) research centre at the University of Cambridge became a strategic partner for this second cycle of research. PEDAL researchers came to give teacher workshops on using evidence into effective playful learning and these discussions fed into lesson study planning work. Teachers also continued to engage with developing dialogic teaching practices by working on a cycle of action research in their classroom with T-SEDA (see Chapter 8), which in turn fed into some research lesson designs.

Challenges with implementation

Planning research lessons

The planning phase of the research cycle provided several challenges:

Time

Lesson study requires a significant investment of time and so could not be seen as an 'add-on'; it needed to be integrated into the design of the school's strategic calendar to allow sufficient time for teachers to collaborate. Things of course differ in Japan, where teachers often meet for many hours over a period of months to plan their lessons; they have a common teacher staff room with desks and they work long hours even when children are on holiday. To match these working hours is undesirable; an effort was needed, however on the school's part to help facilitate time for teachers to have enough time to work together. The school decided to give regular staff meeting times where each research lesson would receive at least two formal collaborative planning sessions. As well as this, teachers chose to meet for working lunches, at times after school to continue their discussions and to plan during in-service training (INSET) days. One strategy we used was to plan in 'check-in' type meeting opportunities over the lesson study cycle to join the two lesson research teams in the school. In these meetings, we could share developing knowledge and steer the direction of implementation in the school; evaluating the success of its different components and agree on adaptations needed.

Use of curriculum/teaching materials (*kyouzai kenkyuu*)

For the first three years, we carried out research lessons across all subjects in the school. While much curriculum support material could be found for the core subjects of maths and English, other subjects were more challenging. For example, when teachers looked in the National Curriculum programmes of study, they would find 79 pages of guidance for English and yet only one for other subjects like art and computing. In the UK system, teachers and schools are given 'autonomy' by being asked to break down this knowledge into six years of study and then to expand each into a coherent sequence of learning. As a school, we subscribed to subject associations where possible but these resources themselves were of variable accessibility. The best materials used were those that supported teachers' subject knowledge, allowing them to begin to anticipate what children's responses and misconceptions might be, but these were unfortunately rare. Perhaps unsurprisingly, the wealth of teaching materials and textbooks available in high-performing countries produced for all subjects appear to have often been developed themselves through approaches such as lesson study. This deficit of high-quality curriculum materials remains an ongoing challenge.

Refining a research question

As with any form of research, honing in on the exact area of focus is an iterative process that takes time. During staff discussion, the design of the research question was identified as a key aspect with which teachers were struggling. While planning groups would begin at the outset with an idea for a research lesson, e.g. the role of play in teaching English, they needed time and discussion to refine their exact focus. In the following example, we can see how the exact type of play and specific aspect of English learning is developed and identified over time:

Version 1: What is the role of play in teaching writing?
Version 2: How can role play support the teaching of writing dialogue?
Version 3: How can children develop characterisation in their writing through the use of role play?

The planning team also became more familiar and skilled at developing questions that helped the observers to collect focused evidence. This again requires thought and calls on support from the planning team and the expert advisor as to which questions may be most pertinent.

Research questions for observers:

■ What aspects of characterisation were developed through the role-play phase of the lesson?
■ What evidence was there that the content of children's role play transferred into their dialogue script?
■ What aspects of teacher and peer modelling were evident in children's development of characterisation skills?

Choice of research lesson subject

In the first few years of implementing lesson study, we let teachers lead on a lesson in a subject they felt most confident with but gradually moved away from this. Lesson study is ultimately concerned with exploring together gaps in teaching knowledge and practice rather than seeking to demonstrate competence (Takahashi, 2010). As the number of lesson study cycles completed increased, teachers began to teach areas they were personally interested in developing.

Outside expertise

In Japan there are three types of '*koshi*' for lesson study: subject specialists, pedagogical specialists (e.g. collaborative learning), and research lesson specialists. Takahashi (2010) lays out three core purposes of expert advisors:

1. To bring new knowledge from research and the curriculum.
2. To show the connection between the theory and the practice.
3. To help others learn how to reflect on teaching and learning.

Without the structures in place as they are in Japan, it could be considered a challenge to gain access to such expertise in England, although local authority advisors, teacher educators and educational consultants could (with guidance or training) potentially take on this role. On approaching researchers, however, it was found that they were generally interested to be contacted and to have an opportunity to visit a lesson in a primary school, hinting perhaps at an untapped potential in relationships between schools and higher-education institutions across the country. Expert advisors were communicated with on their commitment to provide feedback on a lesson plan, attend the research lesson and support the post-lesson discussion.

We most commonly requested educational researchers to be expert advisors for us; some of whom were previously teachers or had involvement in teacher education. Generally, we found that expert advisors had heard of but were not very familiar with lesson study. When inviting them, we would include the lesson study guidance and the specific role of the expert advisor. Where expert advisors added real value to the process was in their contribution to both the planning and post-lesson discussion phases, as an invaluable pair of outside eyes that could question assumptions or decisions made by the planning group. They often were subject specialists who could advise on the content knowledge of lessons. Some helpfully detailed notes on the plans, asking questions of the planning group and challenging them to reconsider aspects. Sometimes their comments were aimed at clarifying the intentions of different parts of the lesson but others would also challenge the sequence of learning, choice of questions or the rationale of the planned task. Key to the sustainability and improvement of lesson study at the school has been developing longer-term relationships with these expert advisors who bring invaluable outside knowledge into the process.

Post-lesson discussion

A common structure for post-lesson discussions was useful for facilitators and teachers to understand how to navigate the data they had collected. Teachers were unfamiliar at first with which information to select and give from their observations of children in the lesson. It became clear that there was a tendency to feedback on unfocused general observations rather than referring directly to the research questions. This highlighted the need for both lesson study facilitators as well as participants to have a good level of understanding about the purposes and principles of such discussions. One simple but effective device that we moved to as a school, recommended by a lesson study leader from Sandringham Primary, London, was writing the research questions on flip-chart paper before the post-lesson discussion and then facilitators scribing on post-it notes whenever evidence was collected, sticking these on the relevant question paper. Useful for the distilling and summarising of themes at the end of the research lesson, this significantly focused discussion and made learning points clear and visible.

An interesting parallel to come out of the focus in the classroom on efficacy and productivity of dialogic interactions between children was mirrored and of equal importance for the post-lesson discussions of the teachers. The 'ground rules for talk', such as making sure everyone was involved, querying, elaborating and building on ideas through exploratory talk, came out during the most insightful post-lesson discussions.

Mobilising knowledge

Sharing the knowledge we gained from research lessons became more challenging as we grew as a school; for practical reasons, we moved from one lesson research group into two in the second year. We began to ask all teachers to complete a research learning summary poster. Lead teachers shared this at the following lesson study staff meeting where it was presented to the other lesson study group whose members had not experienced the lesson. This enabled some cross-fertilisation of initial findings and ideas around how children were responding to different types of lessons. The posters were also shared with teaching assistants and displayed in the staff room for governors and visitors to gain insight into some of the main themes coming out of individual research lessons. A few teachers have now begun to use their experiences of the research lessons to contribute to articles, blogs and chapters to share initial findings more widely.

The future of lesson study in the UK

Conclusion

While lesson study's popularity as a mode of professional development appears to have increased in recent years, there is a danger that it is adopted without a critical perspective on what the conditions for its success might be. The critical features, their complexities and the ongoing challenges of their implementation need careful consideration and likely mediate whether the benefits translate into different contexts. This chapter points to some of the changes that might be implemented at individual teacher, school organisational and cultural level. Our experiences of working with lesson study have suggested significant areas of attention for the UK's education system:

■ Priority and funding given to sustainable and coherent professional development in schools.
■ The role of 'experts' within the school system and building networks between schools and expertise.
■ The degree of inter-school collaboration within a fragmented, mixed system of local authority and academy schools.
■ The role of government, researchers, subject associations and teachers collaborating on developing high-quality curriculum materials for teachers to draw on.
■ The dissemination of school research findings and their role in informing the development of curriculum materials such as textbooks and schemes of work.

Questions

1. How will you bring about the culture change needed for lesson study to function effectively? How will lesson study be differentiated from other performance management strategies?
2. How will lesson study fit into your strategic school and curriculum development plan?
3. What overarching research theme will guide your focus for professional learning? How will findings feed into cycles of enquiry and knowledge mobilisation?
4. What curriculum, teaching and research materials will your teachers have available to them?
5. Which external expert advisors could you work with? What training and understanding of lesson study will they need?
6. How will you schedule lesson study into the strategic and professional development calendar so that it is not considered an 'add-on'?
7. Who will coordinate lesson study in the school? How many research groups will you have in the school and what training will the research group discussion facilitators receive?

References

Barber, M., & Mourshed, M. (2007). *How the world's best-performing schools systems come out on top.* London: McKinsey & Company.

Chokshi, S., & Fernandez, C. (2004). Challenges to importing Japanese lesson study: Concerns, misconceptions, and nuances. *Phi Delta Kappan, 85*(7), 520–525.

Coe, R., Aloisi, C., Higgins, S., & Major, L. (2015). *Developing teachers: Improving professional development for teachers.* London: Sutton Trust.

Godfrey, D., Seleznyov, S., Anders, J., Wollaston, N., & Barrera-Pedemonte, F. (2019). A developmental evaluation approach to lesson study: Exploring the impact of lesson study in London schools. *Professional Development in Education, 45*(2), 325–340.

Guskey, T. R. (2002). Professional development and teacher change. *Teachers and Teaching, 8*(3), 381–391.

Fujii, T. (2014). Implementing Japanese lesson study in foreign countries: Misconceptions revealed. *Mathematics Teacher Education and Development, 16*(1), 1.

Fujii, T. (2016). *What can we learn from the Japanese model of professional growth from novice to expert?* Cambridge, UK: Centre for Mathematical Sciences, University of Cambridge.

Hallgarten, J., Bamfield. L., & McCarthy, K. (Eds.) (2014). *Licensed to create: Ten essays on improving teacher quality.* London: RSA Action and Research Centre.

Isoda, M. (2007). *Japanese lesson study in mathematics: Its impact, diversity and potential for educational improvement.* Singapore: World Scientific.

Lave, J., & Wenger, E. (1991). *Situated learning: Legitimate peripheral participation.* Cambridge, UK: Cambridge University Press.

Lewis, C., Perry, R., & Murata, A. (2006). How should research contribute to instructional improvement? The case of lesson study. *Educational Researcher, 35*(3), 3–14.

Murata, A. (2011). Introduction: Conceptual overview of lesson study. *Lesson Study Research and Practice in Mathematics Education, 1*(12), 1–11.

Sahlberg, P. (2011). *Finnish lessons*. New York, NY: Teachers College Press.

Seleznyov, S. (2018). Lesson study: An exploration of its translation beyond Japan. *International Journal for Lesson and Learning Studies, 7*(3), 217–229.

Steiner-Khamsi, G., & Waldow, F. (Eds.) (2012). *World yearbook of education 2012: policy borrowing and lending in education*. London: Routledge.

Stigler, J. W., & Hiebert, J. (1999). *The teaching gap: Best ideas from the world's teachers for improving education in the classroom*. New York, NY: Free Press.

Stoll, L., & Louis, K. (2007). *Professional learning communities: Divergence, depth and dilemmas*. London: McGraw-Hill Education.

Takahashi, A. (2010). Prospective and practicing teacher professional development with standards. Paper presented at the APEC Conference on Replicating Exemplary Practices in Mathematics Education, Koh Samui, Thailand, March.

Wake, G., Foster, M., & Swann, M. (2013). *Bowland maths lesson study project report*. Retrieved from www.bowlandmaths.org.England/lessonstudy/report.html.

Watkins, C. (2001). *Learning about learning enhances performance* (Research Matters Series No. 13). London: Institute of Education School Improvement Network.

Unlocking coaching and mentoring

Rachel Lofthouse, Colin Lofthouse and Ruth Whiteside

Developing purposeful, powerful coaching and mentoring can be transformational for teachers and schools, embedding a culture of professional learning and development at all levels. In this chapter we will share insights from research and practice that can support you to create, engage with and embed effective practices. We will explore the roles of coaching and mentoring in supporting professional development in the primary context. This will allow us to consider the full career span and range of professional needs and concerns of primary teachers, from trainee and newly qualified teachers to established practitioners through to leaders.

CollectivED working papers as an evidence base

CollectivED: The Centre for Mentoring, Coaching and Professional Learning is a research and practice centre at Leeds Beckett University. Our stated purposes include to expand the available knowledge base on coaching, mentoring and collaborative professional development through research and to make the knowledge base accessible. As one response to this, we publish working papers as an open-access resource.[1] The papers are written with a broad audience in mind: teachers, governors and school leaders, academics and students, members of grassroots organisations, advocates, influencers and policy makers at all levels. The working papers enable a diverse range of informed voices in education to coexist in each publication in order to encourage scholarship and debate. We have drawn on these papers as a key evidence source for this chapter.

Navigating this chapter

As coaching and mentoring can be used to support those working in primary schools at every career stage, this chapter will focus on how and why they can be used to appropriately support both new and experienced teachers as well as those engaging in leadership roles. Evidence will be drawn from practice and research and offered in the form of vignettes, first-person accounts and research summaries. Having given examples of specific named mentoring and coaching practices adopted for each career stage we will then challenge the assumption that the two should be separated by drawing on two case studies where they are deliberately integrated. Finally, we will reflect on research evidence about what can go wrong and consider how we can avoid pitfalls to allow the practices of coaching and mentoring to become powerful tools at our disposal. Not all of our research-into-practice evidence base is limited to primary contexts, partly because of the nature of the available evidence and also because learning from across sectors has genuine benefits. In addition to examples from England, we include an international example from Canada and draw on influences of the Instructional Coaching Group in the United States.

The spectrum of coaching and mentoring in education

Knowing, and living out, the difference between coaching and mentoring in schools is a recurring dilemma and one that seems to get no easier with the passing of time. We are not short of definitions, but we have to recognise that real working worlds and practices do not always conform to rules and characteristics defined in textbooks, research journals or in training. Hence, we are going to discuss coaching and mentoring as existing on a spectrum, and indeed we are going to take note of the fact that this spectrum is itself multidimensional.

One definition of 'spectrum' is as a scale or range between two points on to which we can map or classify things. If we put mentoring and coaching at either end of the scale, it suggests that they are somehow connected but also distinct. It also suggests that we can recognise degrees of variation knowing that real life is often not clear cut. Figure 6.1 is our starting point and is unlikely to offer any significant deviation to what most teachers and leaders in schools would already assume. It is worth noting that if we cross international borders into new school systems and cultures, the meanings of coaching and mentoring do jump around a little, so Figure 6.1 may be more familiar in some places than in others.

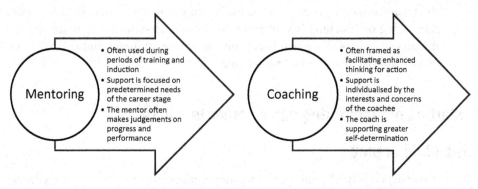

Figure 6.1 An outline spectrum of mentoring and coaching in education

On this spectrum, we can identify differences in the typical purposes of coaching and mentoring. By implication, these position the participants in different roles. For example, in mentoring, the mentor would usually be expected to have relevant experience in the role that their mentee is working towards and to be offering the mentee role-specific and target-orientated advice. Part of their job may also be to ensure that the mentee (e.g. a trainee or early career teacher) has gained sufficient experience and evidence of competency in relation to non-negotiable professional standards and indeed to be reporting on related progress to a line manager or training provider. This frames the mentoring relationship as one of expert and novice and as one in which significant power rests with the mentor.

There are a variety of ways that coaching typically differs from mentoring. While most mentors are internal to a school, some coaches are external. It is possible that a coach will not have the same professional experience or background as the coachee. Rather than working towards a set of established standards or practices, a coach will help their coachee set their own objectives for change. A coach would typically not prioritise giving advice or even suggesting targets, but instead they would be asking the kinds of questions of their coachee that elicit critical, creative and productive thinking. Through generating this thinking, the aim is to impact positively on the coachee, so that they gain confidence, acquire insight and make appropriate plans for action.

In this chapter, examples will be offered to illustrate that, in reality, coaching and mentoring practices exist at many points on this spectrum. Both coaching and mentoring happen over a course of time, although the duration will vary for many reasons. Both are interpersonal practices designed to act in support of professional and/or personal change. Both can be conducted with expertise and significant positive impact, but both can also be weak and even negative experiences. So, the spectrum as 'range' or 'scale' also reflects the variation in the quality and value of both coaching and mentoring seen across education.

So, what about the other definition of spectrum? Let's also focus on it as a band of colours, like those that are separated out in a rainbow but appreciated as a spectacular whole. In this version of spectrum, we notice and appreciate the details of difference, the different coaching and mentoring practices that can be defined specifically through close attention to what they each are and what they can offer in the reality and complexity of schools. When put into practice, each experience of mentoring or coaching has different degrees of refraction from theorised research definitions. Establishing that spectrum can create a vibrant and optimistic culture of professional learning and well-being.

Starting out mentoring early-career teachers

The state of play

Nowadays it is hard to imagine a teacher working in a primary school who has not had a formal or informal mentor. However, for many this might have only been while on placements during their initial teacher training and education course, with no further sustained mentoring as their career moved up a gear when in post. In England, the importance of this role is reinforced by publication of the Department for Education (DfE) 'Mentor Standards' (DfE, 2016) to support practice. The standards indicate that mentoring is deemed to be particularly appropriate for pre-service and early career teachers because it pairs them up with a more experienced colleague, who is working in the same context as them and who can offer authentic advice and provide an essential part of the induction process. In reality, there are some variations in how mentoring is configured in primary schools, and this is no surprise given differences between schools and their staffing structure. For example, for trainee teachers, sometimes the mentor is the class teacher with whom they share a class, sometimes the mentor is a different, perhaps more experienced member of staff whom they meet with at designated times.

Mentoring matters

New teachers often report that their mentor made the world of difference to their success and survival in role. Typical feedback about mentoring is illustrated in Figure 6.2, which is based on trainee teachers' comments gathered during a small research project (Lofthouse, 2018a). Even the shorter quotes given in Figure 6.2 demonstrate the range of ways in which mentors make a difference. They can provide much needed emotional support, give clear and targeted advice and guidance. They can also pay close attention to the trainee's developing practice and ensure appropriate feedback is given. They can exemplify and explain effective practice and also demonstrate professional qualities and practices that new teachers can learn from. That mentors have the capacity to do so is remarkable given how very busy every teacher is in their day job. When it works well, mentoring can create a positive place in what can be a very challenging training or induction year.

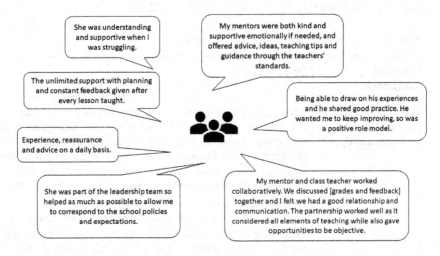

Figure 6.2 Why mentors matter to primary PGCE and BA students

Mentoring in practice is often a strong reflection of the procedures developed by the training provider or school leader and these do differ in terms of observation practices, expectations about how and when to use the Qualified Teacher Standards (QTS) in England, structures of practical support that the mentor is expected to offer (e.g. co-planning or team teaching) and oversight of the mentoring practices and outcomes.

Changing the status quo

When thinking about how research can be used to unlock new practices, it is worth remembering that we can seek to both enhance existing practices and to develop our repertoire. While mentoring can be influenced by cultural norms, we can also consider how it can become routinised in each setting; 'this is the way we do it here' is sometimes worth challenging. Sustaining high-quality teacher training and induction is complex when so much of the training time is spent in schools where teachers' and school leaders' workload is already high and as a result mentoring is often vulnerable (Lofthouse & Thomas, 2014). For teachers acting as mentors and for school leadership teams, there can be a real dilemma about whose learning needs come first; those of the trainee or early career teacher or those of the pupils they are teaching? Schools and teachers are judged on results, and policy changes can mean making tactical decisions about how and what to teach, with potential perceived dips in pupil progress becoming real concerns. On the other hand, giving new teachers support and time and appropriate experience from which to develop is essential if we are going to sustain the profession. One way to address this is to aim to reduce the related dependencies of the mentee and their mentor or class teacher. Another way might be to tweak some of the existing practices. Table 6.1 offers three insights from evidence about how mentoring might be developed differently. The examples are drawn from working papers published by CollectivED in 2018 and 2019.

Table 6.1 Developing alternative approaches to mentoring

Mentoring approach	Description
Live coaching for new teachers (Moyse, 2018)	'Live coaching' is where an experienced mentor or coach, skilled in providing immediate live feedback, works alongside a less experienced teacher while they are delivering a lesson. The coach provides the teacher with live feedback about their teaching so that the feedback is immediate and acted upon rather than being given after the lesson when it is essentially too late (p. 7).
	Frequent live feedback will help enormously … as it has the power to influence the lesson and therefore the learning in the moment, build great habits and also save time on lengthy feedback conversation too which is a real bonus (p. 10).

Table 6.1 Cont.

Mentoring approach	Description
Mosaic mentoring (Gilligan, 2018)	A number of recently qualified teachers … voiced a preference for what is usefully described as a 'mosaic of mentoring'. The participants described the benefits of what amounted to mentoring networks within a setting rather than a singular relationship with a more senior other. This was because with a dyadic relationship there is always the possibility of a breakdown in the relationship, which may cause issues that can have long-term impact … a constellation of relationships may ensure that a mentee receives different aspects of support from a variety of individuals and relationships are therefore less pressured in terms of delivering every aspect that a mentee needs (pp. 17–18).
Group mentoring, a Japanese case study (Briggs, 2019)	Each student [trainee teacher] is placed with three or four others in one class working with the teacher [mentor] for their main placement … When the students are not teaching or observing the teacher teaching they are supporting the student who is teaching, and observing both the children and their fellow student. During each week a trainee's lesson is the focus of the discussion at the end of each day … The class teachers generally facilitate the discussion rather than leading and do not give direct feedback in the early stages of the discussion … On other occasions a critical incident becomes the focus with the group problem-solving around this event unpacking what did it mean, how should they respond to the event and what might they do in future. The intention is that the group collectively share the issues from the observation … positive as well as areas for development, exploring options and problem-solving together. The skilled class teacher/mentor asks questions of the group guiding their discussion (pp. 35–36).

Coaching for enhanced teaching and learning

While mentoring is often required or offered during a teachers' early career to support training and induction, coaching has developed into a wider range of practices, including those that are deployed to develop teaching and learning. Five such approaches are described here through research-informed vignettes, representing the experiences of primary teachers using different types of coaching.

Video-based coaching

Gemma

I volunteered to be part of a research project to participate in video-based coaching. I was coached through six lessons over two terms. My coach Mel is one of my colleagues, although we have not worked together much before. For each lesson Mel and I agreed a focus area and I planned with that in mind. We used an iPad app to video each lesson. Mel was able to observe all the lessons, but what was different was that the video meant I could too. We agreed which video segments of the lesson to focus on (time is always a bit tight). The first time I watched myself teaching was weird, but also reassuring – at least I look like a teacher! After each lesson, we talked in depth in the coaching session and I found that we were able to focus on details that were really revealing and helpful. Mel asked me stuff I would never have thought of. She had watched the video segments too, so it had given her a chance to think about useful themes for discussion. I discovered so much about my teaching, the children's learning and engagement and how I influenced them. This meant that when we discussed targets for the next round of coaching it was really relevant to me and my class. When we shared our experiences with the others in the research project I was amazed to hear Mel talk about what she had learned as well.

Reflection

This vignette is based on research by Marsh (2018). Using video to support teachers in coaching, mentoring, video clubs or personal reflection has gained ground with the advent of new technologies although some schools admit that their equipment lies largely dormant, often because of anxiety about the use of video and the time taken to set up and use the technology.

Instructional coaching

Ben

When our continuing professional development (CPD) coordinator announced we were going to start instructional coaching to improve teaching reading in Key Stage 1, I was quite worried. Would it add to my workload? Would it mean teaching to a formula? Our instructional coach, Sonia, is employed as literacy lead in the Multi-Academy Trust. Instructional coaching is focused on specific teaching techniques and Sonia seems confident in these and wants me to follow particular guidelines. I have had to drop some of my old practices. On the flipside, I am more confident in how I can use these teaching strategies and I understand a bit more about the evidence for them. All Key Stage 1 teachers have been making more use of the same approaches, but Sonia's advice is always centred on me and my class and our discussions are based on that. It feels like the best bits of the mentoring I remember from my Postgraduate Certificate in Education (PGCE) five years ago. The lesson observations and coaching sessions are time-consuming, but I think it is making me more effective in this bit of my planning and teaching.

Reflection

This vignette is based on the practices of instructional coaching (Knight, 2007), which have been developed through the Kansas Coaching Project, over about 20 years and are gaining in popularity in the UK and Australia. 'Instructional coaching' has strong mentoring characteristics, but it is not 'instruction' in the UK sense of the word, as teaching and learning is known as instruction in the United States.

Specialised contextual coaching

Fatima

My school has been one of ten primaries in a DfE-funded Strategic School Improvement project (SSIF) focused on teaching for metacognition in maths. I am the project's lead teacher in my school and have been working with Caroline, who is a lead practitioner and coach employed by the teaching school for this project. Caroline has been in school one day a week, for three terms and most of her time has been spent with me and my class. This involved her modelling teaching, us co-planning new maths lessons, co-teaching and debriefing discussions. Caroline would admit that she had to learn about metacognition to add to her experience as a primary teacher and middle leader. Her knowledge and expertise seemed fresh and I guess we were learning together what it meant in practice. We have seen real changes in how our pupils talk about maths problems and they do seem to have more resilience when they feel stuck. It has also been great to be part of a network of lead teachers. We have been meeting to discuss metacognition in maths and have visited each other and observed teaching. The discussions we have had following those observations, facilitated by Caroline, have helped to clarify and consolidate my understanding from my own practice. This has been the best CPD of my 15 years in teaching. I am also happy to say that I am now applying to be a specialist leader in education – which I never thought I would have the guts to do!

Reflection

This vignette is based on a model of coaching developed by lead practitioners Hannah Munro, Claire Barnes and Kirsty Davies for a specific SSIF project led by Swaledale Teaching School Alliance (Lofthouse & Rose, 2019). Coaching featured in a number of SSIF projects and another interesting example is offered by North Star TSA (Ashley & North Star TSA, 2018).

Teacher coaching

Mateo

Since arriving in London work has been frantic, but I feel lucky to have landed in a school with a coaching culture. It's a big primary school, and three members of staff have been trained as teacher coaches and have time allocated to working with those of us who opt in. As a non-native English speaker, I asked to be coached to support my teaching of literacy as I felt that this might benefit me and my Year 4 class. Tom (a Year 6 teacher) has been coaching me this term, sharing an interest in literacy learning. Each coaching cycle is focused on a lesson. We meet beforehand and have a conversation, which helps me plan the lesson. Tom then observes the lesson and focuses on things we have agreed would be useful. Following that we meet to review and make new plans for more teaching and the next coaching cycle. I would describe Tom as 'helpfully curious' because he asks great questions and we seem to generate ideas together that excite both of us to try out.

Reflection

This vignette describes a model of coaching based on a research project funded by the National College for School Leadership (NCSL) and the Centre for British Teachers Education Trust (CfBT) (Lofthouse, Leat, & Towler, 2010). Of all the models in this section it is the least resource-dependent, but also the one that relies heavily on the school itself ensuring that the teachers acting as coaches are well-enough trained and supported to ensure high-quality sustained practices.

Inter-professional coaching

Cheryl

I have been teaching in early years for nine years and just moved to be phase leader in a multilingual school in the inner city with 80 per cent of children learning English as an additional language (EAL). It's been quite a culture shock and I worried about whether I could teach well here, let alone lead others. One thing that has been helpful is working with Jill, a speech and language therapist. Jill has been coaching me and my team to support us to develop communication-rich pedagogies. Jill started off with a couple of after-school training sessions to explore speech, language and communication development and delay and to bust some myths about EAL learners. Then she worked alongside each of us as a coach, videoing short bursts of us working with pupils (selected by us) and then using the video clip during coaching conversation. Being able to see the interactions between pupils and my own communication habits was fascinating and Jill was able to scaffold my reflections by referring to the training and also asking me more about the pupils involved. These discussions were always on the same day and usually only 20 minutes long, but they were really powerful. I also think it helped me integrate with the team by being coached myself. Now I am thinking about whether we can find an educational psychologist who might work in the same way to help us develop more expertise.

Reflection

This vignette is based on the work of speech and language therapists Jo Flanagan and Bib Wigley through their former company ClarityTec who worked with several primary and nursery schools in Derby (Lofthouse, 2018b; Lofthouse, Flanagan, & Wigley, 2018).

Returning to the spectrum

These vignettes offer insight into the practices and experiences of coaching as CPD for teaching. They do not constitute an exhaustive list, and while technology through the use of video is illustrated as a tool here, web-mediated coaching is also emerging, such as that developed in the 'My Teaching Partner' programme at the University of Virginia,[2] or 'international remote coaching' being developed by ONVU Learning in the UK.[3] As you read the vignettes above you might have been thinking about that spectrum again (both in terms of the overlapping and distinctive qualities of coaching and mentoring) and of the ways that each practice is contributing to a potentially rich professional development landscape. We could argue that they are each characterised by their own curriculum and pedagogy. The coaching curriculum is the scope and detail of the content of the conversations and its links with the teaching and learning context. In some examples above, this curriculum is framed as part of predetermined focus, while in others it emerges from discussions between the coach and teacher. The specific coaching pedagogy includes the roles taken by the participants, the nature of the questions being asked and the way that tools (such as video and pedagogic guidelines) are deployed to support reflection and planning. The coach's and coachee's level of engagement and their personal epistemologies, their understanding of and approach to the professional and conceptual knowledge to be explored, will also influence the potential for coaching as workplace learning.

Growing leaders: coaching and mentoring as part of leadership development

While the focus of this chapter so far has been initial and early career development and supporting teaching and learning, coaching and mentoring are also offered to school leaders. Becoming a school leader may appear to happen when a teacher steps up to that role; but growing into leadership starts much earlier and continues far beyond that first day. Figure 6.3 illustrates some of the ways that coaching and mentoring may form part of leadership development.

- During coaching and/or mentoring conversations a teacher starts to develop their interest in future leadership and becomes more confident in their knowledge and skill base that would support that professional transition

- As a coach or mentor for colleagues a teacher develops skills and knowledge that are transferable to future leadership roles, including communication skills, empathy and the ability to offer professional challenge without creating anxiety

- A new leader is offered mentoring to support their initial development in that role. This provides them with expert guidance and creates an opportunity for them to make more confident and informed decisions

- A leader engages with coaching to give them space to reflect on how their leadership approaches and personal and professional values can be aligned. This helps them to feel greater self-efficacy when facing contextual challenges

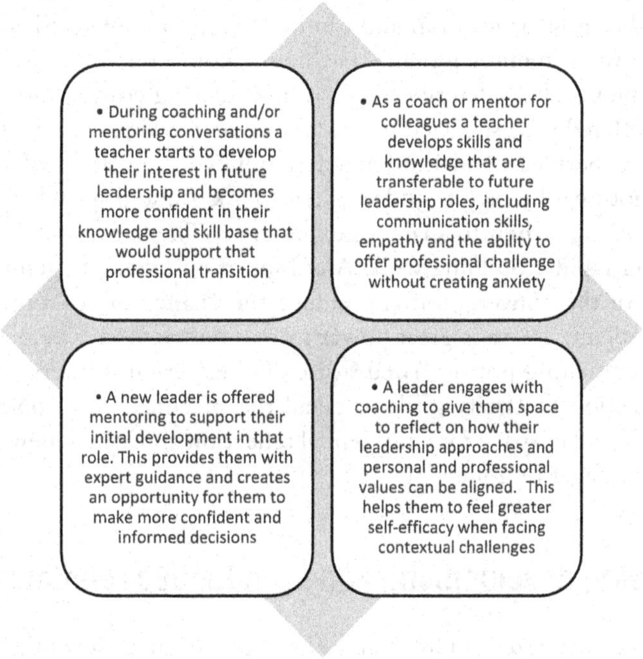

Figure 6.3 Developing leadership through coaching and mentoring

Offering the right support at the right time

Experienced leaders are often asked to support others in leadership roles. Co-author Colin describes how he uses mentoring approaches when supporting others in leadership.

The journey for an early career teacher to knowledgeable expert and middle leader can seem insurmountable and is in part based on gaining legitimacy. Given teacher workload it cannot be assumed that ambition and intrinsic motivation will carry someone through to leadership. School and system leaders have a critical responsibility to grow the leaders needed to sustain leadership and management expertise and capacity. An example of this comes from the support I as a head teacher offered to a teacher who became the school lead for English. In this case, practical actions mattered, for example creating a set of staff meetings for her to have the space in which to present to colleagues and practice her leadership skills. In my role as head teacher, I could provide her with a captive audience and demand their attention. The debrief of these staff meetings was also crucial and was a blend of direct feedback (an aspect of mentoring) and encouragement to reflect on her practice through coaching questions. Another key part of my role was to gather positive feedback from colleagues and share it, a well-timed piece of praise can be highly effective in boosting self-confidence.

I have also had the privilege to mentor a number of head teachers under a range of circumstances. Some have been very experienced heads who have suddenly found themselves in a new and difficult situation. Others have been new to a headship post or location and can be feeling disconnected and alone. Here the lines between mentoring and coaching become further blurred and interwoven in complex ways. I describe these as 'meandering conversations' in which advice is not offered, but suggestions are arrived at through a mutual understanding of pooled experience and thinking. It requires a high level of interpersonal skills and emotional literacy to judge when to ask a question, when to leave space for reflecting and when to share an experience. The success of this kind of support relies on rapidly building trust. Any hint of an exterior agenda can threaten the quality of the conversation and reduce the chance of co-constructing a solution to a problem. There is great power in co-construction where a solution emerges from the melting pot of shared stories and experience interspersed with prompts for reflection to clarify goals or detail the specifics of a problem, allowing for a critical blend of space for confidential reflection and where new ideas can be tested for that nugget of gold.

Experiencing developmental and productive relationships

As already suggested, individual leadership and career journeys can be influenced by coaching experiences. Co-author Ruth reflects on this aspect of her own professional life.

My teaching career has been based on developing coaching in my schools. From very early on, I realised I loved working with the adults in a school as much as I did with the pupils, and this led to me becoming the school-based mentor for trainees and newly qualified teachers (NQTs) from my third year of teaching. An interesting dimension to mentoring has been working with trainees and NQTs who really struggle with the rigours of teaching, particularly as the accountability stakes grow ever greater. That very often became much more of a coaching role as we sought to unpick where the difficulties were and how the trainee/NQT could move forward with new-found confidence.

Within my various coaching roles, I have given instructional coaching as the English subject lead, particularly as we moved through the different versions of the primary English curriculum. With the introduction of the grammar and punctuation paper in Year 6 Standard Assessment Tests (SATs) came a very real need for teaching teachers – teachers at any stage of their career – the grammar curriculum. This led to hours of staff training followed by the requisite hours of individual observations, support and subject-specific coaching.

A pitfall of the coaching model I think is when it is used to address teacher underperformance. A tension arises between what we would like coaching to be and the way it can be subverted. If we take coaching as being a reciprocal practice based on trust and authentic conversations only to then use it to identify how to improve individual teachers' practice, it can become a very blunt tool. Add to this the idea of the coach being a more knowledgeable other – usually a member of the senior leadership team – and we can begin to see how coaching can be abused. Coaching is regarded as a supportive process, rich in dialogue and learning. If it is used as a performance management tool, with targets being set by the coach so that the coachee can improve their practice, it can perhaps be seen as an 'intervention', rather than a conversation. In my naivety, I have been that coach and I found that 'teachers do not resist making changes; they resist people who try to make them change' (Tschannen-Moran & Tschannen-Moran, 2010). My M.Ed dissertation explored these tensions, although when I began it I had assumed I could iron them out (Whiteside, 2017).

Having recently set up my own coaching company, I find myself talking to head teachers who would like to implement coaching to address underperformance. I very quickly talk them out of it! The problem seems to be that even now, not all head teachers understand what coaching actually is. Done properly, it takes time and commitment. This, of course, is not so easy when heads are struggling with reduced budgets and increasingly complex individuals, both adults and pupils. At a time when the mental health of our pupils and teachers is becoming increasingly more fragile, coaching seems a cost-effective and supportive strategy. If we want to develop, retain and celebrate our teachers, we need to offer more in the way of coaching.

Gaining perspective on being a leader

As indicated above, an important question for every education system (at local and national level) is how sustainable school leadership is and a key indicator of this is headship. Some schools find recruiting to head teacher roles difficult; some head teachers experience stress and burnout, many retire early or move outward to other roles that they feel more comfortable in. This is not sustainable on either a human or system level. There is a critical and urgent need to develop an appropriate and multifaceted response to this challenge and there is emerging evidence that coaching may contribute to this. It is possible to think of this with a health analogy. Coaching of school leaders may be an intervention put in place when a problem has been diagnosed (or self-diagnosed). Alternatively, coaching senior leaders might be recognised like a public health programme, promoting a focus on balancing professional life and well-being, supporting good decision-making that has positive knock-on effects and reduces risks of problems emerging. As Campbell and van Nieuwerburgh (2017) make clear, effective coaching in education is not simply about meeting the perceived needs of the coachee (teacher or leader); it also addresses the desired educational outcomes for both their students and colleagues.

Some head teachers are now accessing coaching. For example, the National Education Union has funded a number of head teachers to engage in external coaching over a period of a year. In 2018/2019 CollectivED evaluated this programme. One data set is from interviews with a sample of coaches. Their reflections have a strong overlap with those of the head teachers themselves, gained through questionnaires and interviews. They offer insights into the greater potential of head teacher coaching if it was to become more systemic. It is worth stressing that this programme is provided by a professional coaching company that is led by an ex-head teacher. It is also relevant that the coaches are qualified and experienced coaches who are skilled at asking deep questions and have refined understanding of what coaching is and where the boundaries lie with other forms of support. The coaching is individualised and responsive to needs and preferred styles of the engagement of head teachers. During coaching sessions, the head teachers typically discuss the problems that they face with a recognition that these challenges change but do not necessarily become less substantial over time. They include managing the complex demands that they face as school leaders, both externally (e.g. the Office for Standards in Education, Children's Services and Skills (Ofsted), the budget and the impact of a reduction in other children's services) and internally. In particular, coaching becomes a place where head teachers think through how to build and maintain their relationships not only with government policy, but also with other senior leaders, their wider staff, governors, parents and the community while maintaining a focus on the needs of each child. The coaching conversations often focus on well-being, reduce feelings of isolation and help head teachers in aligning their personal and professional identities. There seems to be an impact on their confidence in their leadership role with a greater sense of self-efficacy and an ability to make more strategic decisions about their school and their own professional role and development. Figure 6.4 is based on quotations from the head teacher interviews.

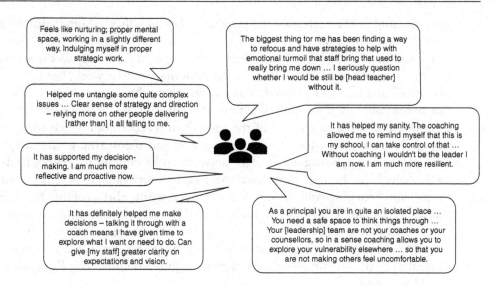

Figure 6.4 What head teachers say about their experiences of being coached

The emerging findings from the research into this model of head teacher coaching support what Whitmore (2002, p. 40) asserts when he says that relationships sit at the heart of coaching, highlighting the need for trust, safety and minimal pressure, allowing the coach to act as a 'sounding board, a facilitator, a counsellor and awareness raiser'.

Gaining ground and avoiding the pitfalls: creating impactful coaching and mentoring

Balancing the workload

It is not always easy to achieve or maintain positive practices and impact of coaching and mentoring in schools, and so it is important to know what can compromise them. It is worth bearing the following issues in mind whether you are a school leader, a coach or coachee, a mentor or mentee. In England, the DfE has acknowledged the need for a strategy to address workload in schools and it doesn't take much imagination to realise that activities like coaching and mentoring can fall victim to this. Some schools try to account for this by allocating directed time to activities like peer coaching, guaranteeing non-contact time can be used for mentoring and coaching (rather than cover), releasing coaches from lessons to allow them to observe colleagues, or expecting that if a student teacher is teaching parts of their mentor's timetable the pressure has been eased. In reality, there are often other jobs that squeeze into these times or it is suddenly deemed more essential that a particular class is taught or a revision session is offered. It is rare that coaching or mentoring are the priority and as such they are often abandoned when the pressure is on.

Coaching or mentoring (particularly when offered internally to the school) can be described as a Cinderella profession; doing essential work, but relatively unnoticed and rarely celebrated. The metrics that schools are measured by are not the number of impactful coaching or mentoring relationships, the career progression secured as a result of the growth of teacher confidence and well-being. There is also a tension when coaching and mentoring gets entangled with performance management. This tension can be difficult for school leaders to grapple with, both if they have the role of coach and if they are trying to manage coaching and mentoring practices while also pushing the individual accountability agenda (Whiteside, 2017). There is, however, emerging research evidence that points to coaching and mentoring having the potential to positively impact on both instruction (teaching) and pupil achievement, as illustrated by the literature review and meta-analysis conducted by Kraft, Blazar, and Hogan (2016).

It is interesting at this point to return to the spectrum of coaching and mentoring and we hope that the explanations and examples given help to clarify the nature of this. Some practitioners and researchers worry intensely about preserving the gap between the two, and while there are existing international professional associations for coaches (not limited to education) and national standards for mentors, this gap may be hard to maintain in practice. One way to acknowledge this is to accept that the practices of coaching and mentoring are different, but they are not wholly distinct, and that both could be valuable means of support to the same teacher or school leader within a similar time frame. It is not impossible to imagine a head teacher (for example) being offered mentoring through their multi-academy trust (MAT) or local authority, while also accessing more personal coaching. It is also quite possible to imagine the two being strategically co-developed within a single CPD offer; in other words – to deliberately mix it up a bit.

To explore how it is possible to rethink this we will conclude with two final examples, one from Canada and one from a special school in England working within a Quaker ethos. Sometimes it is useful to open our eyes to other education systems and cultures and to wonder what we can learn from them.

Mixing it up: making mentoring and coaching part of the culture shift

Our first example of the coexistence of coaching and mentoring is found in the Teacher Induction Programme (TIP) offered to all new teachers joining schools in the Western Quebec School Board (WQSB) in Canada. The TIP has three pillars: professional learning, a mentoring and coaching fellowship (which all teachers joining the schools and their school-based mentor coaches join) and teacher evaluation. Trista Hollweck explains more about this in her CollectivED paper (Hollweck, 2018). Trista was one of the TIP designers, a former TIP consultant and is completing her doctorate on the evidence of impact emerging from the programme. She suggests that 'both mentoring and coaching are viewed as distinct yet interconnected components critical for an effective teacher induction program' (Hollweck, 2018, p. 32). Here Trista explains the features of the mentor coaching fellowship:

> Every teaching fellow[4] is paired in their first year with an administrator-selected[5] non-evaluative mentor coach to collaborate, practice and reflect on new learning in their own environment as a fellowship. mentor coaches are ideally a veteran 'master' teacher from the same school, same grade and same subject area. However, with a fifth of the WQSB's teachers currently in the TIP, distance mentor coaches are often engaged and teaching expertise varies. Each fellowship is provided with two 'fellowship days' that can be used at their discretion, often to observe teachers in different classes and/or schools.

The underlying principle of mentor coaching is that over the two-year induction, a teacher is likely to need both. Through mentoring, they can access ongoing practical advice and guidance specific to the new role that they are in, the school setting and the school board expectations. Through coaching, they gain the opportunity to discuss individual goals, engage in expert discussion and be open to inquiry about their own practice. In the WQSB it is believed that this mentoring and coaching can be provided by the same skilled person who can nuance their approach over time and build an empathetic, trusting and mutually respectful relationship. Trista conceptualises this in a model that has been developed as the TIP programme has evolved (Hollweck, 2018, p. 33). Mentor coaches are provided with ongoing professional development and even with this provision the current TIP consultants believe it takes most of them three years to really develop as experts in this role. As the mentor coach fellowship has evolved and been embedded in practice, the schools are also engaging in the design of their own coaching models and supporting the professional development of their coaches beyond the TIP induction years. The balance of structure and freedom is important.

The second example comes from a special school in England that also chose to develop a coherent 'Coaching and Mentoring' programme. Ann Litchfield describes the journey towards this in her CollectivED paper (Litchfield, 2018). She writes that 'our Quaker ethos underpins all we aspire to build in our students: respect, tolerance, equality, understanding and forgiveness' and that these are 'then obviously extended to our teaching team', with one difficulty expressed as the question 'but what do we do about performance management?' (Litchfield, 2018, pp. 12–13). One of the key aspects of the journey towards changing the culture has been its gentle progress. Rather than hurtling headlong into a new policy, devised and implemented in a hurry, Ann did a lot of thinking and reading and took time to reflect on how to marry up vision and practice. She involved a small team of new and experienced staff from whom to gain more insight, who were involved as a core group piloting the approaches.

The point that they have reached on their journey is based on: an enhanced understanding of the need for both coaching and mentoring (not solely dictated by career stage); a rethinking of the practices and cultures of lesson observation; the involvement of student voices, which teachers are encouraged to gather to help contextualise their discussions with colleagues and support forward thinking; and a focus on a classroom-based project, selected and owned by each teacher and supported through the coaching and mentoring programme.

Final thoughts

When schools thrive, they undoubtedly do so because their staff live and love their job, paying attention to their professional development their professional identity and their sense that they are making a difference without compromising their well-being or their working relationships. Hargreaves and O'Connor (2018, p. 3) use the term 'collaborative professionalism' to describe 'deep and sometimes demanding dialogue, candid but constructive feedback, and continuous collaborative inquiry'. When it works well, coaching and mentoring contribute to collaborative professionalism and thus can help to build an underlying or sometimes overarching culture of support and growth. Prioritising coaching and mentoring means treating all teachers and school leaders as respected individuals with an important contribution to make. It also acknowledges that as professionals, they have the capacity to keep developing the sorts of expertise needed to meet the challenges of complex school communities.

Notes

1 The CollectivEd working paper series is published as an open-access resource on the Leeds Beckett University CollectivED website at www.leedsbeckett.ac.uk/carnegie-school-of-education/research/collectived.
2 See https://curry.virginia.edu/myteachingpartner.
3 See www.onvulearning.com/doon-school/?utm_source=Influence%20Marketing& utm_medium=Andys%20Contact&utm_campaign=Doon%20Campaign%202019.
4 Teaching fellows are teachers in their first two years in a WQSB school, who may be new or experienced teachers.
5 In Canadian and US schools, the term 'administrator' means school leader.

References

Ashley, K., & North Star TSA (2018). Working together: Coaching as the compass in the journey of implementation. A practice insight working paper. *CollectivED*, *5*, 12–16.

Briggs. M. (2019). Mentoring primary trainee teachers: What can we learn from Japan? A research working paper. *CollectivED*, *7*, 35–39.

Campbell, J., & van Nieuwerburgh, C. (2017). *The leader's guide to coaching in schools.* Thousand Oaks, CA: Corwin Press.

Department for Education (DfE) (2016). *Mentor standards.* London: DfE. Retrieved from www.gov.uk/government/uploads/system/uploads/attachment_data/file/536891/ Mentor_standards_report_ Final.pdf.

Gilligan, K. (2018). The benefits of mosaic mentoring for early career teachers. A research working paper. *CollectivED*, *6*, 16–21.

Hargreaves, A., & O'Connor, M. (2018). *Collaborative professionalism: When teaching together means learning for all.* Thousand Oaks, CA: Corwin Press.

Hollweck, T. (2018). A pracademic's exploration of mentoring, coaching and induction in the Western Québec School Board. A research working paper. *CollectivED*, *4*, 31–40.

Knight, J. (2007). *Instructional coaching: A partnership approach to improving instruction.* Thousand Oaks, CA: Corwin Press.

Kraft, M. A., Blazar, D., & Hogan, D. (2016). *The effect of teaching coaching on instruction and achievement: A meta-analysis of the causal evidence.* Brown University Working Paper. Retrieved from https://scholar.harvard.edu/files/mkraft/files/kraft_blazar_hogan_ 2016_teacher_coaching_meta-analysis_wp_w_appendix.pdf.

Litchfield, A. (2018). Developing a coaching model integral to the Quaker educational ethos implementation. A practice insight working paper. *CollectivED*, *6*, 11–15.

Lofthouse, R. (2018a). Mentoring as part of the foundation for career-long professional development and learning. A research insight working paper. *CollectivED*, *5*, 28–36.

Lofthouse, R. (2018b). Supporting children's speech and language development through inter-professional coaching: A case study of collaboration. A research working paper. *CollectivED*, *3*, 10–19.

Lofthouse, R., Flanagan, J., & Wigley, B. (2018). Talking it through: Using specialist coaching to enhance teachers' knowledge from speech and language sciences. *Impact: Journal of the Chartered College of Teaching*, *2*, 85–88.

Lofthouse, R., Leat, D., & Towler, C. (2010). *Improving teacher coaching in schools; A practical guide.* Reading, UK: CfBT Education Trust. Retrieved from www.ncl.ac.uk/media/ wwwnclacuk/cflat/files/coaching-for-teaching.pdf.

Lofthouse, R., & Rose, A. (2019). Developing a model of contextualised specialist coaching to support school improvement. A research working paper. *CollectivED*, *8*, 31–38.

Lofthouse, R., & Thomas, U. (2014). Mentoring student teachers: A vulnerable workplace learning practice. *International Journal of Mentoring and Coaching in Education*, *3*(3), 201–218.

Marsh, B. (2018). Teachers supporting teachers in professional learning and the development of classroom practice: The use of video-mediated peer coaching. A research working paper. *CollectivED*, *3*, 26–32.

Moyse, C. (2018). Live coaching and how it helps new teachers get into good habits quickly. A practice insight working paper. *CollectivED*, *4*, 6–10.

Tschannen-Moran, B., & Tschannen-Moran, M. (2010). *Evocative coaching* (1st ed.). San Francisco, CA: Jossey-Bass.

Whiteside, R. (2017). Is coaching for transformation possible in a culture of performativity? A research working paper. *CollectivED*, *1*, 5–9.

Whitmore, J. (2002). *Coaching for performance: Growing people, performance and purpose*. London: Nicholas Brealey.

7

Look no further: inquiring into learning needs as professional development

Eleanore Hargreaves and Tim Scott[1]

Figure 7.1 'Why?' by Landon, January 2019

Introduction

'How do we come to know ourselves as learners? And how do we un-hide (i.e. dis-cover) the lives of learners in classrooms?' These were Chris Watkins's (2015, p. 324) queries about the hidden experiences of children in classrooms. Free from external pressures (such as those illustrated in Figure 7.1), people tend to be curious and creative. Being enabled to act on curiosity and creativity is accompanied by a sense of fulfilment and well-being especially when this is achieved in the good company of others (Ryan & Deci, 2000). Where people have opportunities to use their agency, to feel that they themselves have achieved something, their curiosity and creativity are likely to flourish and lead to rich learning and further achievements. The nurturing of curiosity and creativity needs to be given pride of place among purposes for schooling – if schools wish to enable rich learning among teachers and students – because rich learning depends on curiosity and creativity. This is tricky because schools in the UK and many other countries have become constrained by business-model accountability, based on instructions and assessments from outside the school itself, into which neither teachers nor pupils make a real contribution. Without their personal autonomy being exercised, without a sense of being free to fulfil one's calling towards children's well-being and learning, curiosity and creativity become stifled and learning is stunted. And when teachers feel constrained, pupils' learning is constrained too. In such a climate, professional development can end up focusing on perfecting techniques that someone else has proposed, working towards ends that others have defined. And yet research into continuing professional development (CPD) suggests that effective CPD is fuelled when teachers use their *own* curiosity and creativity in order to develop professionally (e.g. Hargreaves & Elhawary, 2019).

In this chapter, writing as one academic and one primary teacher, we hope to explore how, despite constraints from outside, teachers can use their curiosity and creativity to find ways of improving the aspects of teaching that they value as learning enhancing. One easily available means for doing this is by teachers being curious about their pupils' true feelings, thoughts and attitudes as a basis for teachers' professional development, as well as for meeting their pupils' real needs as expressed directly by pupils. Interaction with pupils in this way will inspire not only the inquiring teacher her/himself, but the pupils as well. We address this aspect of professional development in the first part of this chapter. Another means, even closer to home, is by teachers being curious about their own true feelings, thoughts and attitudes as professional learners themselves who draw on curiosity and creativity. We discuss this aspect of professional development in the second part of this chapter.

Nell Noddings's emphasis on expressed versus inferred needs

American professor, Nell Noddings (2005), has written very persuasively about the need for teachers to be curious and to be creative in discovering children's expressed needs in the classroom. She describes how most of teachers' work currently focuses on 'inferred' needs, those needs that policy makers and other adults have decided to apply to children in the classroom. Examples of such 'inferring' include assuming that children should focus much more on maths than on art and music, that children will achieve most by sitting in silence and that each child needs the same school diet as the others. The rare research that has inquired into children's 'expressed' needs – that is, what children actually say they need – has suggested that some of these inferences are *misguided*, according to children. Noddings proposes that to be a truly competent teacher who directly helps children learn, one must be curious about children's expressed needs and creative about exploring and meeting them. This is easier said than done. Children become accustomed to hiding behind 'a veil of compliance' at school (Fisher, 2011) and to assuming that at school, a 'correct' answer is required, rather than an honest one. Therefore, teachers need to be creative about 'dis-covering' (or 'un-hiding') children's expressed needs.

One of the issues that makes this a harder task than it might otherwise have been is that feelings, thoughts and interactions have often been excluded from the school learning equation. As recently defined by the Office for Standards in Education, Children's Services and Skills (Ofsted), learning is too often considered only through the cognitive lens. Learning is seen as being about using one's brain to remember things and work things out. The social context of learning and people's diverse responses to stimuli in the environment – including other people – have consistently been excluded. This is where teachers can benefit greatly from considering their own learning first. What really makes the teacher her/himself *want* to learn more? Which conditions lead to the richest learning for the teacher? Which factors block their learning most destructively? By 'meta-learning' about their own professional learning, teachers are in a stronger position to inquire into children's learning.

Curiosity and creativity

Unfortunately, the pressure created by accountability often funnels teacher development in the direction of 'what works' and, in turn, 'what works' becomes defined as that which delivers better data. It is a game of short-term profits and losses, with schools frequently changing their 'what works' strategies in response to the latest test results or changes of personnel. Although all of this happens within the context of 'continual improvement', the timescales are so short that approaches which require long-term commitments (but that may deliver deeper learning) are generally avoided. The pressure to *deliver* each set of results also ensures that, in many schools (especially those with the most deprived cohorts) there is little chance of the yearly CPD calendar being given over to non-subject-specific teaching strategies, especially those that require the development of in-depth understanding. Here, the 'off the peg' and the 'quick fix' almost always wins out. This results in schools adopting superficial versions of important techniques (e.g. tick-box self-assessment slips) in place of the more fully explored evaluations of learning that *do* result in better outcomes. Unsurprisingly, such surface changes rarely last. Equally destructive is the fact that the conveyor belt of superficial fads rarely stops long enough to allow teachers to put their own curiosity and creativity to work.

As the American psychologist Mihalyi Csikszentmihalyi (1996) pointed out, successful creativity is an autotelic process, i.e. the joy of doing the work is the point of the work. It is a process that starts in curiosity about the possible and ends in something that suggests further possibilities. Although it can happen within given constraints, such as the conventions of a writing genre, the point of creativity is to go *beyond* the familiar. In doing so, it implicitly affirms the individual and places them at a critical angle to the world around them. Therefore, in asking adults and children to pursue their curiosity, to be creative and to question accepted norms, we are not only saying that we value them, but that we value them enough to tell us how things around them might be better. One subsequent effect of this is that the sense of relatedness that was referred to in our introductory paragraph emerges naturally through the promotion of creativity and curiosity. Overall, it is hard not to reach the conclusion that, in educational settings, these experiences should be classified as needs rather than luxuries.

Part 1 Inquiring into children's expressed needs: using creative means for encouraging 'expression'

Research into children's own voices regarding schooling is limited. Some adults believe that primary-aged children cannot give sensible answers to inform research. Others find it difficult to talk to children, taking a researcher capacity. Some people rely only on brief interview-style data collection among children, if they engage in it at all. Our own experience is that it takes teachers' creativity, as well as genuine curiosity, to engage children meaningfully in informing research. By research, we mean any data collection that is carried out systematically and with a research-informed theory behind it. This might be formal, or externally funded, research or teachers' own 'practitioner' research. In some ways, the class teacher is in the prime position to collect data by engaging with children in her/his class. In other ways, it may be difficult for the class teacher to switch from teacher to researcher, and this needs creativity and practice. In many cases, the difficulty is also switching from being a controlling, all-knowing adult to being a receptive, non-judgemental, listening inquirer.

In this section, we describe some practices we have engaged in through a formal, externally funded research project, in order to help children express their own feelings and thoughts about all aspects of learning at school. Through these means, we hope to understand better what makes them tick and helps them learn richly so that teaching be adapted appropriately. We also hope to inspire teachers to adapt some of these processes as part of their own teaching practices so that they can learn directly about children's expressed needs.

Children's life histories in primary schools: CLIPS project

In April 2018, a small research team (Eleanore Hargreaves, Laura Quick and Denise Buchanan) began a five-year research project funded by the Leverhulme Trust. We aimed to construct the life histories of 24 children who were in Year

3 (aged 7–8 years) at the start of the project. We chose children who had been identified by their school as attaining relatively poorly in maths and/or writing. Six pupils were chosen from each of four very different schools: two inner-city schools, one suburban and one rural. Our research questions were:

1. How do these primary school pupils experience school, in terms of their personal/social flourishing and their learning, across five years of their school life histories?
2. Which factors influence their experiences?

In order to feel that, as a research team, we were genuinely allowing the children to express themselves and their experiences of personal and social flourishing, we had to be creative in how we approached them. We tried to make the research environment friendly and of course it was always their free choice to come and talk to us. We gained the ethical clearance from teachers, parents and children themselves using the British Sociological Association's ethical guidelines.

Video recording a child in class and asking them to talk through the video

One method we used to understand the 24 children's experiences and needs was discreetly video recording each child in the classroom for a short while and then playing the video back to them afterwards and asking them to talk us through how they experienced the class. In the research literature, this is referred to as 'stimulated recall'. This was as close as we could get to climbing inside their heads during class. It led to some fascinating discoveries about what was going on. For example, one child, Eleanor, found it very difficult to confront the fact that she was struggling in class. *Despite clear video evidence*, she seemed to feel the need to defend herself:

> **Interviewer Laura:** Quite a lot of the time you were looking around and I was wondering how the work was for you … Your face is going like this [*copies the anxious face in the video*] … Yeah, I don't think you look very happy.
> **Eleanor:** I did look happy!
> **Interviewer Laura:** So, there's all those questions with people putting their hands up – you chose not to put your hand up then, can you explain to us?
> **Eleanor:** I did put my hand up!

Eleanor was not alone among the 24 children to try to maintain that all was well when, to us, it was clear that she was struggling. We theorised that perhaps this indicated the burden that some children were carrying around with them every day at school: *pretending* is tiring and takes energy away from other learning.

At the end of the first set of interviews with all 24 children, we decided that the creative and active aspects of our interviews had held the children's curiosity best. We decided to increase these in the next round in order to encourage our richest understanding of their experiences. And so we became more creative in our approaches. We talked to a play and drama therapist, Emily Barlow, for inspiration, and then used our own creativity and many years of experience working with children to craft active, enticing ways of supporting children to express themselves.

Reading quotes on individual coloured cards and asking children to sort them as 'yes', 'no' or 'don't know'

In our second round of interviews, in autumn 2018, we presented each individual child with 15 key quotes from the first round of interviews and asked them to place each one beside a label of 'yes', 'no' or 'don't know' (see Figure 7.2). We explained that real children in this project had said these things and that we were curious to know what they thought.

Figure 7.2 'Yes', 'No', 'Don't know' quotes, January 2019

For example, we offered them quotes such as 'I'm not one of the smart people in my class' and 'Everyone can be successful'. We read each of the 15 quotes out loud to the child. The participants enjoyed this game and it led to some valuable insights. For example, when presented with the quote, 'I'm not one of the smart people in my class', Jake responded, 'I'm a little bit smart'.

Interviewer Laura: What stuff are you smart at? Hard question – I know!
Jake: I don't know, but I'm a little bit smart … because I was just born, um, for – for being – being a little bit smart.
Interviewer Laura: You were just born being a little bit smart. And how do you know you're *not a lot smart*?
Jake: Because my brain is really big and it doesn't know anything.

Jake was a popular class character who was good at fixing computers. But he believed that his brain was empty of the necessary contents. This sense of not knowing *the right things* was a common theme among the children, even when they acknowledged their strengths in other areas. It was by definition a *deficit* model of learning. For example, several of the participants were very knowledgeable about animals and had studied their habits and habitats. However, such knowledge seemed inferior to what they learnt at school. For example, when asked to place the card 'Anyone can be successful', another child, Ben, placed it in the 'no' column. When asked whom he knew who could *not* be successful, he chose himself. He claimed that there were too many things that he did not know, despite his rich knowledge about animals in the Australian outback. He also mentioned that he lived in fear of walking past the head teacher's office, in case he was pulled in and told off for not doing well enough.

Inviting the child to draw facial expressions and put words into thought bubbles

We presented each child with the outline of a face and asked them to draw the facial expression of the child who got 'high marks' at school and the child who got 'low marks'. We then asked them to draw those children's teacher's expression. Because the children did not have to identify with the picture, they could express their true feelings more easily. Eleanor, who had earlier claimed always to be coping well and to be happy, drew a face of the child who achieves low marks. The loneliness, sadness and disappointment were tangible in Eleanor's picture (see Figure 7.3).

Figure 7.3 'The loneliness of the low-marks child', by Eleanor, October 2018

She explained:

Eleanor: This one's feeling really lonely.
Interviewer Laura: Lonely?
Eleanor: Lonely and sad and very disappointed. I think that's it.

The *isolation* of the 'low-marks child' became a theme we followed up with other children. We know that a sense of relatedness or belonging is essential for rich learning (Ryan & Deci, 2000). In a different exercise, we noted that one pupil, Jeff, described the 'friendship bench' in the playground as the place he felt most cared about because 'nice people' would come and ask him if he wanted to play with them.

Bearded Dragon (his own choice of pseudonym, because of his deep interest in lizards) portrayed the *teacher's view* of the low-attaining child (see Figure 7.4). The teacher he portrayed was saying, 'Stop it you stupid!' and she was so angry she had steam coming out of her ears.

Figure 7.4 'Stop it you stupid!', by Bearded Dragon, October 2018

One striking aspect of this portrayal was the fact that this child had probably never been spoken to harshly at school. He was given particular care and attention in fact, due to his difficulties with concentration. However, this seemed to be the meaning he made for himself about being someone who struggled with some school subjects.

Inviting children to imagine how others see them

We first asked children to represent themselves in plasticine, magnetic sticks, paint or felt-tip pens. Alternatively, they could choose one of our emojis or toy animals to represent them. For example, Anna chose a panda because she said, 'I'm a little bit spiteful'. This was the only time she referred to herself as anything other than funny and talented. Landon was keen to portray in detail his school crest, using plasticine (see Figure 7.5).

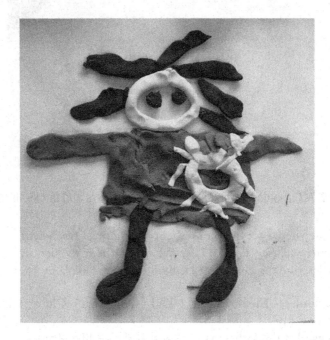

Figure 7.5 Plasticine self-portrait, by Landon, January 2019

Saffa was keen to include her Muslim identity in her painting by drawing herself in *hegab*. Jeff portrayed himself using magnetic sticks, holding a sword (to defend himself?) (see Figure 7.6).

Figure 7.6 Self-portrait magnet model with sword, by Jeff, January 2019

Figure 7.7 Cut-outs to represent children's teachers and family, January 2019

We prepared a set of coloured cut-out figures: teachers, family and friends of the participant (see Figure 7.7). We asked them to identify how each of these would describe the child. For example, Chrystal explained as follows.

> **Interviewer Eleanore:** If I said 'Oh, what's Chrystal like?' what would people say?
> **Chrystal:** I think they would say that she's – like – rude.
> **Interviewer Eleanore:** Rude? Yeah?
> **Chrystal:** Yeah, I'm not really rude, it's just that *I'm standing up for myself.*
> **Interviewer Eleanore:** Yes I see, I see yeah.
> **Chrystal:** And I think they would say I am kind of nice, like a nice girl, and I should be people's friend because of how nice I am. I think that's it.

Chrystal's need to stand up for herself, despite being a 'nice girl', indicated to us a struggle that was hard for her to describe directly. Later, she also depicted her teacher as calling her a very, very hard worker, again suggesting that Chrystal had some shame around her difficulties with concentration as well as difficulty with relationships. We know that some children find it harder to sit and 'concentrate' than others, but this knowledge is not always acted upon by the teacher. And research has consistently illustrated how damaging a sense of isolation, separateness and not fitting in can be for rich learning.

Inviting children to assess their relatedness to others

Because of the key place of good relationships for rich learning, we explored relatedness further. Using the same googly-eyed figures (see above), we invited each child to place their self-portrait or self-representation in the middle of a set of concentric circles on an A1 piece of cardboard, each circle getting further away from the child at the centre. We asked them to place each cut-out person on to the board, according to how close they felt to them (see Figure 7.8).

Figure 7.8 Arrangement of relatedness, January 2018

While some placed family and friends close, teachers tended to be further away. One child, however, did not place anyone close to himself, indicating the isolation or loneliness already highlighted (see Figure 7.9).

Figure 7.9 Arrangement of distant relatedness, January 2018

Asking children to take photos around the school to illustrate particular emotions

Most recently, drawing on Laura's interest in Boal's 'Theatre of the Oppressed', we asked some children to take a photo, using a mini iPad, of somewhere in school where they felt excited, bored, unhappy, anxious or cared for. Previous research has indicated that it is hard to learn richly when feeling bored, unhappy, uncared for or anxious. People learn best when they feel interested or excited about a topic (Moore, 2013). The range of responses was staggering, suggesting that school is a very different place for different children and recognising their social and emotional needs was a complex challenge. For example, Chrystal took her photo of the playground and explained it was where she felt unhappy because no one played with her. In contrast, Anna chose the playground as the place she felt most cared for – while her seat in the classroom made her feel stressed because the seat was too hard.

The place of excitement could be the child's place in class or in a particular subject such as hockey, clay modelling or computers; and some children showed us the most remote area of the playground, where wild bushes and grasses grew, as the most exciting place in school.

For boredom, the assembly hall was singled out a couple of times and Bella surprised us by saying that she was never bored at school. By giving the children the camera and letting them loose in school, we gained some illuminating insights to guide our future actions. We came to understand better how diversely people respond to similar environments. What may help one child's learning, may block another's.

Conclusion to Part 1

The thoughts in Part 1 are not based on any systematic analysis of our research data. They are presented only to illustrate some activities we created in order to better understand how children experience school – so that teachers could attune their teaching more finely to such children's needs. We are in the early stages of our five-year research project and we plan to keep devising more creative ways of illuminating children's experiences at school. Part 1 is intended to illustrate some of the issues that can be present when researching with primary children and some ways around these. So far we have learned that children competently provide sophisticated insights into their school experiences. We look forward to learning still more richly from them. To refer back to the quote by Chris Watkins (2015) at the start of this chapter, 'How do we come to know ourselves as learners? And how do we un-hide (i.e. dis-cover) the lives of learners in classrooms?' Our answer so far is inquiry, based on being curious and creative, to improve our own and our students' learning.

Part 2 Turning it inwards: teachers as learners

Earlier, it was suggested that in order for teachers to understand the needs of their pupils it was important for them to show equal levels of curiosity about their own experiences of learning. We gathered together the reflective writing of some MA students at the UCL Institute of Education. These were experienced teachers from a range of countries of the world. The essays and meta-learning journals of these postgraduate students on the Guiding Effective Learning and Teaching module highlight the impact that such a commitment to exploring one's own learning can have. In fact, one of the characteristics that defines these texts is the degree of affect they express (i.e. feelings, emotions). Often emerging as a sense of regret about previous practice as a teacher, these emotions are indicative of three things: (1) the high degree of relatedness felt by the students during this module (without which this degree of personal exposure would not be possible), (2) the connection between changes in understanding and changes in feeling and (3) the absolute centrality of emotions to the embedding of long-term change. There is little evidence here of changes in technique imposed from above or of superficial commitments to superficial ideas; the professional development experienced by these studying teachers is rooted in heartfelt values, curiosity and the will to be creative. As Shota, one student (and teacher from Japan), put it: 'I was able to feel the moment when my autonomy was facilitated by a variety of activities in the classroom. I strongly believe that such experience as a learner will tremendously influence my teaching in the future.'

The teaching that led to these developments embodied the principles mentioned in Part 1 of this chapter, as well as some new factors and approaches singled out by teachers as making an important contribution. These included the use of collaborative learning strategies to promote agency within a supportive climate, the provision of choice to balance inferred and expressed needs and the use of meta-cognitive strategies to develop self-regulation. It is also worth noting here that, in many instances, an increased sense of agency evolved into the critical creativity mentioned in our introduction.

In contrast to Eleanor, the pupil (described in Part 1) who felt it shameful to admit that all was not well, the teachers on the MA module openly expressed feelings of anxiety. However, this was not automatic. Drawing on Alex Moore's work, Tanvee (a teacher from India) wrote:

As I did not want to lose her [the teacher's] approval of me as a bright student, I just kept nodding to pretend that I understood. I struggled with the desire to be popular with my teacher, and peers, and I believed [that] to gain the love, affection, the acknowledgement of my teacher, I must conform to their image, which in turn must be my image, of the good (enthusiastic, academically able) student, by whatever means I can.

(Moore, 2013, p. 277)

For all its hard-won honesty, this description of uncovered emotions illustrates how difficult it is for teachers to gain access to the inner worlds of their students or for trainers to know how trainees are experiencing their learning. It is also a description that many of us know all too well as it is symptomatic of the cultures we have lived in during our schooling and professional lives. Plenty has been written about how cultures of high-stakes accountability create falsification and, in this instance, it is possible to recognise how these cultures create inauthenticity – it is through the fear of being compared with others and found wanting. This, in turn, is felt on a personal level as a loss of love, relatedness and even identity, which raises the stakes even further. In this way, these cultures set individual against individual, restrict autonomy and erode the possibility of creative risk-taking. This strong sense of normativity is also a barrier to critical creativity as the individual is caught up in a wholly one-sided power relationship. As Tanvee's words show, these responses can become so deeply embedded that they can become habitual and be carried forward into situations in which they are counterproductive.

Carol Dweck (2006) might also argue that this face saving is a characteristic of the fixed-mindset thinking that can be so destructive to learners. In her research, she argues that, where intelligence is seen as a series of skills that can be developed through effort, resilience in the face of challenge follows but, where intelligence is seen as a fixed given, resilience is weak and challenge is avoided (i.e. to admit to finding something difficult is to admit to being less than a genius, which must be avoided at all costs, even if it means avoiding the task entirely). In this way, all challenges to social standing and identity are also avoided. Fixed-mindset thinking also tends to express itself in competitiveness and face-saving behaviour as it draws its strength from a sense of innate superiority. For example, in the instance above, to admit to the need to learn is to admit to the possibility of being temporarily inferior and, therefore, becoming unworthy of social recognition. From this, it is tempting to speculate that one of the reasons that corporate accountability cultures stifle creativity is that fixed-mindset thinking is deeply embedded within them.

In the light of all this, it is remarkable that the teachers on the course managed to move beyond the constraints they brought into the classroom. A key factor identified in many of the texts was the use of collaborative learning strategies such as 'diamond nine' sorting activities and jigsawing – a range of similar strategies can be found in the Northern Ireland Curriculum's 'Active Learning' resource books. As several students pointed out, these approaches were seen to contribute to a sense of connectedness, especially when groupings were sensitively thought out. As Shota observed, choosing to sit beside a familiar face allowed him to feel relaxed and to seek help when needed, but it was also felt to limit the range of perspectives that he was exposed to. Groupings arranged around choices of review articles or pedagogic themes allowed increased relatedness within the group and exposure to more varied points of view. Shota also noted the importance of group sizes, commenting that:

If the number of people in one group was ... three, including me, I would tend to actively engage with the discussion ... because I was feeling a responsibility for making the discussion valuable in cooperation with others.

In contrast, within larger groups, he noted that he tended to rely more on others' input and that, in this situation, 'my listening was also less effective ... because I was not expected to respond to someone's idea'. However, if working in a pair, to avoid conflict he would tend to agree with his partner's opinions, making the discussion 'superficial'. This self-analysis is useful in that it is as applicable to adult learning as it is to children and it provides one of many instances where insight from learning may be carried over into practice. It could be said that these experiences may help with the future identification of pupils' unexpressed needs. It is also worth adding that these small, fluid groupings can alleviate the peer pressure that causes face-saving behaviour while also strengthening relationships that are supportive of learning. As several students stated, fluid groupings also allow tentative, risky ideas to be tested in a safe context. In this way, they encourage independence and allow for the rehearsal and filtering of contributions to more public discussions.

The pieces of MA writing illustrated that student choice played a large part in the development of agency within the group. Although the course had confines (as all courses must) there was a wide range of focus areas on offer, all of which were modelled through the teaching itself. This last point must be stressed as it is a point that many in tertiary education and CPD provision do not seem to grasp. Within the accountability culture, teachers work to extremely tight requirements. For instance, Fumiko (another teacher originally from Japan) describes how, prior to undertaking her studies, her entire understanding of quality of teaching was drawn from extrapolations of the Ofsted descriptors of effective teaching. Again, this is a very common experience within the profession and one of its effects is that the criticality that teachers work within tends to be used to evaluate others. Therefore, if they participate in professional development that is transmissive in nature, they inevitably question the credibility of those delivering the training. To put it bluntly, teachers are required to perform at very high levels and they expect those who advise them to do likewise – for many teachers, a *lecture* on effective education is oxymoronic. As the teaching on the MA module, however, was conveyed through a range of promoted techniques, it had credibility enough to convince and also demonstrated how the lived experience of participating in learning is always superior to being a passive recipient of it. Reading the texts produced by the students, it is very clear that the high levels of interactivity during the module produced a wider range of emotions than any passive experience might have. It could also be argued that it is this engagement at an emotional level that secures these students' commitment to long-term change. While the provision of choice from within the module curriculum (with specialised reading lists for independent study) encouraged students to follow their curiosity, it appears likely that engagement with the ideas at an emotional level added the passion required to transfer theory into future practice. It is also worth bearing in mind that it is easier to recognise unexpressed needs in others if they have been felt first-hand.

For many of the teachers, their first real encounter with meta-learning (or metacognition) was when they were asked to create a metaphor that expressed what they are like when they are learning effectively, an idea drawn from Sarah Nixon (2013).

Figure 7.10 'A blood-hound, scenting, hunting and capturing ideas. It takes time! I don't give up. I close in on my ideas and pin them down!' by MA student, Nic, November 2017

For example, MA student Nic described herself when learning at her best, as like 'a blood-hound, scenting, hunting and capturing ideas. It takes time! I don't give up. I close in on my ideas and pin them down!' (see Figure 7.10). In line with Chris Watkins's ideas, these metaphors allowed the students to start developing a narrative awareness of their own learning by encouraging them to think about the conditions in which it thrives. It is also significant that these descriptions were expressed in the students' own terms, allowing for accurate, individualised expressions. The discussion of the metaphors uncovered expressed needs and also allowed students to recognise elements of their own learning that they had not been aware of. Again, the honesty called for assisted in the creation of a warm, supportive, growth-mindset climate; it is difficult to persist with a façade if the rest of the group are being open about their own shortcomings.

Subsequent sessions saw the introduction of private meta-learning journals (in which students recorded their experiences of feeling, learning and interacting).

Fumiko's reported that 'initially I thought it would feel like self-assessment, but it did not have the feature of judgement, and therefore it motivated me to keep recording my learning'. This sense of ownership extended into the assessment process itself, with students providing peer feedback on essay drafts and co-constructing success criteria for their essay submissions. Several students noted that this refocused attention away from final grades and on to the process of learning itself, neatly inverting the accountability system's means–ends hier-archy and focusing on the autotelic value of learning. This sits equally well within Carol Dweck's research as grade-centred thinking is another character-istic of fixed mindsets: to refocus on the process of developing understanding is to emphasise that 'intelligence' is an acquired set of skills rather than a birthright.

Conclusion to Part 2

While this combination of effective unearthing and addressing of needs, pro-motion of agency and meta-learning laid the foundations for expressions of curiosity and creativity, it also opened doors into wider social issues. As stated earlier, creativity in itself can be read as having an essentially critical core and it is interesting to note that this MA module encouraged many of us to look closely at the reasons why so many children experience education as a series of acts of stifling denial. In a sequence of moving interviews with pupils in India, teacher and MA student Vignesh described the unforeseen outcomes of a well-intended governmental policy that left disadvantaged pupils alienated and, at times, open to violence, symbolic or otherwise. As one child, Gaurav, observed: 'I think the problem exists everywhere. You get shouted at in the house, sometimes by your friends outside the school and every day by your teachers.' In tracking outwards from the expressed needs of these children, Vignesh identified the role schools play in modelling violent interactions for children and the tendency for idealistic trainee teachers to become inducted into this culture against their better instincts. It is in this increased ability to see social forces played out within the classroom that many of us have discovered a convergence of curiosity, need and creativity, and this is a great gift to take back into educational institutions. The alternative, as Tanvee describes it, is 'an endless loop … in which students are no longer interested in what is being taught, and educators need to superficially control students to ensure learning occurs'. Whose needs can that serve?

Summary

We hope that this chapter has illustrated some potential areas through which teachers and researchers (as well as teachers as researchers) can draw on their own curiosity and creativity in order to become more supportive – and more ful-filled – in their role as educators of children. We have suggested that the nurturing of curiosity and creativity, in collaboration with others, needs to be given pride of place among purposes for children's school learning. We have also illustrated some strategies for exercising curiosity and creativity in inquiring into children's learning needs – including all the social and emotional aspects that underpin these and deeply influence cognitive functioning.

We have also explored what happens to teachers when they feel constrained: their learning can be stifled, deprived of the curiosity and cre-ativity it needs to flourish. In turn, this hinders the development of supportive and transformative teaching. We have illustrated that teachers' effective CPD is fuelled when teachers use their curiosity and creativity in order to develop pro-fessionally by examining and monitoring – in a creative way – the social, emo-tional and cognitive aspects of their own learning, as well as their pupils'. They can examine learning within the professional context or from outside, but the ultimate aim is to use this curiosity and creativity to 'dis-cover' or 'un-hide' what makes each individual learn richly in order to flourish. Look no further: profes-sional development starts here.

Note

1   We are hugely grateful to all the pupils who are taking part in the CLIPS project and their teachers and parents who are facilitating this. Thank you so much to Laura Quick and Denise Buchanan for their input into the CLIPS research and this chapter. Thanks also to teachers Fumiko, Nic, Shota, Tanvee and Vignesh who allowed us to use their MA writing as part of this chapter.

References

Csikszentmihalyi, M. (1996). *Creativity: The work and lives of 91 eminent people*. New York, NY: HarperCollins.

Dweck, C. (2012). *Mindset: Changing the way you think to fulfil your potential*. London: Hachette.

Fisher, H. (2011). Inside the primary classroom: Examples of dissatisfaction behind a veil of compliance. *British Journal of Educational Studies, 59*(2), 121–141.

Hargreaves, E., & Elhawary, D. (2019). Professional development through mutually respectful relationship: Senior teachers' learning against the backdrop of hierarchical relationships. *Professional Development in Education, 45*(1), 46–58.

Moore, A. (2013). Love and fear in the classroom: How 'validating affect' might help us understand young students and improve their experiences of school life and learning. In M. O'Loughlin (Ed.), *The uses of psychoanalysis in working with children's emotional lives* (pp. 285–304). Lanham, MD: Rowman & Littlefield.

Nixon, S. (2013). Using metaphors to aid student meta-learning: When you're learning at your best your like what? *Creative Education*, *4*(7), 32.

Noddings, N. (2005). Identifying and responding to needs in education. *Cambridge Journal of Education*, *35*(2), 147–159.

Ryan, R. M., & Deci, E. L. (2000). Self-determination theory and the facilitation of intrinsic motivation, social development, and well-being. *American Psychologist*, *55*(1), 68.

Watkins, C. (2015). Metalearning in classrooms. In D. Scott & E. Hargreaves (Eds.), *The Sage handbook of learning* (pp. 321–30). London: Sage.

8

Teachers as 'natural experimenters': using T-SEDA to develop classroom dialogue

Ruth Kershner, Kate Dowdall, Sara Hennessy, Hannah Owen and Elisa Calcagni

Introduction

Teachers have long been encouraged to use and apply research in their professional development, and the 'teacher as researcher' notion has gathered momentum over more than four decades. In this chapter, we write about a professional development approach that involves embedding teacher inquiry in day-to-day practice within a context of whole-school development. The central focus for teachers is on the investigation and enhancement of classroom dialogue between teachers and pupils. Productive classroom dialogue involves participants in critically and respectfully taking account of others' perspectives in constructing knowledge together (Kim & Wilkinson, 2019; Mercer, 2000). Teachers are encouraged to create a supportive classroom ethos and opportunities for multiple students to participate in classroom activity and learn together. In the past, this dialogic approach has rarely been observed in classrooms, despite increasing evidence of its association with student learning and attitudinal outcomes (Alexander, Hardman, Hardman, Rajab, & Longmore, 2017; Howe, Hennessy, Mercer, Vrikki, & Wheatley, 2019). However, there is growing interest in developing dialogic pedagogy among practitioners and educational researchers.

The inquiry at the centre of this chapter took place in one primary school in eastern England. It was undertaken by a Year 6 teacher (Kate Dowdall) with the support of her professional development leader who took a wider whole-school development perspective (Hannah Owen, deputy head teacher). Kate's inquiry involved the use of an extensive, research-informed professional development resource called the Teacher Scheme for Educational Dialogue Analysis (T-SEDA). T-SEDA was developed in the Cambridge Educational Dialogue Research (CEDiR) group of the University of Cambridge Faculty of Education, by a team including the three other authors of this chapter (Sara Hennessy, Ruth Kershner and Elisa Calcagni).

After outlining T-SEDA in the next section, we then look in detail at Kate's T-SEDA inquiry. This took place in guiding reading lessons that she audio recorded and coded classroom dialogue using T-SEDA, taking a critical and reflective analytical approach to her own role. Her strategies included use of talking points, ground rules, sentence stems, 'think, pair, share' and withholding evaluation, as explained later. These led to students giving lengthy and well-justified opinions about a text, building on others' ideas, challenging and agreeing with each other during rich discussions – all key elements of productive dialogue and learning. Kate's inquiry was one of several dialogue-focused inquiries that took place across the school, facilitated by Hannah in her role as deputy head. During the previous year, Hannah had aimed to develop more dialogic approaches in all year groups and she had taken steps to engage teachers in using inquiry for their own professional development. So the T-SEDA project fitted well with what Hannah already had in mind for school development. In the final section of this chapter, we draw on a discussion that took place after Kate's inquiry had finished with a view to writing this chapter collaboratively. This dialogue allowed us to share our different perspectives on how the use of T-SEDA worked in this school context and the general issues it raises about linking research and practice. In our conclusion, we reflect on the role of T-SEDA in potentially supporting the development of an 'inquiry stance' by teachers that lies at the core of effective professional learning, valuing teachers as 'natural experimenters' in practice.

The Teacher Scheme for Educational Dialogue Analysis (T-SEDA)

The Teacher Scheme for Educational Dialogue Analysis (T-SEDA) focuses on key features of classroom dialogue, highlighting those that are known to be productive for learning and sharing them in an accessible format. It is intended to provide a highly flexible, research-informed tool for teachers and teacher educators to actively engage with, and lead, professional development that is driven by teachers' reflective inquiries into their own practice. The main T-SEDA resource pack includes a self-audit, a dialogue coding framework, inquiry planning templates, systematic live observation tools, case studies and video exemplars; it is freely downloadable from the website at http://bit.ly/T-SEDA, along with editable templates. The three tools at the heart of the T-SEDA pack are depicted in Figure 8.1.

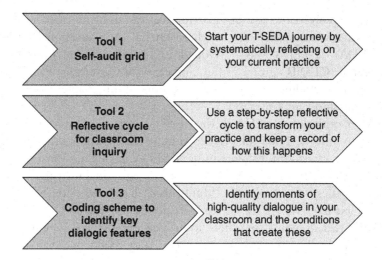

Figure 8.1 Three core T-SEDA tools

While the self-audit and the reflective cycle for inquiry may be fairly familiar parts of practitioner action research, the T-SEDA approach has a distinctive element in the focus on systematic observation and coding of classroom dialogue. The coding scheme is given in Table 8.1. This research-based scheme is adapted from an earlier, more fine-grained tool called SEDA (Hennessy et al., 2016). It draws attention to the different ways in which teachers and pupils may contribute to spoken dialogue. These 'talk moves' are signs that dialogue is developing in ways that are likely to be productive for learning. For instance, it was found in a recent study by Howe et al. (2019) that learning gains in Year 6 (ages 10–11) were associated with talk in which contributors built on each other's ideas (code B) and challenged other speakers' views respectfully (code CH). This research also showed that this sort of productive dialogue was strongly linked to active pupil participation, which is supported by the explicit use of ground rules for talk, as negotiated with pupils (Mercer, 2000).

Table 8.1 Coding scheme for classroom dialogue

Dialogue categories	Contributions and strategies	What do we hear? (key words)
IB – invite to build on ideas	Invite others to elaborate, build on, clarify, comment on or improve own or others' ideas/ contributions	Can you add What? Tell me Can you rephrase this? Do you think? Do you agree?

Table 8.1 Cont.

Dialogue categories	Contributions and strategies	What do we hear? (key words)
B – build on ideas	Build on, elaborate, clarify or comment on own or others' ideas expressed in previous turns or other contributions	It's also That makes me think I mean She meant
CH – challenge	Questioning, disagreeing with or challenging an idea	I disagree But Are you sure? … different idea
IRE – invite reasoning	Invite others to explain, justify, and/or use possibility thinking relating to their own or another's ideas	Why? How? Do you think … ? Explain further
R – make reasoning explicit	Explain, justify and/or use possibility thinking relating to own or another's ideas	I think Because So Therefore In order to If … then It's like … Imagine if … Could
CA – coordination of ideas and agreement	Contrast and synthesise ideas, confirm agreement and consensus; invite coordination/synthesis	Agree To sum up … So, we all think that … Summarise Similar and different
C – connect	Make pathway of learning explicit by linking to contributions/knowledge/experiences beyond the immediate dialogue	Last lesson Earlier Reminds me of Next lesson Related to In your home
RD – reflect on dialogue or activity	Evaluate or reflect 'metacognitively' on processes of dialogue or learning activity; invite others to do so	Dialogue Talking Sharing Work together in the group/pair Task Activity What you have learned I changed my mind

(continued)

Table 8.1 Cont.

Dialogue categories	Contributions and strategies	What do we hear? (key words)
G – guide direction of dialogue or activity	Take responsibility for shaping activity or focusing the dialogue in a desired direction or use other scaffolding strategies to support dialogue or learning	How about Focus Concentrate on Let's try No hurry Have you thought about … ?
E – express or invite ideas	Offer or invite relevant contributions to initiate or further a dialogue (ones not covered by other categories)	What do you think about … ? Tell me Your thoughts My opinion is … Your ideas

Another key feature of the T-SEDA approach is that users choose their own inquiry focus and appropriate tools and ways to explore it, adapting the approach to their own settings and prior knowledge about dialogue (see Figure 8.2). So T-SEDA does not offer a fixed programme of intervention or a 'recipe' for dialogic pedagogy. It is academic and research-informed but actively practitioner-led. The T-SEDA pack has itself been developed in response to feedback from teachers. This is ongoing; indeed, at the time of writing in June 2019 it had reached Version 7c.

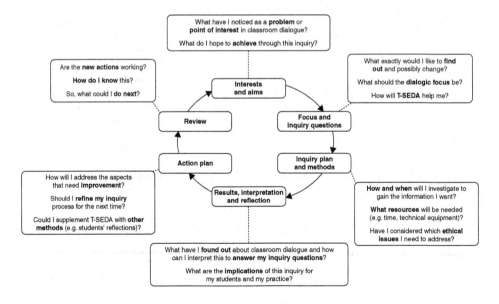

Figure 8.2 The reflective cycle for classroom inquiry

T-SEDA was designed to be relevant to teachers in any phase of education with application in any curriculum area. During 2018–2019 T-SEDA was trialled by 81 practitioners in seven countries (England, New Zealand, Israel, Mexico, Spain, Pakistan, Hong Kong), spanning early years to postgraduate students. This trial indicated that T-SEDA has a wide range of possible uses in diverse educational contexts. It proved to have distinctive potential for helping teachers to tune into classroom talk by undertaking detailed and systematic analysis of the quality of classroom dialogue and its impact on learning. Evidence from pre- and post-inquiry surveys, lesson video recordings, teacher reports and interviews, including individual teacher case studies, showed that significant, concrete changes in practice took place: dialogic activities and strategies were formulated, 'talk rules' were generated and used and students engaged more with their classmates' ideas. The trial helped us to identify several ways in which academic–practitioner research partnerships developed in different contexts, including school networks and in-service courses in higher education as well as the in-house teacher professional development initiated by school leadership that we are writing about in this chapter. In most cases, we found that local facilitators and research leaders held a crucial role in enabling practitioners to work productively with the T-SEDA materials, selecting and adapting tools as appropriate for their own purposes and contexts. Facilitators took on an important translating and brokering role between different stakeholders, resolving tensions such as managing conflicting aims and expectations. Reports and other feedback from teachers and facilitators contributed directly to our growing knowledge about dialogic pedagogy, manifesting the two-way dialogic approach for building knowledge between practitioners and researchers that was embedded in the original T-SEDA design. In the next section we expand on this experience of using T-SEDA from practitioner perspectives.

Using T-SEDA in practice: teacher inquiry in the context of whole-school development

In this section we present Kate's case example, looking closely at what she did with T-SEDA. Kate's inquiry was supported by her deputy head teacher, Hannah, in her role as professional development leader with a wider whole-school development perspective. The setting is an urban primary school where over a third of pupils are eligible for additional funding for disadvantaged pupils. Hannah gives her perspective first, then Kate describes her project.

Hannah

In Summer 2015, our school was defined as 'coasting' according to government metrics. Improving the quality of teaching and learning was imperative but rather than snatching at quick fixes, as senior leaders, we were keen to develop an approach that would be sustainable over time and outlast changes in personnel.

Therefore, we sought research-based solutions to the various areas for development that we identified.

Investment in teacher learning was essential in order to raise pupil outcomes and over the years has taken many different forms, including traditional professional development courses, coaching and mentoring and support from external consultants. We have committed to providing an ongoing programme of professional learning activities that staff can engage with and that will support them to reflect upon and develop their own practice. We have also been continually seeking to develop a culture within the school of 'continuous improvement' and encourage teachers to take risks, seek and try out new ideas and strategies and discuss their own work openly so that they feel confident to collaborate with and learn from each other.

However, my own personal research into teacher learning, undertaken for my master's qualification, has highlighted the need for professional development that not only gives teachers a range of ideas and experiences but also the opportunity to develop their skills for systematically and critically examining their practice (Cordingley et al. 2015; Kazemi & Hubbard, 2008; Opfer & Pedder, 2010; Pedder, 2006). Being 'natural experimenters' requires teachers to move beyond reflecting on their past and current practice and to develop a 'critical mindset' that weighs up the benefits of alternative approaches and uses the evidence collected to think reflectively and reflexively about the consequences of particular choices.

As a school, we have adopted a layered approach to identifying and meeting professional development needs. First of all, quality assurance practices by senior and middle leadership across the school highlight areas of development that need to be addressed. The quality of classroom talk was one such area identified in this way. Over time, as senior leaders, we had become aware that while talk was being promoted in the classroom as an instrument for learning, it was not always being implemented as effectively as it could be. Although the idea of 'dialogic talk' had been introduced as part of our professional development conversations around the teaching of reading, through further discussion with teachers, it became evident that there was a lack of clarity about what constituted good quality classroom dialogue and how it could be promoted effectively across the curriculum and school.

Having pinpointed a particular need, the senior leadership team normally reflect on the possible options for bringing about change. These options can include the following:

- A *'blanket' approach* in which all staff engage with a series of development activities to discuss the modifications that we need to make to our practice across the school.
- An *optional approach* in which we offer developmental activities that staff can opt into, with a view to personalising their professional development and so allow them to follow their own interests.
- A *directed approach* in which we work with particular teachers and provide them with opportunities for specific developmental support through coaching and mentoring.

As we were discussing our options, we were alerted to the T-SEDA impact trial that was being conducted by the CEDiR group at the Faculty of Education. The invitation we were sent invited us to participate in a 'teacher-led inquiry' on the quality of dialogue in the classroom. I had become aware of the work of this particular research group and knew that the focus of the project aligned with the needs that we had identified. In addition, the focus on 'teacher-led inquiry' also promoted the systematic and critical examination of ideas that we valued as an important part of teacher learning.

However, while we felt that engagement in the project would be beneficial for all, we were aware that additional expectations might possibly be placed on teachers through their participation in the project. As a result, we decided that an optional approach would be best and advertised the opportunity to all staff yet with no expectation of their involvement. When eight teachers expressed an interest, we discussed with Sara and Ruth the possibility of conducting a workshop in school as part of a school in-service training (INSET). We requested that part of this workshop be open to all teachers, so that they could all be introduced to the principles of dialogic talk. We felt that this would raise the profile of classroom talk across the school and develop a school-wide understanding that would, in turn, support the transfer of knowledge from individual inquiries to whole-school practice.

Kate

After attending Ruth's T-SEDA workshop on dialogic talk, I was very interested in the opportunity to be involved in the development of this teaching strategy in our school and was keen to be a case study. Initially, my inquiry centred around students developing their discussion skills by encouraging them to question and challenge each other's ideas to make their reasoning clear. First, I tried a few discussion activities in which my children were encouraged to use question stems such as, 'Can you … ?' 'What if … ?' 'Why … ?' in order to probe each other's thinking to draw out their reasoning. However, it soon became apparent to me that the children in my class found it hard to take on the questioner role. This led me to think that the children were still at the stage of needing an adult to support and guide them to deepen discussions during dialogic talk.

As the year progressed, I became further interested in the impact that using dialogic talk in the classroom could have on outcomes in English and in particular, guiding reading. As the school English leader, I had been developing whole-class reading, focusing specifically on the reading skills that the children needed to acquire and develop in Key Stage 2 (ages 7–11); dialogic talk seemed to complement what we were trying to achieve in this subject in order to raise standards. I particularly felt that dialogic talk really supported the development of student's inference-making skills, allowing them to become better at justifying their opinions and ideas about a text by referring to evidence. Dialogic talk also provided the students in my class with the time and space to discuss and develop their opinions of a text before engaging in written work.

A verse from 'The Highwayman' by Alfred Noyes

Dark in the dark old inn-yard a stable-wicket creaked
Where Tim, the ostler, listened – his face was white and peaked
His eyes were hollows of madness, his hair like mouldy hay,
But he loved the landlord's daughter
The landlord's black-eyed daughter;
Dumb as a dog he listened, and he heard the robber say:

Following the workshop, I identified several strategies that I was keen to trial. One of these was using 'talking point' statements as a stimulus for dialogic talk as I felt this would work well in the English context with my own class. I implemented this into a plenary for an English lesson on Alfred Noyes's poem, 'The Highwayman'. In this lesson we focused on the verse about Tim the Ostler: we inferred that he was the person who alerted the red coats to the fact that the highwayman could be found at the inn. We looked at various visual representations of Tim the Ostler and discussed his character and other character's opinions of him in the story before launching into a plenary class discussion about the statement 'Tim the Ostler is an evil character', which I recorded. Figure 8.3 illustrates some of these discussions.

Next we worked in pairs to think about Tim's feelings at different points in the story and how other characters' might treat Tim both before and after Bess's death.

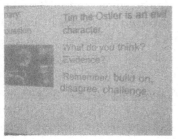

Finally we had an in-depth class discussion about the statement:

Tim the Ostler is an evil character.

We built on each other's ideas, disagreed respectably and even challenged each other's views.

Figure 8.3 Photos documenting dialogue around the character of Tim the Ostler

After the lesson I transcribed and coded this discussion (see Table 8.2). Through this process, I found that students were making good use of the sentence stems I gave them to discuss the statement, and were able to provide justifications when prompted. Students were engaged and eager to take part. Some children with additional needs who were usually reluctant writers, took important roles in the discussion (Callum, David and Cory in this transcript).

Table 8.2 Discussion about Tim the Ostler's character

Line no.	Speaker	Code (see Table 8.1)	Turn
1.	T		So my statement is 'Tim the Ostler is an evil character'. What do you think? Why do you think that? Do you agree with everybody? Let's start over here with S1.
2.	Callum	CH	I would like to challenge you because um Tim is just jealous and um sad and that can make you grumpy and when you're sad and jealous all it does is fill your mind with um grief and so you can't think about anything else but what you want – so it's not necessarily evil.
3.	David	B	I agree with Callum because like I don't think he's an evil character I just think jealousy took over his mind and he just really wanted Bess for himself.
4.	T	IB	Ok so you don't think he is evil you just think the jealousy has warped his mind. I like that idea. Anybody want to build on or challenge that?
5.	Cory	CH	I disagree because I think Tim is an evil character because he put the girl that he loved in danger and he could (1) lose his job and (2) he could never see the woman that he loves again.
6.	T	CI	So you think he actually is evil because what he's done has actually put Bess in danger and that's the woman he is supposed to love.
7.	David	CH	I challenge you because um well I don't think he didn't actually know that Bess was going to get hurt or killed or anything so I have to disagree.
8.	T		OK so you think he did that without having any knowledge that that was going to happen. I like this conversation.

I was pleased by how the students were usually able to give lengthy and well-justified opinions about the text, challenging and agreeing with each other. Although I was involved in the discussion, I tried to refrain from giving my own opinions (withholding evaluation) and took the role of the questioner, encouraging the children to justify their opinions. It was interesting to note how one vocal student, after listening to others' ideas, was able to acknowledge a shift in his own opinion about the character, showing how dialogic talk encourages children to really listen to each other as well as share their own thoughts:

> **Callum:** I've changed my mind because everyone who is saying Tim the Ostler is evil is persuading me because he did put his – the person he loved – in danger and if he did truly love Bess, he would have left her and he may have known how horrible the red coats may have been because he may have seen them in action before.

Taking part in the T-SEDA enquiry powerfully supported me to reflect on and change the role I take in classroom dialogue; it moved me to better allow children to develop the discussion through expressing their opinions and thoughts without my intervention. Furthermore, anlaysing children's written responses to inference-type questions suggested that the dialogic talk had had a positive impact on their understanding of texts. I particularly noted a correlation between children's developing inference skills and their ability to answer comprehension questions using evidence from the text, their written responses appearing to echo the preceding classroom talk. Figure 8.4 gives one example of a child's increased ability to write justifications in a clear and concise way developed through the use of high-quality dialogic talk in guiding reading lessons.

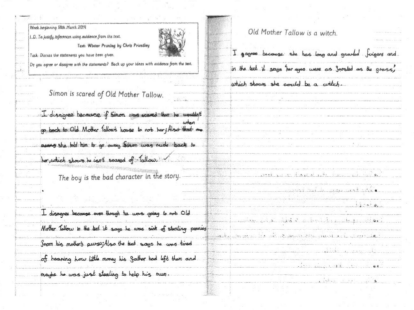

Figure 8.4 Example of written outcome in a child's guiding reading journal

This particular lesson was videoed and the faculty research team compared it to another I had taught earlier in the year, before encountering T-SEDA. Elisa led this process, outlined in Figure 8.5.

Video rating process
I divided the lessons into shorter activity segments. I rated each segment using the four criteria explained below, assigning a 1 or a 0 and adding them up for a maximum aggregate rating of 4

1. Pupils' lengthy contributions
At least two students take turns of seven or more words

3. Teacher using dialogic categories
The teacher uses one or more of the T-SEDA dialogue categories, excluding 'G' and 'E'

2. Pupils' engagement with other's ideas
At least two students engage with other's ideas by building, challenging or asking questions

4. Teacher guiding dialogue
The teacher actively shapes the form or contents of dialogue by giving directions or feedback

Figure 8.5 Elisa's account of her video analysis rating of classroom dialogue

The proportion of lesson time with different ratings was compared pre- and post-inquiry using ELAN software (ELAN, 2018), to assess whether dialogic segments (rated 2 and above) had increased. As shown in Figure 8.6, 75 per cent of the initial lesson time had low levels of dialogue, which fell to only 35 per cent in the final lesson. This was in comparison to the final lesson where around a third of the time was considered to have dialogue of 'medium' quality and another third was considered 'high' quality. This increase related to the number of lesson segments that were rated positively under criteria (1), (2) and (3) but not under (4), i.e. the dialogic talk increased with a reduced amount of teacher guidance.

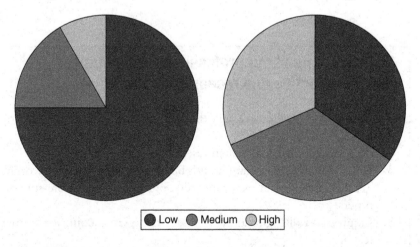

Low   Medium   High

Figure 8.6 Proportion of lesson time with different levels of dialogue from initial (left) to final lesson (right)

It appeared that the areas of focus – 'talking points', ground rules for talk and use of sentence stems such as 'I disagree … ' – proved very fruitful. Observers noted in the videos a shift in the classroom dialogue norms from short answers to discussions in pairs followed by whole-class discussion segments where students gave lengthy and well-justified answers, building on and challenging each other's ideas. The latter was especially rare in the initial lesson, indicating that students were taking on the new practices and ultimately able to successfully contribute to rich discussions.[1]

Thinking together about supporting and valuing teachers as 'natural experimenters'

To reflect further on Kate's inquiry, and with reference to Hannah's perspective as a senior leader, we now draw on a dialogue between four of the authors of this chapter about how T-SEDA worked in this school context and the wider lessons that might be drawn from this experience. To structure this discussion, we used the 'talking points' method, as already referred to by Kate. Dawes's (2012, p. 1) explanation of talking points illustrates why this approach seemed so suitable for our own purposes, bringing together our different perspectives:

Talking points are statements that encourage children to talk to one another about a topic, sharing what they know and understand … They help children to focus on the topic in hand, and to compare their point of view with that of others … The statements might be right or wrong; they might suggest interesting or unusual ideas, or simply stimulate discussion that will elicit children's current thinking … Talking points are not questions. They require creative, analytical or evaluative thinking; they require children to provide reasons for what they say.

Talking points about professional development, dialogic practice and research partnerships

1. Schools and teachers are very different in their professional development needs.
2. There's a big divide between research and practice.
3. Research partnerships are useful, but they add to teachers' workloads.
4. Teachers are natural experimenters, but some need more support than others.
5. Inquiry and dialogue are two sides of the same coin, for learners and teachers.

6. Systematic observation of classroom dialogue calls on teachers to learn and apply new skills.
7. Teachers' professional development doesn't work without a whole-school approach.
8. It is difficult to translate research into practice.
9. The most effective forms of professional development are ...
10. Collaboration can be useful, although professional development works very well when teachers work individually.
11. It requires a school-wide effort with all involved for teaching to become more dialogic.

Opening up this conversation about professional development, dialogic practice and research partnerships enabled us to reflect together on T-SEDA with our multiple perspectives on research and practice. Analysing the transcript of this discussion then helped us to identify some key aspects of what is involved in supporting and valuing teachers as 'natural experimenters' in developing classroom dialogue, as seen in the extracts that follow (with key ideas in italics):

Extract A: creating conditions for teacher experimentation: using tools and sharing ideas.
Extract B: identifying and embedding dialogic talk.
Extract C: increasing awareness of dialogue through engagement with systematic observation and coding.
Extract D: perspectives on research partnership and collaborative professional learning.

Extract A highlights an idea at the centre of this chapter: teachers as 'natural experimenters'. The discussion also raises three key elements involved in supporting teacher experimentation: the professional conditions that make purposeful experimentation possible, the tools that can be used in experimentation and the importance for teachers of having opportunities to share ideas that can guide experimentation.

Extract A Creating conditions for teacher experimentation: using tools and sharing ideas

Ruth: I think it was you, Hannah, who came up with the phrase 'teachers are natural experimenters', which we immediately grabbed and made the title of our chapter.

Hannah: Yes. That is what I said I wanted.

> **Ruth:** That is what you wanted. So, that is something to grab on to.
>
> **Hannah:** Teachers to be natural experimenters. That is the approach I want teachers to have.
>
> **Ruth:** But that means you have got to create the conditions in which teachers can follow their inclination.
>
> **Hannah:** Yes.
>
> **Kate:** I think I agree with Hannah. *There is that element of experimenting as a teacher: you want to try new things out, but I think, also, you need to get ideas as well and then experiment with ideas and twist them and turn them and use them in ways, in your own class, perhaps, that they haven't been used before. So, I think the sharing is actually massively important towards teachers then having ideas to go and experiment with.* Does that make sense?
>
> **Ruth:** Absolutely.
>
> **Hannah:** So, then, in that respect, the T-SEDA worked, because, actually, that gave us the tool and the ideas for us to then go and experiment with.

In Extract B we see how the use of tools, like systematic observation and coding, can help to clarify the focus and goals of inquiry: experimentation needs clear identification of what we are looking for in classroom dialogue and how we know whether changes have happened. This is important, also, in seeing whether children are generalising their learning to other contexts (such as in art with Hannah) and, as Kate says, beginning to 'do it naturally'.

> ## Extract B Identifying and embedding dialogic talk
>
> **Hannah**: Yes. I am using the T-SEDA within lesson study … I am coding my teacher transcript using the T-SEDA coding, to see whether their talk is dialogic as well.
>
> **Sara**: Wow! That is great.
>
> **Ruth**: Great!
>
> **Hannah**: But, what has been really interesting, I think, for me, was having that coding meant you understood what was meant to be, what you would consider as part of classroom dialogue to be dialogic and what you wouldn't, because *I think that we all know that talk goes on in our classrooms, but actually knowing which of the bits that I really want to be promoting, as opposed to the bits that actually aren't going to be as useful for the children's learning, is actually quite a good thing to open people's eyes to. And I think the coding, particularly the sentence stems with that, helped as well.*
>
> **Kate**: Yes, the sentence stems are brilliant.
>
> …

Kate: I put them on my interactive whiteboard and we talk about them, but they kind of know them, to be honest, now. So, it is quite, I suppose, embedded.

Hannah: It is, because I did art in your class the other day. I asked them: 'What is art?'

Kate: Oh yes.

Hannah: And I gave them loads of pictures, and then said, 'So, tell me, what is it?' and then we were having this big conversation about it, and they were like, 'But I'd like to just build on what So-and-so was saying.'

Kate: They do it just naturally.

Hannah: Yes.

Kate: And that is really good. What I like about it is because they are actually listening to each other, which, I think, with a lot of classroom dialogue, the children just want to tell you. And this is definitely lower down, when you are teaching infants [ages 4–7], they just want to tell you what they know because they just all want your attention. But, for them to be able to take part in dialogic talk, they almost have to listen to the other person, otherwise they can't participate. So, it forces them to listen.

Extract C goes further in reflecting on systematic observation, and the skills required in this approach. The discussion develops towards consideration of the potential effects of systematic observation in 'stopping time' and increasing awareness of the signs of productive dialogue.

Extract C Increasing awareness of dialogue through engagement with systematic observation and coding

Kate: Let me have a look. What about: 'systematic observation of classroom dialogue calls on teachers to learn and apply new skills'?

Ruth: OK, there we are. Right. Sara, what do you think?

Sara: I am all for systematic observation. I like the notion of being systematic. I think it goes back to what Hannah was saying earlier, actually, about her experience of coding; that you have got talk in a classroom and you think that is all great, but you are not exactly sure which bits of it might be productive for learning. So, if you look at it systematically and code it, you can then emphasise those bits a bit more. And I think it is maybe not something that teachers have often done before. It is not

something in the training and it is not expected. So, maybe it is new, in which case I think it does require very new skills. Not complex skills.
...

Hannah: I would say that I have had to learn a whole new set of skills, if I am thinking back to last year and this year, in terms of doing educational research in school, I have had to learn a whole load of new stuff, which has been quite exciting.

Ruth: What have you had to learn?

In Extract D, the discussion extends to more general thinking about research partnerships and collaborative professional learning. As can be seen in this extract, we were sharing conceptualisations of the meaning of 'research partnership', including its dynamic and cyclical nature in creating knowledge and understanding.

In Extract D, the discussion extends to more general thinking about research partnerships and collaborative professional learning. As can be seen in this extract, we were sharing conceptualisations of the meaning of 'research partnership', including its dynamic and cyclical nature in creating knowledge and understanding.

Extract D Perspectives on research partnership and collaborative professional learning

Ruth: Are there any other ways in which you understand the meaning of research partnership, what that would mean? What do we mean from our perspective, Sara, research partnership? Sometimes these words trip off the tongue, don't they? What do we mean by research partnership? It doesn't mean we are doing the same thing. A partnership can be people with different goals, ultimately, but working together to achieve those different goals or creating something new in doing that. That is interesting, isn't it, that you get more from the partnership than you do from separate partners working independently.

Kate: In a way, I have viewed this almost like a picture, and then you have got you in the middle and then we will be like a leg of your spider and then there will be lots of other legs with other schools I know you are working with. So, I would see us as a tiny little part of all of the research you are doing, and then you will take that research and, basically, organise it and decide what has worked well, what hasn't worked well and you would share that with us, and then we would be able to move forward even more. I don't know. That is how I would see it.

Ruth: I am seeing that in my head.

Kate: But we are a tiny little bit of what you are doing and that, by being that tiny little bit, we might learn more things that, in the future, we will be able to put into place.

Ruth: That is also a process you have described, isn't it? It is not just a one-off. It is not a static thing.

Kate: Yes.

Hannah: Yes. So, it comes back and it keeps going on. It is a cycle, isn't it?

Kate: Yes. That is what you would hope. It wouldn't just be, 'We have done this and that is it, and I will go off into the sunset.'

Hannah: Which doesn't happen with all projects.

Kate: 'I am never going to dialogic talk again. Forget the sentence stems!' But, actually, there would be some sort of continuation.

Hannah: But I wonder whether that depends on the nature of the project.

Kate: Yes.

Hannah: Because I think some of the ones we get involved in are testing something, and, therefore, actually, there is a finite end point, whereas, actually, this is more infinite.

Sara: Yes. Maybe those ones are less of a partnership and more just you being involved in research.

Hannah: In facilitating that.

Sara: Yes. I think, for me, the term 'research partnership' means that both parties are getting something out of it. So, we are learning from it as well. So, although your diagram is fairly accurate, in a way, that we have lots of other schools, but all of the parts are really important, especially case studies are even more important because we go in more depth with those and with certain sites and people. So, we learn even more from those.

So, we learn about how dialogue can be used in the classroom, how resources can be used to help support that, but also we learn about the process; so, just having this conversation now, having had the interviews and so on, helps us learn about the whole process of sharing our other research with teachers and with schools in a way that makes it helpful for practice.

Kate: And, I think, part of it, if I had just read about dialogic talk and T-SEDA or somebody had just told me about it, I wouldn't have had the knowledge, perhaps, that I have after two and a half terms of actually having a go at using it. So, I think, from my point of view, it has really been useful in that it has definitely deepened my understanding of what dialogic talk really is and how you can use it in your classroom effectively. So, I have definitely got a lot out of it.

Conclusion

From a research perspective, T-SEDA was developed as a resource that is both inquiry-focused and dialogue-focused. It encourages teachers to take the 'inquiry stance' that lies at the core of effective professional learning, valuing teachers as 'natural experimenters'. The idea of 'inquiry stance' has roots in the work of influential scholars like Lawrence Stenhouse, pioneer of action research, who described the importance of teachers' willingness to take a 'research stance' (Stenhouse, 1975, p. 156).

As highlighted in the previous section, supporting teacher experimentation requires attention to the conditions that make purposeful experimentation possible, the tools that can be used in experimentation and the importance for teachers of sharing ideas that can guide experimentation. One of the key areas of support in this case lies in the clear identification of what dialogic talk is (and what it isn't). This then allows teachers like Kate to review the quality of talk in their own classrooms and identify which parts they need to develop. Specific approaches emerge as distinctively important in this area, not only from Kate's case but from the wider international T-SEDA trial findings. These include:

- video or audio material to reflect on;
- sentence stems to promote dialogic talk;
- opportunities and willingness for reflection with a self-critical and reflexive approach;
- a framework for structuring inquiries over manageable periods of time, possibly including agreed deadlines and opportunities for 'supervision' discussions about progress.

The T-SEDA trials so far have helped to identify different levels of activity at which researchers can engage with practitioners to make 'impact' happen collaboratively and dynamically. In this case, the initial whole-school approach involved all teachers in the first workshop before encouraging some teachers to conduct individual inquiries. This meant that other teachers were also challenged to develop the principles too and all staff had a common language. So discussions about dialogic talk could continue elsewhere in the school, not just among those teachers who were involved in the T-SEDA project.

In thinking about the role of research partnerships in professional development, we conclude with a quote from Kate, based on her T-SEDA inquiry experience. This encapsulates many of our conclusions about the constructive ways in which professional change can happen:

> Personally, I think really effective forms of professional development within schools are, from a teacher point of view, collaborative. I think, when people work together, when you share ideas, when people get a chance to observe

each other, I think that is really, really powerful, but it, obviously, has to be chosen carefully so that people are going to observe with a goal in mind, and that you have identified something specific that you want them to take on, when you have that shared planning time, and it has to be supported as well ...

I think the T-SEDA definitely does have elements of that. So, the fact that you get observed and you can watch back your lesson, although that can be stressful, actually, if you go in with the right frame of mind, with reflecting on it and no one is judging you, then it is really, really powerful. I think having the discussions about it ... and having that time to reflect and then go away and squirrel away and do something else and notice areas that you need to improve on, but do it without that pressure, 'Oh my God, I've got to do this', is really, really powerful.

Note

1 Three video clips from Kate's final lesson are available to view online at https://sms. cam.ac.uk/media/3212641.

References

Alexander, R., Hardman, F., Hardman, J., Rajab, T., & Longmore, M. (2017). *Changing talk, changing thinking: Interim report from the in-house evaluation of the CPRT/UoY Dialogic Teaching Project.* York: University of York.

Cordingley, P., Higgins, S., Greany, T., Buckler, N., Coles-Jordan, D., Crisp, B., ... Coe, R. (2015). *Developing great teaching: Lessons from international reviews into effective professional development.* London: Teacher Development Trust.

Dawes, L. (2012). *Talking points: Discussion activities in the primary classroom.* New York, NY: Routledge.

ELAN (2018). [Computer software]. Nijmegen, the Netherlands: Max Planck Institute for Psycholinguistics. Retrieved from https://tla.mpi.nl/tools/tla-tools/elan.

Hennessy, S., Rojas-Drummond, S., Higham, R., Márquez, A. M., Maine, F., Ríos, R. M., ... Barrera, M. J. (2016). Developing a coding scheme for analysing classroom dialogue across educational contexts. *Learning, Culture and Social Interaction, 9,* 16–44.

Howe, C., Hennessy, S., Mercer, N., Vrikki, M., & Wheatley, L. (2019). Teacher–student dialogue during classroom teaching: Does it really impact on student outcomes? *Journal of the Learning Sciences, 28*(4–5), 462–512.

Kazemi, E., & Hubbard, A. (2008). New directions for the design and study of professional development: Attending to the coevolution of teachers' participation across contexts. *Journal of Teacher Education, 59*(5), 428–441.

Kim, M. -Y., & Wilkinson, I. A. G. (2019). What is dialogic teaching? Constructing, deconstructing, and reconstructing a pedagogy of classroom talk. *Learning, Culture and Social Interaction, 21,* 70–86.

Mercer, N. (2000). *Words and minds: How we use language to think together.* London: Routledge.

Opfer, V. D., & Pedder, D. (2010). Benefits, status and effectiveness of continuous professional development for teachers in England. *Curriculum Journal, 21*(4), 413–431.

Pedder, D. (2006). Organizational conditions that foster successful classroom promotion of learning how to learn. *Research Papers in Education, 21*(2), 171–200.

Stenhouse, L. A. (1975). The teacher as researcher. In L. A. Stenhouse (Ed.), *An introduction to curriculum research and development* (pp. 142–165). London: Heinemann.

William Blake Quotes (n.d.). Retrieved from www.brainyquote.com/quotes/william_blake_378669.

9

Inspiring a love of reading: professional learning to develop a culture of reading for pleasure

Teresa Cremin and Aimee Durning

Introduction

Whether children read for pleasure – that is choose to read – within and beyond school matters. Not only because 'the will influences the skill' as research repeatedly reveals, but because reading for pleasure (RfP), for exploration, relaxation, imagination and making connections, is a worthwhile activity in its own right. It is mandated in England, Ireland, is expected to be required in the new Welsh curriculum and is central to the First Minster's Reading Challenge in Scotland.

Teachers and schools across the UK are working to enhance children's desire to read, and most schools participate in a myriad of book activities, including Book Week, World Book Day, author events and literacy parents' evenings. Many have also refurbished/reclaimed their libraries; purchasing reading sheds and double-decker buses and adding cushions and sofas to enrich classroom reading corners. Such activities and spaces demonstrate to families, governors, inspectors and the children that the school values reading. But is this institutional positioning of RfP enough?

To avoid being sucked into 'performing RfP', some schools and teachers draw on research to underpin their pedagogic practice; they move away from 'doing' reading activities and instead they engage in serious continuing professional development and learning (CPDL; Cordingley et al., 2015). They review their professional knowledge and understanding about what counts as RfP and develop research-informed, sustained and embedded practice – creating an RfP ethos that runs through the school. Some schools also document the difference their new practices make to children's identities as readers and their desire to read.

This chapter demonstrates the value of schools embarking on such research-informed RfP journeys, and the salience of staff exploring research and practice in collaboration with one another and evidence-based resources. Initially we explore the benefits of RfP, and the challenges and tensions involved; then we turn to relevant research and ways to mediate this through professional development. We focus on a CPDL course run in one school for local teachers as an example of the road travelled, highlight the new research–informed understandings developed, the pedagogic and community consequences and the impact on children's (and teachers') identities as readers. We also offer ways to get involved.

The challenges involved in fostering RfP

There is strong evidence from multiple international studies that the will to read influences the skill and vice versa. For example, drawing on the large data set offered by the British Cohort study, researchers have shown an association between childhood reading and increased attainment in literacy and numeracy in adolescence, with marked progress in vocabulary (Sullivan & Brown, 2013). In addition, other studies have shown, somewhat unsurprisingly, that RfP has other benefits such as wider general knowledge, enriched imagination and narrative writing and that when children choose to engage in reading in their leisure time beyond school, they have opportunities to explore who they are or might become and to develop an empathetic awareness of others.

Yet despite these benefits, reading in school tends to be framed as a cognitive activity and teaching children to decode and comprehend texts is prioritised. Yet while necessary, this is not enough to develop confident readers who not only can but *do* choose to read. Reading also encompasses behavioural and motivational characteristics that deserve professional attention if we are to develop readers for life. In England, however, in the recent Progress in International Reading Literacy (PIRLS) study, it was evident that children's attitudes to reading are comparatively low compared to their skills and that in English-speaking countries, England had the lowest ranking for enjoyment and the lowest for pupil engagement in reading (except Australia) (McGrane, Stiff, Baird, Lenkeit, & Hopfenbeck-Oxford, 2017). In such accountability cultures, the backwash of assessment places pressure on teachers, reducing the time available to support RfP. This often constrains the experience of struggling readers, particularly boys (Hempel-Jorgensen, Cremin, Harris, & Chamberlain, 2018). With the best of intentions, the teachers in this study of 10-year-old boys, prioritised skills practice and consequently the boys' experience of reading focused solely on technical aspects. Their reader identities, habits and interests beyond school were neither known nor built upon and their teachers' perceptions not only of them as 'boy readers', but also of their social class and ethnicity further constrained their engagement (Hempel-Jorgensen et al., 2018). Arguably they were trapped in a circle of underachievement and poor pedagogy.

The Teachers as Readers (TaRs) (Phase 1) research also showed that teachers' knowledge of children's literature is dominated by Roald Dahl and other 'celebrity' authors and is arguably insufficient to support reader development (Cremin,

Mottram, Collins, Powell, & Safford, 2009). This finding was underscored by a later National Literacy Trust survey (Clark & Teraveinen, 2015). Despite the six-year difference in these surveys, the results were very similar. Teachers relied upon their own childhood favourites and were over-reliant on a narrow range of children's authors. Roald Dahl was the unrivalled favourite in both surveys. In addition, as only 4 per cent of the 9,115 children's books published in the UK in 2017 featured Black or minority ethnic characters (CLPE, 2018), it is particularly important that teachers seek such texts out and widen their repertoires. Without such subject knowledge teachers cannot cultivate children's personal preferences and practices. Furthermore, the new digital library systems that are very popular in primary schools tend to position teachers as librarians, curators and monitors of children's reading. This significantly undermines their potential roles as listeners, mentors and co-readers (Kucirkova & Cremin, 2017).

In sum, there are tensions and challenges for time-poor teachers who wish to nurture children's RfP. They may feel obliged to keep reading skills centre stage, may have limited knowledge and may be positioned as monitoring children's reading not supporting them as co-readers. Arguably the goal of reading instruction is for each child to achieve the reading level deemed appropriate by current policy. Whereas the goal of RfP is not only for each child to develop positive attitudes and dispositions towards reading, but for them to become lifelong readers (see Table 9.1). This conceptualisation, while visually creating a dichotomy between RfP and reading instruction, does not seek to polarise, rather it recognises the significance of these different orientations, the interplay between the skill and the will and the vital necessity of working towards a balance between them.

Table 9.1 Distinctions between reading instruction and RfP

Reading instruction is oriented towards …	RfP is oriented towards …
Learning to read	Choosing to read
The skill	The will
Decoding and comprehension	Engagement and response
System readers	Lifelong readers
Teacher direction	Child direction
Teacher ownership	Child ownership
Attainmnet	Achievement
The minimum entitlement:	The maximum entitlement
The 'expected standard'	A reader for life
The standards agenda	The reader's own agenda

Source: Based on Cremin et al. (2014, p. 157).

Research focused on fostering RfP in school

The TaRs Phase II research, undertaken with 43 teachers from 27 primary schools in five areas of England, focused on RfP across a school year (Cremin, Mottram, Powell, Collins, & Safford, 2014). The research team tracked teachers' knowledge and practice, the impact on children's identities as readers and later observed the creation of RfP pedagogy, the development of Reading Teachers (capital 'R', capital 'T') and communities of engaged readers (see Figure 9.1). Each of the findings from this work is now addressed in turn, as these were the basis of the RfP CPDL work discussed later in the chapter.

The research identified that teachers need a wide knowledge of children's literature and other texts, and a working knowledge of the reading practices and identities of those young people in their classrooms to effectively nurture RfP. The young people benefitted from having a teacher who could tailor their text recommendations to different individual's interests and who as role models voiced their passion and pleasure in reading. Such focused support not only increases the chance of young readers finding books that satisfy them, but also leads to significant 'book blether' – critical text conversations between readers that helps sustain and nourish readers.

A coherent RfP pedagogy was also identified. This encompassed reading aloud, book talk, inside-text talk and recommendations and the provision of quality time for independent choice-led reading, all offered in a social reading environment. However, these can become little more than routine pedagogic procedures (see Hempel-Jorgensen et al., 2018). The effectiveness of any pedagogy depends on teachers' subject knowledge and knowledge of their children, and in the case of RfP pedagogy, professional understanding of reading, as social, relational and affectively engaging. With a richer understanding of reading and of themselves as readers, teachers can more sensitively shape their RfP pedagogy. This fourfold pedagogy, endorsed by the National Union of Teachers (NUT) (2016), needs to be embedded and sensitively sustained in order to foster children's autonomy as readers, readers who exercise discrimination and choice within and beyond school. Key to this pedagogy is the extent to which it is LIST, that is:

- **L**earner-led
- **I**nformal
- **S**ocial and with
- **T**exts that tempt.

In planning reading-aloud provision across a school, for example, the research indicates that teachers need to consider the extent to which the time set aside is reader-led: who makes the choices of what to read, who reads aloud and how often and are opportunities planned within English and across the curriculum?

How might this vary across the primary years and to what extent are these opportunities informal and social? Research suggests that with the pressure of time and curriculum coverage, reading aloud is often shelved, tends to be teacher-led and may be misappropriated as a space in which reading instruction is foregrounded, reducing its potential to inspire (Hempel-Jorgensen et al., 2018). The social nature of reading can be supported though pairs of children reading aloud (e.g. Year 3 and Year 5), the creation of reading buddies, time with volunteers, children reading aloud to friends and staff running 'You Choose Fridays' when children select which teacher's read-aloud session to attend. Finally, the texts chosen must tempt readers to imagine, be curious, debate issues and want to hear more. The TaRs research indicated that reading aloud to young people, without attendant work, is a key pedagogic practice in fostering RfP (Cremin et al., 2014). It is not an optional extra, but every child's right to hear fiction, non-fiction and poetry read aloud with passion and pleasure.

In addition, if independent reading time is heavily constrained, by silence, formality, limited choices and ability-assigned texts, it is likely that indifferent or negative attitudes will be fostered. If the teacher requires children to sit in their assigned seats and uses the time for preparation of later lessons, this will further limit child volition, relaxed engagement and opportunity for critical conversations and reader-to-reader recommendations. It is clear the ways in which RfP pedagogy is shaped by practitioners can constrain or empower readers and will prompt different responses, impacting upon children's desire to engage as readers. The relaxed social nature of the reading environment and the extent that the pedagogy LIST is used is critical.

Research also suggests that those teachers who develop as Reading Teachers make a positive difference to children's identities as readers and their pleasure in reading (Cremin et al., 2014). While all teachers are readers, only some develop as Reading Teachers, who are not only motivated and enthusiastic fellow bookworms (with a rich repertoire to draw upon), but are thoughtful and interactive reading role models. Such teachers do far more than share their enthusiasm for reading, they investigate their own experiences of reading and consider the classroom consequences in order to support children, they also develop new understandings of the social, relational and affective experience of reading. The project showed that new and highly productive relationships between such teachers and children were forged that impacted positively on children's attitudes to and pleasure in reading. If teachers are willing to position themselves as fellow readers, share their own reading histories and experiences and invite the children to share *their* everyday encounters with reading and their perceptions of themselves as readers, then it is possible for reciprocal relationships to emerge and reading communities to be created (Cremin et al., 2014).

Through developing their knowledge of children and texts, an RfP pedagogy and as Reading Teachers, the practitioners in the TaRs research gradually built interactive and reciprocal reading communities in their classrooms (Cremin et al., 2014). In these new relationship-strong communities (see Figure 9.1) new spaces were created for children and teachers to participate and talk about their reading, and children were encouraged to bring their cultural knowledge and lived experience of reading to school and make more of their own choices as readers. This fostered more personal involvement and commitment and a shift in the locus of control around RfP.

Some teachers also blurred the boundaries between home and school reading and began to involve parents and community members more fully. However, this is not without challenge as recent research has shown that once children can read, parents tend to stop reading to their children; reading may become 'an orphaned responsibility' (Merga & Ledger, 2018) such that both teachers and parents assume it is the other's role to provided sustained support and encouragement. Thus children are left to fend for themselves as readers. In addition, as the study undertaken by Orkin, Pott, Wolf, May, and Brand (2018) indicates, schools too often seek to foster RfP by offering extrinsic rewards to children or families for completing reading homework or for the number of books read for instance. Such reading for recognition, for grades and for competition focuses on extrinsic motivation, which can have a detrimental effect on reading comprehension and readers' engagement. It is widely known and underscored by Orkin et al.'s (2018) study, that RfP is closely associated with intrinsic motivation, desiring to read for its own sake rather than reading for rewards. Orkin et al. (2018) found that the presence of incentives to read were ineffective in encouraging readers, and that those readers who were supported to find their own pleasure in reading and became intrinsically motivated, demonstrated increased engagement in the reading tasks offered and extended their skills in the process.

The research is clear: if teachers are to develop children's RfP, they need, as Figure 9.1 indicates, to enrich their knowledge of texts and of children, and to develop an RfP pedagogy, one that is, as noted earlier, learner-led, informal, social and with texts that tempt (LIST), as well as a personal stance as a Reading Teacher. They will then be in a position to build communities of readers within, and potentially beyond, the classroom.

Mediating RfP research through professional development

The CPDL framing

Fostering children's pleasure in reading is more complex than introducing an intervention or programme; building reader-to-reader relationships and a reading culture takes time; it is an ongoing commitment. The continuing professional development (CPD) course, 'Reading for Pleasure' on which this chapter draws, was organisationally framed around the research-based recommendations made by Cordingley et al. (2015) about CPD and its essential focus on CPDL (i.e. CPD and learning). The course sought to ensure that the teachers were actively engaged in reviewing their practice, identifying individual starting points and working with

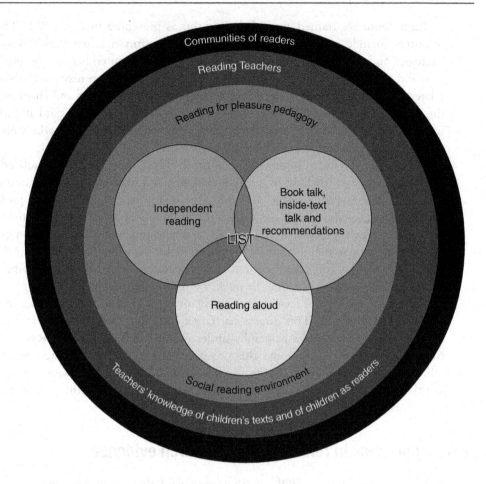

Figure 9.1 Research insights regarding effective RfP

Source: Based on Cremin et al. (2014).

facilitators who in a responsive manner sought to develop the teachers' subject and pedagogical content knowledge, helping them to apply their learning from sessions and explore and evaluate their work back at school in order to support the younger learners.

It was designed in partnership with academics from the Open University (OU), Cambridge University and teachers from the University of Cambridge Primary School (UCPS). Ten teachers from local schools were recruited, two staff from UCPS also attended, one learning coach lead and one classroom practitioner. Some course members were English leaders in their schools. Over the course, they worked together, shared their learning journeys and development work back in school. This was central to each of the six three-hour sessions. The programme made extensive use of a new practitioner website informed by the TaRs research, which shares the findings in an accessible classroom-focused manner. This has multiple resources framed around the insights as presented in Figure 9.1. These resources include: self-reviews, focused research summaries, practical classroom strategies and over 100 examples of practice, written by members of the profession and informed by the research. Additional features on top texts, authors and related blogs serve to support practitioner enquiry and full papers and chapters on the work are available.[1] RfP was foregrounded, but the course also paid attention to comprehension. Tutors included two teacher members of the OU website advisory board and three academics, all ex-teachers.

The sessions included inputs, workshops, feedback on gap tasks that related to auditing practice in the light of research evidence and working on a small number of practitioner enquiries, either individual or whole school. In addition, professional reading, establishing a baseline in the chosen area and the development of research-informed practice were key. Each teacher's journey was undertaken as an enquiry and course members were invited to make clear their aspirations for their children as readers and document any differences occasioned by their changes to practice. They worked not only to track the impact of their work, capturing and exploring outcomes, but shared their resultant work on the OU RfP website as 'examples of practice'. This directional target sought to prompt practitioners to distil their learning and the principles underpinning their approach to RfP. In the final session, teachers presented these examples to each other and to attending school leadership team members from their schools. The examples were structured as title and name, school context, research inspiration, aims, outline, impact and reflections.

Auditing practice in relation to the research evidence

As a core part of the CPDL, teachers reviewed their practice using research-informed audits on the OU website. This helped identify areas of strength and areas that would benefit from development. The most common areas of strength were reading environments, although some saw these as reading corners alone and not the wider school social reading environment. Several teachers identified a need to develop their own (and their staff) knowledge of texts for children ('I simply cannot name any picture fiction authors beyond the most popular and I realise now this is holding me and the children back'), while others sought to reinstate reading aloud or their provision for independent reading ('It's just dropped off the timetable and so many of our children don't read at home'). Reviewing was a two-stage process: step one was an overarching audit that enabled the teachers to identify an area of need; step two was a focused audit, also derived from the OU website.

Stretching intellectual muscles through professional reading

Reading relevant research to stretch professional understanding and discussing the extent to which this challenged or confirmed current practice was key. Course members were both set and set themselves research reading challenges, they read around their area for RfP development, both research summaries on the OU website and other material.

For example, the learning coach lead at UCPS came to read *The Book Whisperer* by Donalyn Miller (2010), *The Reading Environment: How Adults Help Children Enjoy Books* by Aidan Chambers (2011), *Developing Critical Thinking Through Picture* books by Mary Roche (2014), *Understanding Reading Comprehension* by Wayne Tennant (2013), the OU website article 'More Research Details' (based on the TaRs research)[2] and the paper 'Understanding Boys' (Dis)engagement with Reading for Pleasure' by Amelia Hempel-Jorgensen, Teresa Cremin, Diane Harris and Liz Chamberlain (2017). Her area of focus was to improve staff and children's knowledge of children's literature and to create more social interactive spaces to profile RfP. These readings helped her on her journey, offering underpinning arguments around the value of text talk, teachers' knowledge of children's texts and the explicit sharing of this knowledge in ways that would tempt and engage the children.

The reading and discussion supported the teachers as they began to shape up their own enquiries and worked to enrich their knowledge and practice. It caused them to ask questions, debate issues, engage with robust and often challenging material; each piece of which was not always closely aligned and sometimes needed mediation. In retrospect, however, these discussions might have been more effectively summarised if the teachers had been invited to represent their understandings visually and if more 'research texts in common' had been set by the course team. Careful selection and setting of one or more of the listed texts in the references of this chapter could be of value in future CPDL for RfP to read, discuss and represent. Balancing the setting of more and less demanding readings can also be effective. It is also always useful to set at least one text that deals in detail with the applied consequences of the research and attends to the consequences for children's knowledge, skills, understanding or attitudes.

Establishing a baseline, desired outcomes and methods to evaluate impact

Having reviewed their RfP knowledge and practice, chosen an area for development and widened their understanding of related research, course members sought to involve the children, staff and/or parents as appropriate and give space to their voices. Some also drew on other forms of baseline data. An English leader in their school for example, involved all staff in completing the OU audit of teachers' knowledge of children's texts. They often found that, as in the studies reviewed above, that staff were reliant on texts from their own childhood or those written by celebrity authors (Clark & Teraveinen, 2015; Cremin, Mottram, Bearne, & Goodwin, 2008). Another course member invited all staff to bring their term's read-aloud books to a staff meeting and found that all but one of these had been published before 2000. So both these teachers, working to enrich staff knowledge, focused on broadening staff repertoires of more contemporary texts.

Some staff, seeking to find out children's attitudes to reading, used the OU survey.[3] In one case, when all the data was analysed across a school, staff were concerned to learn that over 70 per cent of their children preferred reading at home than in school. This resulted in a development focus on teachers' knowledge of the children as readers and a school development plan that prioritised practices that sought to make school-based reading more relaxed and enjoyable. Another course member who used the survey wanted to enrich her reading-aloud practice and found to her consternation that children were somewhat indifferent to this practice. This underscored the need to enrich her reading-aloud provision and prompted her to reshape her pedagogy and ensure she used the pedagogy check (LIST). For example, she sought to involve the children in making more of the read-aloud choices, offered time for them to talk informally about the texts read and, through reading more widely herself and purchasing texts recommended by leaders and members, tried to make wiser more discerning choices to read aloud. As the year progressed, this teacher documented the difference that her altered pedagogy made to the children's attitudes and interests as readers. Other data sources used by teachers to establish an initial baseline from which to document difference included observation of a small number of case study children (those who could but didn't choose to read), library borrowing records, Office for Standards in Education, Children's Services and Skills (Ofsted) reports and parents' perspectives written as part of the inspection process.

Discussion of desired reader outcomes revealed that members felt that if children were seen to be visibly enjoying any activity, this was an endorsement and justification for such. Robust discussions ensued about the value of tracking more closely the impact on children's development as readers (behaviourally, affectively or cognitively) and the group were introduced to the National Literacy Trust's tripartite conceptualisation of reading, based on the Organisation for Economic Development's (OECD) (2016) new definition of reading (see Figure 9.2). This led to focused discussions on a professional need to develop ways to track (not measure) subtle identity shifts and the frequency with which children choose to read, which in turn resulted in a research review and the production of a summary document to support the profession. This showcases the interplay between research and practice.[4]

Developing, documenting and sharing research-informed practice

Diverse development work emerged. One of the English leaders who had identified teachers' knowledge of children's texts as an area for whole-school development, used the OU PowerPoint on this with staff, set up a teachers' book box in the staffroom and made personal recommendations to staff in order to promote reading and book talk. She also created a space for book recommendations and

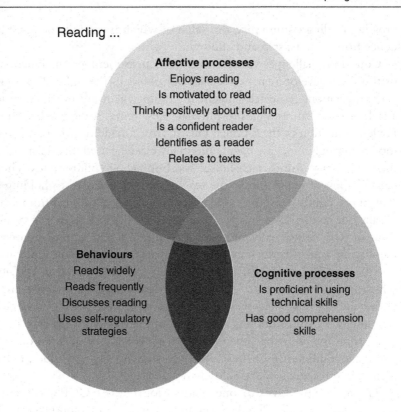

Reading ...

Affective processes
Enjoys reading
Is motivated to read
Thinks positively about reading
Is a confident reader
Identifies as a reader
Relates to texts

Behaviours
Reads widely
Reads frequently
Discusses reading
Uses self-regulatory
strategies

Cognitive processes
Is proficient in using
technical skills
Has good comprehension
skills

Figure 9.2 Top-level tripartite conceptualisation of what we mean by 'reading'

Source: Based on Clark and Teraveinen (2017).

requests and encouraged staff to follow keen readers on Twitter. The staff trip to a local Waterstones where the bookshop staff shared the nominations and winners of the Costa Book Award was particularly successful, and staff were inspired and enabled to select texts for their own classes. In her summary of this work, which also aimed to ensure staff were modelling a love of reading across the school, the leader notes that there was an increase in book blether around the school, with adults suggesting texts for children and each other.

Another English leader sought to develop an enthusiasm for reading among parents and children since the parent voice perspective analysed from the school's Ofsted data indicated that like some teachers, they tended to perceive reading as book and proficiency bound. RfP was not widely valued. The leader deployed several strategies, the most successful of which she perceived were pop-up reading picnics. These had a relaxed homely feel with blankets and cushions, food and a wide range of texts, chosen by staff for their year groups to enjoy. Children were buddied up (e.g. Year 1 and Year 3) and responding sensitively to feedback on the initial picnics, adjustments were made. These half-termly events for each paired year group have since become an established part of school life, a marker of a growing reading community, the value of which is carefully documented via evidence from parents, staff and children.[5]

Common challenges experienced by course members included time to prioritise their development work back in school in the light of external pressures and expectations (especially salient for those who were not literacy leaders) and a lack of financial resources to purchase new texts. Some teachers applied to the Foyle Foundation or the Siobhan Dowd Trust for additional funding, others raised money through in-school events and many teachers used their salary to supplement the class library. Another challenge was honouring children's text choices, as this created a loss of control for some teachers who were used to holding the reading reins more tightly. In some cases, there was a lack of support from senior leaders, usually due to their own levels of over-commitment and a lack of awareness of the value of RfP. Additionally, some teachers found it hard to remain focused, despite identifying a priority for development; many sought to introduce multiple RfP initiatives related to several research findings. This resulted in activity overload, which meant the impact of the work on staff pedagogic practice and principled understanding was not as secure. In addition, this RfP activity orientation meant less time was spent examining the impact of these activities. In turn this meant that while time and effort had been put in to supporting readers, no one was sure this had made a difference to the children as shifts in their attitudes, behaviours and identities as readers were not closely documented.

The focus now turns to one school's journey. At UCPS, where strong head teacher support was offered, development work was undertaken to enrich staff knowledge, enhance book talk and strengthen the wider reading community. Under the first of these areas for development, individual teachers within UCPS worked to enhance their reading repertoires and share this with the young learners.[6]

One UCPS teacher, a science specialist, following the stage two audit, set herself the challenge of reading more widely and using this new subject knowledge to help reluctant/vulnerable readers find pleasure in reading. She established a self-set non-negotiable task of reading to the class each day, made a bookshelf of texts she had read (and could therefore discuss and recommend), created loan sheets for some of these texts and for the first time set aside time for reader-led informal discussion of texts and recommendations. She went on to establish a lunchtime book club for the less keen readers, affording them ownership of this relaxed time in which they read alone and together, and engaged in drawing and illustrating texts (or other activities they could suggest) in 'a super informal reading atmosphere'. Her final website sharing of research-enriched practice highlights the impact of these sustained initiatives on the children, many of whom had begun to see the possibilities in reading, and on her own understanding and practice.[7]

The school also began an OU/United Kingdom Literacy Association (UKLA) teachers' reading group. This group, alongside a parent book club, continues today and is run by the learning coach lead, is open to local area teachers, teaching assistants (TAs) and librarians and represents a new platform to develop research-informed RfP practice. The aim of the group, one of 80 nationally supported by the OU, is to foster children's RfP through supporting teachers'/members' own RfP and research-informed practice, support the profession by building a professional community around RfP locally and online and share teachers' resultant development work on the OU RfP website. The OU/UKLA group meets six times a year, mostly at the hotel across the road from the school, with the head teacher often in attendance. It is a rich opportunity to step away from the hustle and bustle of school, to blether about books, read research and enrich RfP practice. However, as the learning coach lead acknowledges, with the demands on teacher workload, it can be difficult to attract regular attendance and fiction tends to dominate, sidelining non-fiction and poetry. Recognising such challenges are important first steps towards addressing them.

Drawing on the OU TaRs research findings, the school action plan also sought to connect children's home and school reading lives and at an RfP parent workshop, the TaRs research findings and a selection of contemporary children's books were shared. This inspired a regular parent book club, which seeks to foster shared understanding around the benefits of RfP and situate reading as a practice beyond technical proficiency. The club, as an initial offer, has produced a school-wide RfP newsletter as it seeks to reach out to all parents.

Within high-stakes accountability cultures, the described RfP development work can be demanding, requiring changes to not only timetables and responsibilities, but also to mindsets. The course members' final evaluations indicated that they recognise this is not a tick-box exercise. It has to be lived, sustained and embedded over time, a thread running through primary education, connecting children to each other and their teachers though RfP. In some of the schools, the ongoing development of RfP was integrated into school development plans and now features in policy and practice. At UCPS, the learning coach lead documented this as a 'reading for pleasure tree' representing the school's many spaces and practices that foster a love of reading (Durning, 2018). RfP is a feature of the school's curriculum design with a reading pedagogical framework laying out in more detail how a text-rich curriculum can enable spaces that foster agency and support the emergence of a reciprocal reading community. But the tree needs nourishing and constant care.

Conclusion

Professional development that builds sustained partnerships between academics and teachers focused on children's learning has the potential for mutual benefit, enriching pedagogic practice, identifying new areas for research enquiries and, most significantly, positively influencing children's learning. In the context of RfP, there is a need for such partnership work to attend to evidence and to engage in both reflection and action. This can support the development of subject and pedagogical content knowledge, which, research indicates, is crucial in order to effectively engage and foster keen young readers (Cremin et al., 2014). While the professional learning journeys of teachers will be unique, process commonalities were recognised and seen to include: attention to identifying needs, classroom or whole-school intent, reading research and drawing on it in order to implement changes and flexibly and sensitively shape and reshape research-informed practice. The OU RfP website resources – from surveys, to research summaries, ideas and video clips, as well as examples of other teachers' research-informed practice – offer strong support on the journey from intent to impact. Critically, the influence of the implemented development work on the children, staff and parents needs to be documented. This remains an area for development both for research and for professional learning nationally.

Notes

1 See https://researchrichpedagogies.org/research/reading-for-pleasure.
2 See https://researchrichpedagogies.org/research/theme/teachers-knowledge-of-childrens-reading-practices.
3 See https://researchrichpedagogies.org/research/page/developing-reading-for-pleasure-in- your-school.
4 See https://researchrichpedagogies.org/_downloads/Documenting_Childrens_Reading_for_Pleasure_FINAL_.pdf.
5 To read more, see https://researchrichpedagogies.org/research/example/the-pop-up-reading-picnics.
6 For a summary of this work overall, see https://researchrichpedagogies.org/research/example/the-potential-of-good-read1.
7 See https://researchrichpedagogies.org/research/example/the-potential-of-good-read1.

References

Centre for Literacy in Primary Education (CLPE) (2018). *Reflecting realities report*. London: CLPE. Retrieved from https://clpe.org.uk/library-and-resources/research/reflecting-realities-survey-ethnic-representation-within-uk-children.

Chambers, A. (2011). *The reading environment: How adults help children enjoy books*. Stroud, UK: Thimble Press.

Clark, C., & Teravainen, A. (2015). *Teachers and literacy: Their perceptions, understanding, confidence and awareness*. London: National Literacy Trust.

Clark, C., & Teraveinen, A. (2017). *What it means to be a reader at age 11*. London: National Literacy Trust.

Cordingley, P., Higgins, S., Greany, T., Buckler, N., Coles-Jordan, D., Crisp, B., ... Coe, R. (2015). *Developing great teaching: Lessons from the international reviews into effective professional development*. London: Teacher Development Trust.

Cremin, T., Mottram, M., Bearne, E., & Goodwin, P. (2008). Exploring teachers' knowledge of children's literature. *Cambridge Journal of Education*, *38*(4), 449–464.

Cremin, T., Mottram, M., Collins, F., Powell, S., & Safford, K. (2009). Teachers as readers: Building communities of readers. *Literacy, 43*(1), 11–19.

Cremin, T., Mottram, M., Powell, S., Collins, R., & Safford, K. (2014). *Building communities of engaged readers: Reading for pleasure.* London: Routledge.

Durning, A. (2018). Reading for pleasure tree. Retrieved from https://researchrich pedagogies.org/_downloads/UCPS_Reading_For_Pleasure_Model.pdf.

Hempel-Jorgensen, A., Cremin, T., Harris, D., & Chamberlain, L. (2017). Understanding boys (dis)engagement with reading for pleasure: Project findings. Retrieved from https://researchrichpedagogies.org/research/understanding-boys-disengagement-with-rfp.

Hempel-Jorgensen, A., Cremin, T., Harris, D., & Chamberlain, L. (2018). Pedagogy for reading for pleasure in low socio-economic primary schools: Beyond 'pedagogy of poverty'? *Literacy, 52*(2), 86–94.

Kucirkova, N., & Cremin, T. (2017). Personalised reading for pleasure with digital libraries: Towards a pedagogy of practice and design. *Cambridge Journal of Education, 48*(5), 571–589.

McGrane, J., Stiff, J., Baird, J., Lenkeit, J., & Hopfenbeck-Oxford, T. (2017). *Progress in International Reading Literacy Study (PIRLS): National report for England.* London: DfE.

Merga, K. M., & Ledger, S. (2018). Parents' views on reading aloud to their children: Beyond the early years. *Australian Journal of Language and Literacy, 41*(3), 177–189.

Miller, D. (2010). *The book whisperer: Awakening the inner reader in every child.* San Francisco, CA: Jossey-Bass.

National Union of Teachers (NUT) (2016). Getting everyone reading for pleasure. Retrieved from www.teachers.org.uk/sites/default/files2014/reading-4-pleasure-10561.pdf.

Organisation for Economic Cooperation and Development (OECD) (2016). *PISA 2015 assessment and analytical framework: Science, reading, mathematics and financial literacy.* Paris: OECD Publishing.

Orkin, M., Pott, M., Wolf, M., May, S., & Brand, E. (2018). Beyond gold stars: Improving the skills and engagement of struggling readers through intrinsic motivation. *Reading & Writing Quarterly, 34*(3), 203–217.

Roche, M. (2014). *Developing children's critical thinking through picture books: A guide for primary and early years students and teachers.* London: Routledge.

Sullivan, A., & Brown, M. (2013). *Social inequalities in cognitive scores at age 16: The role of reading.* CLS Working Paper 2013/10. London: Centre for Longitudinal Studies.

Tennent, W. (2014). *Understanding reading comprehension: processes and practices.* London: Sage.

10

Teachers as writers

John-Mark Winstanley and Lisa Moule

The teaching of writing in the primary phase is a complex process that requires a range of higher-order pedagogical skills and professional competences; it is also an 'artistic event' (Freire, 1985, p. 75) that demands a teacher to be brave, creative and knowledgeable. It is our view, based upon our own experience and our reading of research evidence, that those who teach writing should write themselves, in front of their pupils, so that they can provide an authentic example of how texts are created. Drawing upon Flower and Hayes's (1981) view of writing as a process of distinctive choices that are taken during the act of composing, we argue that teachers should have regular and frequent first-hand experiences of this process so that they can develop a deeper knowledge of this discipline and be able to articulate the 'writer's craft' to their students.

This chapter provides a case study of a professional development programme that supported a group of 27 teachers to develop their practice in this area. The course was developed in response to our concern that, within an ever-more prescriptive system, the meaning and purpose of writing is becoming distorted. The introduction of the 2014 National Curriculum marked an increased focus on transcription, grammar, spelling and accuracy. Our work with a number of teachers across a variety of schools in England tells us that, as a result, English lessons have become dominated by a technical view of writing. This has been exemplified in many of the lessons we have observed, where writing is regularly presented to children as a pre-prepared product that they are required to analyse and dissect from a technical perspective, often leading to the production of success criteria that dictate which word, sentence and text features children should incorporate into their own 'independent' work.

While we acknowledge that this approach has some benefits, our fear is that it comes at the expense of developing children's imagination and sense of self. Our key concern is that pressures within the current education system limit opportunities to inspire meaningful writing among primary pupils and we argue that teachers should be aware of the implicit messages that this approach sends to their pupils about writing. We believe that children need to develop an understanding of writing as a much more nuanced and creative process in which they have to learn to balance the demands of creativity and technical accuracy. After all, a piece of creative writing cannot communicate anything if it is not decipherable. Likewise, technically accurate writing achieves nothing if it does not engage the reader. As such, we advocate for the role of the teacher as a writing role model who can personify how to navigate and balance these two interdependent domains.

As this chapter will go on to explain, assuming the identity of a writing role model within the classroom is by no means an easy feat and is something that many teachers struggle with. We provide a case study of the Empowering Young Writers programme, a series of six twilight continuing professional development (CPD) sessions aiming to support teachers to develop this identity. First, the chapter will provide an overview of what defines a teacher's writing identity and then outline the key factors that evidence suggests may affect this. Following this, a summary of the literature underpinning the programme will be described before an overview of the content and structure of the programme is provided. Finally, drawing upon data collected from our wider research into the effects of this programme, the chapter will reflect upon the participants' experience and present some of the key findings identified.

Throughout the chapter, we invite the reader to reflect upon the key themes raised by engaging in reflective tasks. We hope that these reflective tasks will provide the reader with an opportunity to critically reflect upon the teaching of writing within their own setting and, through engaging with the questions and tasks suggested, identify implications for their own future practice.

Teachers' writing identities

What is a teacher's writing identity?

The nature of working as a primary teacher is often referred to as a role that requires wearing 'many hats'. As such, teachers are cast into multiple identities within any given day: mathematician, historian, scientist, poet, musician, social worker, peace negotiator to name but a few. The skills required to embody many of these identities should not be underestimated; theorists argue that teachers are actively engaged in the process of building their identity throughout their entire careers (Beijaard, Verloop, & Vermunt, 2003). When it comes to the teaching of writing, teachers are expected to enact a multitude of identities, often affected by the specific text type and genre of writing they are attempting to teach (see Figure 10.1). This is complicated further by the way in which many of the qualities and dispositions associated with being a writer can contradict those traditionally associated with being a teacher. For example, when modelling the writing of a diary entry, a teacher may be required to articulate a sense of vulnerability or emotion that they may consider to compromise their status or professional persona. This may explain the fact that – despite teaching writing daily – many teachers do not perceive themselves as writers and, in turn, possess a negative writing identity.

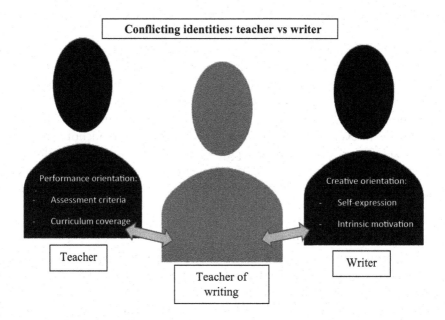

Conflicting identities: teacher vs writer

Performance orientation:
- Assessment criteria
- Curriculum coverage

Creative orientation:
- Self-expression
- Intrinsic motivation

Teacher

Writer

Teacher of writing

Figure 10.1 A visual representation of the conflicting identities of teacher and writer

The small field of research that focuses on this phenomenon frequently conceptualises teachers' writing identities from a sociocultural perspective as a positional, relational and thus multiple construct. Cremin and Baker (2010, p. 7) confirm the complexity of this phenomenon when they state that these identities 'are constructed in relation to the young people, other teachers, teaching assistants and parents' that teachers work with, suggesting that their identities are shaped not only by how they see themselves, but also how they perceive others see them.

Such research also identifies the consequential marked degree of pressure and challenge for professionals who, in order to support young writers, are required to assume the identity of a writer within the classroom. Cremin and Baker (2010) provide a helpful exploration of this through use of the terms 'teacher-writer' (taking a position that aims to meet the demands of a performative system) and 'writer-teacher' (adopting a more authentic and personal position). In defining these two positions, the authors draw attention to the tension between the act of writing on a personal and public level, concluding that teachers' writing identities 'constantly shift and are emotional, relational and conflictual', going on to describe them as 'a complex and interwoven mix of jostling interpersonal, institutional and intrapersonal influences' (Cremin & Baker, 2010, p. 27).

In this chapter, we define teachers' writing identities as constructs that are subject to personal, social and cultural factors. In line with this, we consider this term to embody not only who a teacher is as a writer (both in the past and present), but also what they know and do as a teacher of writing. We argue that, in order to act as the writing role models that pupils need, teachers require support to overcome the potential identity crisis that being a teacher of writing can bring. Key to this support is understanding the issues that may affect teachers' writing identities.

What factors affect teachers' writing identities?

Conflicting paradigms surrounding the teaching of writing

As Chamberlain (2016, p. 14) points out, for the past 30 years, the recommended pedagogy for classroom writing has adopted various models: 'the workshop approach (Graves, 1983); the skills-based approach (Berninger, Cartwright, Yates, Swanson, & Abbott, 1994); genre theory (Snyder, 2008); and, more recently, a return to the skills-based approach within a more prescriptive and accountable framework'.

As a result, a sense of ambiguity in both conception and policy surrounding what constitutes effective teaching of writing has emerged within schools. In line with this, there does not appear to be a significant body of evidence or policy that details the pedagogical skills, or knowledge, that a primary teacher of writing should possess. Green (2006, p. 111) argues that this has resulted in the emergence of 'dichotomous paradigms' surrounding English within schools, suggesting that each of these paradigms are attached to 'associated pedagogies, all of which enshrine their own particular purposes, codes and political agendas'. It is argued that this has left many teachers feeling unsure of how to teach writing effectively, thus affecting their identities as teachers of writing.

Teachers' own writing histories

A number of ethnographic and sociocultural studies (e.g. McKinney & Giorgis, 2009) have found that teachers' own previous experience of learning to write may be a key influencing factor over their subsequent identity. Our own research tells us that many teachers recall negative experiences of writing, describing lessons that placed a great deal of emphasis on transcription and correctness over composition and imagination. The significance of the link to previous writing experiences is explained by Lortie (1975, p. 63), whose work suggests that many teachers of writing may recreate the same type of writing opportunities and activities that they themselves experienced as learners through drawing upon 'their own apprenticeship of observation'. This is a particularly salient point when we consider the fact that many teachers will have been educated within the past 30 years – a period previously described to have been affected by conflicting messages surrounding best practice. Evidence suggests that this has had a negative influence on the identities of teachers as writers (Cremin & Baker, 2014).

Teachers' low self-efficacy as writers

We also believe that a psychological perspective on identity should be taken into account, particularly surrounding the concept of self-efficacy. As Bandura (1997, p. 382) explained, self-efficacy should not be confused with a teacher's confidence to teach: 'Whereas confidence is a nondescript term which refers to strength of belief, it does not necessarily specify what the certainty is about. Conversely, self-efficacy refers to belief in one's own capabilities that one can produce given levels of attainment.'

Research highlights the significant demands placed upon a generalist primary teacher in England, compounded by the fact that many teachers train to teach through a one-year postgraduate course (e.g. Alexander, 2010). While such teachers have no doubt been required to write as part of their previous academic experience, little time is afforded to explore what it means to be a writer or how to approach the complexities of writing different genres of texts for a multitude of purposes and audiences. Consequently, it is no surprise that many teachers express a lack of preparedness to teach writing effectively, resulting in a low sense of self-efficacy as both a writer themselves and as a teacher of writing.

Reframing identities through professional learning

With the latter issues in mind, a rather bleak picture emerges surrounding the state of teachers' writing identities. Notwithstanding, it is important to bear in mind the extent to which literature surrounding teachers' writing identities signposts them as social constructs that can change, depending on context and collaboration with others within professional learning experiences.

Lessons learned from national writing projects

A key theme that emerges from research surrounding teachers as writers is the positive effects that 'communities of practice' can have on teachers' writing identities. Wenger-Trayner and Wenger-Trayner (2015, p. 1) describe these as

> formed by people who engage in a process of collective learning in a shared domain of human endeavour ... In a nutshell, they are: groups of people who share a concern or a passion for something they do and learn how to do it better as they interact regularly.

Such groups have become central to national writing projects in the UK, United States and New Zealand where teachers' writing groups have been established.

The basic premise of these groups is that teachers can come together to write together and to learn more about the teaching of writing and there is a growing amount of evidence that can be largely assessed as signposting their potential.

Smith and Wrigley (2015, p. 4) argue that these groups allow teachers to find new understandings about the teaching of writing by providing communities of practice in which teachers can transform their identities 'in relation to their school community and that of the writing group ... absorbing new perspectives and gaining agency, translating personal knowledge into professional knowledge'.

The power of reflection

Smith and Griffiths (2014, p. 37) stated that teachers' writing groups provide teachers with a valuable opportunity for reflection – to 'pause and have the space and mutual encouragement to define who they are and what they do'. Moreover, it may also be the case that the transformational power of being able to be silent and think is maximised through the act of writing itself. This comes to light through a Vygotskyian body of thought, which suggests that writing, as a repertoire of social practice taking material form in text, has the capacity to change the way we think. Ong (1982, p. 78) argues that 'without writing, the literate mind would not and could not think as it does', going on to state that 'more than any other single invention, writing has transformed human consciousness'. With this in mind, it emerges that being positioned as a writer may lead to significant identity development as it establishes a semantic and emotional base that encourages reflection.

Improved subject knowledge

Research on CPD in writing also identifies the transformational impact that positioning teachers as writers themselves can exert. The rationale underpinning the belief that teachers should write is that through such activity, teachers can establish new understandings that can potentially reshape the epistemological assumptions that underpin their practice. A range of research details the positive effects that occur when teachers, through sustained engagement in writing and reflection within communities of practice, assume identities as writers and enact this identity with their students. This is reinforced by Locke (2015, p. 3) who explains that this transformation occurs because, through direct experience of writing, teachers 'develop a new found understanding of what pedagogical practices around writing actually work'. A visual representation of how knowledge is gained through being positioned as a writer is provided by Gardener (2014), whose work explores how to develop subject knowledge in the student teachers he has worked with (see Figure 10.2).

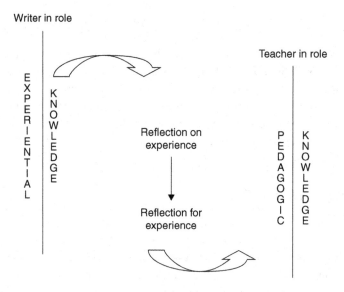

Figure 10.2 Knowledge gained from CPD in writing

Source: Gardener (2014).

The Empowering Young Writers programme

Inspired by the research previously outlined, the Empowering Young Writers programme was centred upon our belief that teachers need to have first-hand writing experiences that develop their own identity as writers and, as a result, improve their teaching of this subject (see Table 10.1). The design of this programme was also heavily influenced by Andrews (2008, p. 5), whose work asserted the following principles:

- To teach writing, you need to be able to write.
- Students should respond to one another's writing.
- The teacher should act as a writer alongside the students and be prepared to undertake the same assignments as the students.
- There is research about the teaching of writing that needs to be considered and applied, where appropriate, in the classroom.
- Teachers can be their own researcher in the classroom.
- The best teacher of writing teachers is another teacher of writing.
- Various stages in the writing process need to be mapped and practised: these include pre-writing, drafting, revising, editing, conferencing and publishing.

Table 10.1 An overview of the Empowering Young Writers programme

Focus of session	Key research explored
Session 1: Modelling The session modelled what aspects of the research explored might look like when incorporated into a 'model lesson'. Delegates adopted the role of pupils and programme leaders assumed the role of the teacher. Once the 'model lesson' had been delivered, delegates were asked to reflect upon the pedagogical approach of the lesson and to identify implications for their future practice.	Flower and Hayes (1981)
Session 2: Balancing the author and secretary The second session explored the implicit teaching of spelling, punctuation and grammar (SPAG) within the teaching of writing as a process model. This was again delivered through a 'model lesson' where delegates assumed the role of pupils. Once the lesson had been delivered, delegates were asked to reflect upon the pedagogical approach of the lesson and to identify implications for their future practice.	Flower and Hayes (1981) Johnston (2004) Ready and Bearne (2013)
Session 3: Who am I as a teacher of writing? Delegates reflected upon and discussed the challenges that writing/modelling writing and teaching writing presents. Following this, they were given time to 'practise' modelling the text type that they were going to teach the following week with a colleague and were then asked to reflect upon and discuss their experience. After this, practical strategies about how to model writing were generated through discussion and modelled by course leaders and delegates. Questions surrounding pupil engagement during modelling were discussed and practical strategies to address this were generated.	Cremin (2006) Cremin and Baker (2010)
Session 4: Modelling and developing creativity Delegates were required to engage in a variety of written activities that centred around developing creativity in writing. Following each piece of writing, delegates were asked to reflect upon and discuss their emotional response, as a writer, to each piece of writing and, from this, to discuss and identify implications for their future practice, as a teacher of writing. Delegates were invited to choose three activities that they wished to 'try out' with their own pupils, which they then reflected upon in the following session.	Cremin (2006) Barrs (2000b)

(continued)

Table 10.1 Cont.

Focus of session	Key research explored
Session 5: Drafting and crafting Delegates took part in a writer's workshop where they explored the planning, writing and drafting of a text with the use of a high-quality text as a stimulus. Delegates were asked to bring their own pupils' writing to the session and to reflect upon the opportunities given to children to engage in the full writing process. Following this, delegates worked in pairs to plan a sequence of lessons that would allow children to plan, write and draft a text. This was to be reflected upon in the next session.	Barrs (2000a)
Session 6: Who was I as a writer? Who do I want to be? Delegates reflected upon their own writing history and discussed how this may have shaped their identity as a writer and as a teacher of writing. Following this, participants took part in a structured conversation about their teaching of writing and reflected upon areas of strength and development. Finally, participants generated an action plan where they set themselves targets for how they aimed to teach writing in the future.	Locke (2015)

Lessons learned from participants' experiences

As part of the wider research project exploring the effects of the Empowering Young Writers programme, a series of questionnaires, self-efficacy measures and interviews were carried out before, during and after the programme. Overall, findings from this study provide evidence that participation may have resulted in some positive changes to participants' identities as writers. Teachers reported increased self-efficacy, confidence and competence as teachers of writing following their completion of the programme. They also spoke about how writing – both in and out of school – offered a valuable opportunity to articulate their emotions and improve their sense of well-being. Participants' responses often echoed previously mentioned research that their development came as a result of being part of a community of practice wherein they could reflect deeply upon the complexities of teaching writing.

Key headlines
Increased pedagogical content knowledge
Feedback from the teachers involved in the programme suggests that they benefited from significant gains in their understanding about the teaching of writing.

For some, this appeared to challenge their view of writing itself: 'I suppose before the course, I was so blinded by spelling and grammar that I had forgotten writing was supposed to be about expression, audience and purpose.' Moreover, a number of the participants indicated that they now have a greater understanding of the difficulties surrounding the writing process, indicating that this has significantly affected the way in which they approach the teaching of writing:

> I think actually writing myself has made me realise just how difficult it is. I know it sounds daft, but I just expected the children to write no problem before I did this course. I'd forgotten how hard it was to actually get the words from your head to the page and to actually make them make sense and there's no way I'd underestimate that again after sitting there all stuck in those sessions.

Participants' responses also reflected an increased empathy with their children as writers, reaching new understandings about the following:

- The importance of talk at all stages of writing – not only between teachers and pupils but between the pupils themselves.
- The way in which attention to detail and accuracy may be affected during the act of composition (i.e. new understandings that insisting upon 'best' handwriting and spelling at all points may be unrealistic).
- The role of the teacher in providing reassurance and boosting morale.
- The need for children to stop, reflect and read aloud, rather than writing constantly without time to think about how their writing is developing.
- An increased understanding of the value of editing and redrafting.

The importance of modelling

Findings from data collected also reveal the importance that participants attributed to modelling as a pedagogical tool significantly increased as a result of taking part in the programme; they now appear to model writing more regularly in front of their classes and reportedly feel more competent when they do so. This marks a significant shift in participants' understanding of how to teach writing, as summarised in the following comments:

> 'I never realised just how much the children get out of me modelling!'
> 'I feel like the children's writing is so much better – they're making so much better choices as writers because they've seen how to do it from me.'
> 'Their use of key vocabulary is so much stronger after they've seen me use it in context as a writer.'

The constraints of the system

While there were many positives highlighted by the teachers who took part in the course, it proves important to reflect upon some of the barriers that may constrain practice from their perspective. Before taking part in the course, questionnaires completed indicated that the majority of participants stated that they either 'sometimes' or 'never' enjoyed teaching writing. While this picture did improve post-CPD, many participants still expressed that the focus of the curriculum and assessment framework were key factors that deeply affected their enjoyment and practice in the teaching of writing. A typical response in both pre- and post-questionnaires was: 'It's just teaching a checklist, there's no joy or creativity'. From this, it is clear that the influence of performativity on teachers' writing identities is significant, supporting Grainger's (2005, p. 76) argument that teachers of writing perceive their role to have been 'reshaped and oriented towards instruction, explication and coverage of the specified writing curriculum'.

Subject knowledge and self-efficacy

Another key issue highlighted by data collected was the implication of an increased focus on technical accuracy within the National Curriculum in 2014. This appears to have resulted in high levels of anxiety for participants:

> 'There's just so much to teach and I don't know where to start – how do I get all of the children to write accurately? I can barely use a semi-colon.'
>
> 'I hate the focus on spelling and grammar, I just don't feel like I know how to explain it.'
>
> 'I don't understand half of the things in the curriculum, so how can I expect my children to?'

Data collected surrounding this issue is also clouded by a sense of accountability; participants felt vulnerable and anxious that their lack of knowledge in this area would lead others to doubt their efficacy as a teacher.

Conclusion

A key theme that emerges from this chapter is that to be an effective teacher of writing within the current system demands a robust writing identity. While findings suggest that the Empowering Young Writers programme may have had a positive influence on the writing identities of participants, evidence also indicates that, on its own, the programme may not be enough for changes to practice to be sustained. Our experiences have suggested to us that performativity discourses may have distorted the profession's understanding of the nature and purpose of composition and this may have a very limiting effect on how teachers view themselves as writers, teachers and teachers of writing. This serves as a call to action that teachers would benefit hugely from sustained professional development opportunities where they can continually develop their writing identities. Other important implications to consider from this chapter are to understand to what extent do we give opportunities for:

- teachers to pick up their pens and write;
- teacher educators and school leaders to challenge teachers' beliefs surrounding what constitutes 'real writing' through questioning the subjectivities they may have developed from their own writing histories or from the discourse surrounding literacy policy;
- CPD designers to establish supportive communities of practice where teachers can engage in meaningful dialogue and share their expertise;
- policy makers to reconsider the narrow focus of writing within the 2014 National Curriculum and the reductive nature of its assessment.

Moving forward, we feel more inspired than ever to continue providing meaningful professional development opportunities to support teachers to develop their identities as writers. A renewed focus of our work will be to continue to challenge the demands and rhetoric of the system through providing teachers with the opportunity to stop, think and write. Our aim is that, through providing these regular opportunities, the teachers we work with will be able to develop their own professional voice, self-efficacy and confidence through the texts that they write. In turn, we hope that they will feel empowered to assume the role of writer within their classrooms and provide their pupils with the creative, risk-taking and confident writing role model that they need.

References

Alexander, R. (Ed.) (2010). *Children, their world, their education: Final report and recommendations of the Cambridge Primary Review*. London: Routledge.

Andrews, R. (2008). *The case for a national writing project for teachers*. Reading: CfBT Education Trust.

Bandura, A. (1997). *Self-efficacy: The exercise of control*. New York, NY: W. H. Freeman & Company.

Barrs, M. (2000a). The reader in the writer. *Reading, 34*(2), 54–70.

Barrs, M. (2000b). Talking and writing. In T. Grainger, K. Goouch, & A. Lambirth (Eds.), *Creativity and writing: Developing voice and verve in the classroom* (pp. 46–61). London: Routledge.

Beijaard, D., Meijer P. C., & Verloop, N. (2003). Reconsidering research on teachers' professional identity. *Teaching and Teacher Education, 20*, 107–128.

Berninger, V. W., Cartwright, A. C., Yates , C. M., Swanson, H. L., & Abbott, R. D. (1994). Developmental skills related to writing and reading acquisition in the intermediate grades. *Reading and Writing, 6*(2), 161–196.

Chamberlain, L. (2016). *Improving writing in primary schools*. Exeter: Sage.

Cremin, T. (2006). Creativity, uncertainty and discomfort: teachers as writers. *Cambridge Journal of Education, 36*(3), 415–433.

Cremin, T., & Baker, S. (2010). Exploring teacher-writer identities in the classroom: Conceptualising the struggle. *English Teaching: Practice and Critique, 9*(3), 8–25.

Cremin, T., & Baker, S. (2014). *Teachers as writers: Implications for identity.* Sydney: PETAA.

Flower, L., & Hayes, J. R. (1981). A cognitive process theory of writing. *College Composition and Communication, 32,* 365–387.

Freire, P. (1985). Reading the world and the word: An interview with Paulo Freire. *Language Arts, 62*(1), 15–21.

Gardener, P. (2014). Becoming a teacher of writing: Primary student teachers reviewing their relationship with writing. *English in Education, 48*(2), 128–148.

Grainger, T. (2005). Teachers as writers: Learning together. *English in Education, 39*(1), 75–87.

Graves, D. H. (1983). *Writing: Teachers and children at work.* Exeter, UK: Heinemann Educational Books.

Green, A. (2006). University to school: Challenging assumptions in subject knowledge development. *Changing English, 13*(1), 111–123.

Johnston, P. H. (2004). *Choice words: How our language affects children's learning.* Portland, ME: Stenhouse.

Locke, T. (2015). *Developing writing teachers: Practical ways for teacher-writers to transform their classroom practice.* New York, NY: Routledge.

Lortie, D. C. (1975). *Schoolteacher: A sociological study.* Chicago, IL: University of Chicago Press.

McKinney, M., & Giorgis, C. (2009). Narrating and performing identity: Literacy specialists' writing identities. *Journal of Literacy Research, 41,* 104–149.

Ong, W. J. (1982). *Orality and literacy: The technologizing of the word.* London: Methuen.

Ready, D., & Bearne, E. (2013). *Teaching grammar effectively in primary schools.* London: UKLA.

Smith, J., & Griffiths, R. (2014). Writing spaces, professional places: How a teachers' writing group can nurture teaching identities. *Forum, 56*(1), 131–138.

Smith, J., & Wrigley, S. (2015). *Introducing teachers' writing groups: exploring the theory and practice.* Abingdon, UK: Routledge.

Snyder, I. A. (2008). *The literacy wars: Why teaching children to read and write is a battleground in Australia.* Crows Nest, NSW: Allen & Unwin.

Wenger-Trayner, E., & Wenger-Trayner, B. (2015, 15 April). Communities of practice: A brief introduction. Retrieved from http://wenger-trayner.com/introduction-to-communities-of-practice.

11

Developing collaborative problem-solving in our classrooms

Ems Lord, Emma Fuller, Gary Casey, Becky Moseley, Tom Oakley and Tracey Sandhu

If you want to go quickly, go alone. If you want to go far, go together.

(African proverb, Anonymous, n.d.)

How collaborative are our classes?

Imagine asking a group of pupils to draw a picture of a 'typical' mathematics lesson. What do you think we might see? Perhaps a busy classroom where fully engaged pupils are working together to solve a rich mathematical problem? Maybe not. Sadly, research tells us that far too many pupils draw themselves sitting alone at their desks, working away on a problem, with little or no interaction with others (Borthwick, 2011). Nevertheless, the ability to work together to solve problems is arguably more important than ever before. Current developments such as driverless cars and deliveries by drones signpost an increasingly automated environment; to manage these changes we need to refocus our attention on tasks where humans can thrive. We need to be able to problem-solve and, perhaps even more importantly, develop our skills to problem-solve as members of a team. Our pupils will be entering universities and workplaces that will demand the ability to work together, even though our curriculum and assessment system seem destined to produce individuals without the training or inclination to do so. It does not need to be this way.

It is essential that we understand how to support our pupils to develop their collaborative problem-solving (CPS) skills. Nevertheless, CPS has a complex set of requirements that we need to fully understand to plan and deliver effective professional development to enable CPS in the classroom.

Things are slowly changing. The highly influential Organisation for Economic Cooperation and Development (OECD), which also publishes the international performance comparisons known as PISA tables, beloved of policy makers and politicians worldwide, has begun publishing international comparisons of CPS skills (OECD, 2015). These international performance tables have brought CPS to the attention of a much wider audience. As a result, countries are responding by commissioning research to identify their own status as CPS nations and establish their next steps. In the UK, this led to the publication of *Solved! Making the Case for Collaborative Problem-Solving* (Luckin, Baines, Cukurova, Holmes, & Mann, 2017), resulting in a collaborative project between the Cambridgeshire Maths Team and many of the county's primary schools with the NRICH team (https://nrich. maths.org/) to explore ways to maximise the potential of our resources for nurturing CPS in the mathematics classroom. In this chapter we'll use classroom-based feedback to identify some of the challenges facing teachers addressing CPS and share some of the effective ways that they have addressed those issues, which are useful to consider when planning professional development for colleagues. Before we explore those findings, let's clarify our understanding of CPS.

What CPS is *and* what it isn't

To help us define CPS, let's do some mathematics together. It's a task called Shape Draw, which involves drawing a shape by following a set of eight clues, one clue at a time. Our first clue calls for a shape with 'two pairs of parallel sides'. Which shapes could we draw? Perhaps it's a quadrilateral; if so, and we don't know that it is yet, then we could sketch a rectangle and a rhombus yet both of our answers would satisfy the first clue. However, the shape might also be a hexagon … Already the power of this activity is becoming apparent as we compare our sketches and realise the wealth of possible answers satisfying this single clue. Our next clue adds a further requirement, it asks for a shape with four right angles as well as the two pairs of parallel sides. Suddenly, one of our sketches needs to change since the rhombus no longer satisfies our criteria. As the task continues, further refinements call for more revisions to our original shape. It becomes increasingly apparent that a willingness to refine our answers, draw on our combined prior knowledge and learn from one another are the essential skills for successfully addressing the challenge. These types of problems, where working together enables our pupils to reach a shared goal, are at the heart of CPS and a highly effective starting point for launching a professional development programme for colleagues focusing on CPS.

Collaborating and solving problems

There are clearly two interpretations to clarify at this point, our interpretations of collaboration and problem-solving. Let's begin with problem-solving, which is one of the three key focuses of the Department for Education's (DfE) 2013 mathematics curriculum (alongside reasoning and fluency). Mathematics education writer and researcher John Mason (2017) argued that, 'If you don't get stuck on a problem, then it can hardly be called a problem!' In schools, we often use routine problems to rehearse skills and embed new facts, such as retrieving times tables facts. Such tasks are ideal for developing procedural fluency. However, mathematical fluency arguably demands far more than pupils demonstrating merely their procedural fluency. It is very worthwhile exploring the different interpretations of mathematical fluency with colleagues before embarking on a professional development programme promoting CPS. One approach towards mathematical fluency that we shared with teachers during our project was proposed by Jeremy Kilpatrick and his colleagues in their *Adding It Up* report (Kilpatrick, Swafford, & Findell, 2001); they suggested that mathematical fluency also requires a positive attitude towards non-routine problems with pupils demonstrating a willingness to solve and pose problems as well as the ability to convince others of their ideas.

The importance of non-routine problems for CPS

Non-routine problems enable our pupils to develop their mathematical fluency, rather than just their procedural fluency. However, when we pose non-routine problems, we arguably place a much greater demand on our pupils because they must also decide how to address each problem on its individual merits. It is generally acknowledged that the teaching of problem-solving varies from school to school as well as from class to class, with some pupils experiencing more non-routine problems than others. This can therefore be a worthwhile professional development topic with colleagues. Developing pupil confidence addressing non-routine problems supports them to successfully make the transition from school mathematics to real-world mathematics, where they might be asked to calculate how much paint they will need to paint their kitchen or the number of paving slabs for a new patio in their garden.

Collaborating or cooperating?

Although our current curriculum and assessment regimes test both routine and non-routine problem-solving, the assessments are usually sat by individuals in rooms where their familiar groups of tables are reorganised with the desks set apart from another, their bags are left at the door and their colourful classroom displays are hidden from view. Asking teachers to learn more about their pupils' view of classroom mathematics by encouraging their classes to sketch themselves doing mathematics can reveal the extent that they regard mathematics as a solitary or collaborative activity. In real life, we rarely need to face problems alone. Many employers now require their potential employees to demonstrate their teamworking skills as well as their academic qualifications during their selection processes. This brings us to the difference between collaboration and cooperation. Collaboration arguably extends beyond cooperation, although the two terms are often used synonymously. For example, one of the teachers in our project gave the example of a production line in a biscuit factory where individual workers perform their tasks that, when combined, lead to the production of a box of biscuits ready for transportation to shops far and wide. They compared the biscuit factory scenario with a different challenge where a group is stranded in a remote forest where they must support one another to reach safety as quickly as possible and simply completing one individual task each may not be sufficient to get rescued. Their two scenarios highlight the differences between cooperation and collaboration, but also their similarities. Clearly, collaboration requires cooperation, but it also requires much more. Collaboration requires everyone to pull together to reach a common goal rather than achieve individual goals – the concept of a common goal is a key aspect of CPS. Nevertheless, too many activities are often labelled as collaborative when perhaps they would be better described as cooperative. Moreover, there appears to be a lack of suitable mathematical resources for classroom collaboration as well as serious concerns to overcome regarding its successful implementation in our schools. Let's explore some of those concerns raised by the teachers in our project.

What are the potential barriers to embedding CPS?

Canvassing the views of almost 100 teachers we found several recurring themes that included negatively held attitudes towards teamworking, insufficient access to high-quality teaching resources, concerns regarding the tendency of some pupils to dominate problem-solving groups as well as some of the other pupils struggling to make meaningful contributions. Other issues raised by the teachers addressed the possibility of increased noise levels in the mathematics classroom and justifying the allocation of teaching time for CPS. It was important to recognise such concerns at the outset of the professional development programme and address them during the training for the teachers. We will address each of these concerns in turn, beginning with attitudes towards teamwork.

Barrier 1: negative attitudes towards CPS

Although an ability to work effectively as a team is valued by many educators and employers, not every teacher or pupil enjoys teamwork. Moreover, we must be aware that some pupils (such as those on the autistic spectrum) may require additional support during CPS sessions. Indeed, we should acknowledge that some individuals make highly effective contributions to their workplaces by working alone and only occasionally seeking out others to test their ideas before retreating for further study and reflection. Nevertheless, CPS activities help to prepare pupils for future challenges that often require teamwork.

Barrier 2: curriculum pressures

Teachers face ever-growing demands on their limited teaching time. Moreover, the impact of high-stake tests can seriously impact on the capacity of teachers to fully address CPS skills in their classrooms. Time is clearly an issue; teachers in our project expressed concerns that lessons which address collaboration and problem-solving may require more time than other sessions focusing on procedural fluency. Teachers need to feel confident that they can devote sufficient time to nurturing CPS skills and that those skills are valued by all stakeholders including governors and senior leaders.

Barrier 3: excessive noise levels

It is often claimed that teachers change their lessons according to whether they are being observed and that the more unpredictable, possibly noisier CPS lessons are best left to times when teachers are left alone with their charges and feel more confident to experiment with new ideas. Nevertheless, concerns about noise levels are important and need to be addressed through our project, especially if they prevent the wider use of CPS in the classroom and lead to missed opportunities to showcase teaching skills to both your classes and senior managers.

Barrier 4: dominant pupils

Concerns about pupils dominating a group were one of the most frequently voiced concerns raised by teachers regarding CPS. Clearly, if one pupil dominated then the others in the group either did not get the chance to share their ideas or, when they did get their chance to speak, it had taken so long to arrive that they had completely forgotten the point that they wanted to make! In such situations, it became a self-fulfilling prophecy as the other pupils tended to remember that a pupil had not contributed and they became even more reluctant to let them speak in later sessions. The teachers in this project felt that concerns regarding individual pupils dominating a lesson were one of the key barriers for schools not engaging with CPS.

Barrier 5: 'invisible' pupils

Whether or not a group had a domineering pupil, the teachers noted that they may have had one or more pupils who did not contribute towards their team goal. Those non-contributing pupils might have been very aware of the set challenge, and understood what they needed to do, but they did not actively engage with the group. They become 'invisible' pupils during group work. As a result, they missed out on opportunities to explain their ideas and develop their reasoning skills. Our project actively explored ways to support those pupils to become more effective team members.

Barrier 6: lack of resources

If a topic or skill (such as CPS) does not feature explicitly in the curriculum, there is a tendency for the manufacturers of teaching resources not to offer suitable resources related to this topic or skill to their schools. Thankfully, a growing awareness of the need to develop CPS skills should lead to a wide range of materials for schools over the next few years.

Maximising the potential of CPS in the classroom

Having established some of the issues surrounding CPS, the NRICH team worked more closely with a group of ten Cambridgeshire schools and the Cambridgeshire local authority's mathematics team to explore ways to address some of those concerns. We began by examining more closely the work of Rose Luckin and her team based at University College London (UCL) who had identified the following five key elements for effective CPS tasks (Luckin et al., 2017, p. 35) and shared them with mathematics subject leaders at their termly briefing events:

- *Positive interdependence*: the task cannot be completed by one person alone. Group members must synchronise their efforts.
- *Promotive interaction*: members are willing to support each other to complete the task.
- *Individually accountable*: pupils must undertake their share of the work and feel responsible for the group's success.
- *Interpersonal and group skills need to be developed/supported*: we cannot assume pupils naturally have (or will use) high-level collaboration skills.
- *Group processing*: members reflect on the quality of their working relationship and seek to improve it through personal and joint effort.

At these subject leader briefings, we found that those five key elements of successful CPS resource design identified by Luckin's UCL team were reflected in several of the concerns raised by the Cambridgeshire teachers. The teachers also liked the recognition that CPS skills needed constant nurturing in the classroom. However, since existing resources did not specifically address each of those five key elements of CPS, we encouraged the schools to revisit several existing NRICH resources and maximise their potential for developing CPS. We recruited project schools from across the county so that they could share their findings with local schools at subsequent meetings. Each of our project schools investigated ways to adapt several resources for their classes to address the five key elements. A member of the NRICH team visited each of the ten schools and collated their feedback to identify which were the most effective ways to adapt the resources to promote CPS in the classroom, which were shared at a later round of briefings. Several common themes, and some unexpected results, emerged across the schools, which we will explore in the next section. This highlights key strategies to share during professional development for schools by exploring how the schools adapted the shape activity known as Stringy Quads (Figure 11.1) and the number activity Five Steps to 50 (Figure 11.2).

Stringy Quads

Age 7 to 11
You will need a loop of string for this activity and three other friends.

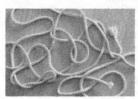

Stretch the string out so that each of you is holding a corner to make a quadrilateral.

Try to make one that has exactly one line of symmetry.
Is it possible?
How could you convince someone else that your shape has just one line of symmetry?
Can you make any other quadrilaterals with just one line of symmetry?

Try again, but this time answer the same questions for a quadrilateral with exactly two lines of symmetry.

Try again, but this time answer the same questions for a quadrilateral with exactly three lines of symmetry.

Try again, but this time answer the same questions for a quadrilateral with exactly four lines of symmetry.

Figure 11.1 NRICH String Quads task

Source: Used with permission of NRICH, University of Cambridge.

Professional development key point 1: encourage interdependence

The teachers reported that Stringy Quads addressed the need for positive interdependence because it offered an example of a task that could not be completed alone since it required several pupils to hold a length a string to create the different quadrilateral shapes. By rethinking a symmetry task, which was often worksheet-based and required pupils to draw mirror lines of redrawn shapes, we maximised its potential for teamwork. The schools trialling this activity found that increasing the group sizes, from the initially recommended number of four pupils in our teacher notes and raising that total to five or even six pupils, increased the opportunities for positive interdependence. More specifically, they found that having four pupils holding the corners of the string to create the shapes meant that there was no one left to record their ideas or reflect on their approach. This caused problems during

Five Steps to 50

Age 5 to 7
This challenge is about counting on and back in steps of 1,10 and 100.

Roll a die twice to establish your starting number – the first roll will give you the tens digit and the second roll will give you the units digit.
You can then make five jumps to get as close to 50 as possible.
You can jump forwards or backwards in jumps of 1, 10 or 100.

Compare your strategy with a friend.
Did you jump forwards or backwards?
Can you land on 50 exactly?
How far from 50 were you?
Could you do it another way?
Could you get even closer?
Which numbers can get you to 50?
Which can't?

Roll the die again and have another go!

For example:
I roll a die and get a 2 then a 3, so my starting number is 23.
I make the following jumps to get as close to 50 as possible:
Starting number is 23
Jump one is +10 to get me to 33
Jump two is +10 to get me to 43
Jump three is +10 to get me to 53
Jump four is −1 to get me to 52
Jump five is −1 to get me to 51

Figure 11.2 NRICH Five Steps to 50 task

Source: Used with permission of NRICH, University of Cambridge.

the feedback part of the lesson since most groups lacked any supporting notes for their answers. In one of the schools, where a teacher had removed all of the desks to leave just stools and clipboards when the pupils returned from their lunch break, they reported increased pupil engagement, 'I just knew that something exciting was going to happen', explained one of their pupils when they discovered the new layout of their classroom. Adapting the classroom environment for different CPS tasks seemed a very positive approach. More importantly, the schools told us that ensuring their pupils took turns recording their ideas, holding the string and observing the group was essential towards nurturing CPS skills in the classroom. Clearly one key aspect of ensuring positive interdependence was identifying several tasks within the wider group challenge and allowing time for every pupil to take their turn at each of those tasks.

In contrast to the group activity Stringy Quads, the number activity Five Steps to 50 was intended to be played in pairs and many of the learners really enjoyed that aspect of the activity. This was usually because the pairs approach ensured that there were two distinct roles for the learners, which they felt made it fair because, in most cases, one pupil rolled the die and the other recorded their answers before swapping roles. Many pupils reported that they were able to work together without having the issues of trying to get heard within a larger group. They also found it easier to stay on track when working in pairs and not get disturbed by others. Nevertheless, the importance of carefully planning the modelling aspect of a lesson arose several times during discussions with teachers who were aware that some of their pupils would try to dominate their group, even if that group only had one other member. So, they modelled taking turns with the die and recording the task, not assuming that those pupils would automatically take turns. Their approach reinforced the importance of continuing to address the need to nurture CPS skills, even for paired activities.

In some classes, there were pupils who preferred to work alone on this activity. In one class, the teacher managed the situation by allowing a pupil to initially work alone but ensured that they shared their answers with a partner at regular intervals. The individual pupil began by using the same wipe board recording approach as his peers, but he quickly realised that a 100 square might be more helpful and willingly shared his efforts with his partner (Figure 11.2). The pupil had discovered a very effective visual approach towards representing his pattern spotting. 'Another way of thinking about this problem,' he reflected, 'is that you can move five spaces across or down.' This realisation led to the different patterns on his worksheet. Can you follow his reasoning? It might help knowing that his class used a set of dice numbered from one to six.

The other pupils in his class quickly realised that they could swap their number lines and wipe boards for 100 squares too. Although the pair did not work together all the time, their teacher found a highly effective way of managing their pairing to the benefit of the whole class and hopefully, this will develop their CPS more fully over an extended period of time.

Professional development key point 2: encourage group work

Our project schools shared two key approaches towards encouraging promotive interaction. Their first approach was curriculum linked; they noticed that successfully encouraging pupils to work together mathematically partly depended on the mathematical strand of their chosen activity. When teachers presented their classes with activities exploring either shape, space and measures (such as Stringy Quads) or the statistics strands of the curriculum, some of their pupils tended to be more willing to work together than when they were presented with number-based activities. Several pupils raised their concerns about working with others on collaborative number tasks, some even suggesting that it was a form of cheating. Reflecting on their comments, the teachers felt that their pupils' views were possibly influenced by the assessment regime, which increasingly prioritised number and calculation skills. However, those pupils did positively engage with Stringy Quads. This engaging geometry task certainly gained their initial attention, but the project schools reported that it maintained their attention through its 'low-threshold, high-ceiling' design. In other words, the task was designed to ensure that it was easily accessible to all pupils, but it offered a hidden level of challenge as they worked through the task.

Similarly, Five Steps to 50 is a very engaging problem. It might be inadvertently dismissed as an activity for young children yet its potential for promoting pattern spotting in the mathematics classroom led to its inclusion in sessions for older learners. In many cases during this project, we found that teachers wanting to focus on nurturing CPS skills often lessened the mathematical requirements of a lesson by choosing an activity from a lower key stage. This often worked extremely well and with Five Steps to 50 teachers reported that their older pupils often stayed on the task into their break time and continued exploring their ideas later in the day.

The classroom environment was just as important as it was for Stringy Quads. Several teachers ensured that their pupils had access to a range of useful resources such as number lines, Numicon and bead strings on their desks, with dice and wipe boards also easily accessible in most classes.

Professional development key point 3: ensure individual accountability

One of the major concerns surrounding group work among the teachers was the potential for pupils to distance themselves from the group task and consequently make little or no progress during the lesson. The project schools found several ways to address this concern when they were using the activity Stringy Quads. For example, some schools modelled listening to each pupil's suggestions before choosing together the next shape to try. Even more effective was stating very early in the session that any member of a group might be expected to share their findings with the rest of the class. Those teachers found that their pupils invariably made a much greater effort to understand their team's approach and solution.

In most classes, the teachers trialling Five Steps to 50 encouraged their pupils to choose a partner who they thought they would work well with on the given task. In the subsequent reflection sessions, several pupils admitted differentiating between partners they would choose in a mathematics lesson and those they would choose to spend their break time with afterwards. This showed a developing awareness of the requirements for successful CPS and teamwork among the pupils. To help their pupil pairs to feed back to their classes and reinforce the point that they would need to do so, some of their teachers provided each pair with a recording sheet. However, most of the teachers in this project encouraged pairs to develop their own recording approaches.

Whisper Maths

The teachers in this project found that Whisper Maths was a useful first step towards embedding CPS in their classroom. Whisper Maths came about after a colleague returned from a study trip to Hungary where she witnessed a very different approach towards problem-solving in their high-performing mathematics classrooms. Rather than pose a problem and set their classes to solve it in groups (an approach adopted by many UK-based schools), which often leads to concerns about raised noise levels as well as issues regarding dominating pupils and others not contributing towards the team goal, Whisper Maths offered a structured, much quieter approach, which in turn could lead towards developing CPS in the class-room. Here's how it worked: once the teacher had shared the problem with their class, the pupils returned to their tables that had large sheets of paper on them. No one spoke at that point and, adopting an approach that mirrored the more familiar 'think, pair, share' often seen in English lessons, the pupils returned to their desks to jot down their initial thoughts on the portion of paper in front of them. Some noted key facts, other drew diagrams or began some exploratory working out of their initial ideas. When they were ready, they shared their thoughts with their partner, using their jottings as an aide-memoire – this really helped to support the less confident pupils to share their ideas. Finally, the group had an opportunity to share their ideas and record their agreed solution in the centre of the paper. Teachers in our project found that the use of the large sheet of paper in their own Whisper Maths sessions enabled their more reluctant speakers to participate when they had a prompt, and the time allocated for personal thought at the start of the session prevented the more excitable pupils from dominating the group. Pupils appreciated the initial thinking time too and, after several sessions using the Whisper Maths approach, they seemed to grow in confidence.

Professional development key point 4: nurture interpersonal and group skills

Across our project we found that the level of CPS skills varied between schools and between their classes. However, several of the teachers found that it was just as important to model working collaboratively as it was to model mathematical procedures in the classroom. For Stringy Quads, the teachers explained that they focused on ensuring that their pupils understood the need to rotate around the different roles. More importantly, they ensured that every member of the group could articulate their team goal. For Stringy Quads, that objective was very clear since their pupils simply had to list shapes with the different number of lines of symmetry and justify their reasoning. Understanding was key to successfully embedding CPS in the classroom. Unless pupils fully understood the team goal, they struggled to support their group no matter their level of enthusiasm and willingness to work together.

Bringing the pupils together to reflect on their CPS skills on a regular basis enabled their teachers to help them to compare their paired skills during activ-ities, such as Five Steps to 50, compared with the group skills needed for tasks like Stringy Quads. There was a strong preference among the pupils for working in pairs rather than groups. Some of the pupils expressed the difficulties that they often faced getting their voice heard within a larger group. Others noted that in group-work sessions they tended to forget what they wanted to say if they had to wait too long for their turn to speak, making it somewhat embarrassing when they finally got their turn to talk but had nothing to say!

Professional development key point 5: encourage group reflection

Many of the teachers in this project reported that the approach that would have the most lasting impression on their future teaching was the inclusion of reflection time in their planning. In our study, we gathered together a group of pupils and asked them to rate their CPS skills in front of their fellow team members. At first, the teachers noticed that some pupils overestimated their CPS abilities and lacked the empathy to support others. 'I just told them what to do' was a frequent comment from those individuals who perhaps needed to nurture their teamworking skills to maximise the potential of Stringy Quads. By listening to the reflections of others, and their future targets, those pupils who initially tried to dominate sessions became more aware of the need to support others to learn too. Others admitted the frustration of knowing several shapes that their group could try during Stringy Quads while acknowledging that they needed to allow the other pupils time to think for themselves and express their own ideas. However, by stressing the need to justify their ratings and listen to the comments of others, it quickly became apparent during the project how much the pupils benefited from regular opportunities to reflect on their CPS skills and identify their possible learning goals.

Although enabling the pupils to experience such group reflection sessions often demanded additional time, the teachers reported that it was time well spent. Towards the end of the project, several teachers reported that the pupils who had focused solely on their own teamworking efforts and mathematical knowledge began to comment on how they supported other members of their group rather than simply telling them what to do. Moreover, several schools reported that they intended to continue the approach by embedding reflection sessions in their regular timetable.

When pupils reflected on their experiences of working together on Five Steps to 50, most reported that they had enjoyed working with their partners, but some were less positive about paired work for number challenges such as this one. More specifically, they felt that number work was far better suited for individual tasks and stated that they would have preferred to work alone. When prompted, they admitted that having a partner might be helpful if they got stuck but were reluctant to work that way if at all possible during number sessions.

Discussion

Throughout this collaborative project between the Cambridgeshire Maths Team, its county schools and NRICH, we found that the teachers were very willing to incorporate CPS skills in their mathematics lessons but those lessons required careful planning and often additional teaching time too, which are key messages for anyone planning to deliver professional development addressing CPS. Most pupils preferred paired work over group tasks, but a significant number would choose to work alone whenever possible. The key reasons for preferring paired work were the opportunity to support one another when they got stuck and the benefits of being able to share their thoughts more easily than when they were members of a larger group. However, the finding that some pupils felt that CPS sessions in mathematics were paramount to cheating demands further investigation. To embed CPS in the classroom, we need to fully understand the reasons behind such views.

School leaders also need to recognise that CPS sessions require more teaching time than conventional mathematics lessons, but that their teachers regard the additional time as time well spent. Moreover, supporting effective CPS requires resource designers to go much further. They need to offer teachers ways to use their activities to promote individual responsibility as well as a group ethos. If they have access to suitable resources, and strategies such as those discussed in this chapter, then pupils should develop the CPS needed to thrive in their increasingly automated environment.

This project has helped to bring CPS to the wider attention of teachers through NRICH presentations, blogs and research articles and you can explore some of these yourself by following the links in the reference section of this chapter. We hope that our findings offer useful insights for planning your own professional development promoting CPS with young children. If you would like to focus on CPS outside the classroom, the Cambridgeshire Maths Team have developed a series of freely available Maths Trails.

References

Borthwick, A. (2011). Children's perceptions of, and attitudes towards, their mathematics lessons. *British Society for Research into Learning Mathematics, 31*, 37–42.

Kilpatrick, J., Swafford, J., & Findell, B. (Eds.) (2001). *Adding it up: Helping children learn mathematics*. Washington, DC: National Academy Press.

Luckin, R., Baines, E., Cukurova, M., Holmes, W., & Mann, M. (2017). *Solved! Making the case for collaborative problem-solving*. London: Nesta. Retrieved from https://media.nesta.org.uk/documents/solved-making-case-collaborative-problem-solving.pdf. https://nrich.maths.org/

Mason, J. (2017). Solving the problem of problem-solving. Retrieved from www.hoddereducation.co.uk/igcsemathematicsblog2.

Office for Economic Cooperation and Development (OECD) (2015). *Collaborative problem-solving*. Retrieved from www.oecd.org/pisa/pisa-2015-results-volume-v-9789264285521-en.htm.

12

Creative ways of learning: using therapeutic arts to inspire professional learning

James Biddulph and Jodie Cariss

Introduction

This chapter is not concerned with professional learning about subject knowledge or skills. Instead, it seeks to explore how the development of teachers and teaching assistants as human beings with agency, with the capacity to deepen awareness of themselves, can lead to richer, more wholesome school communities. In so doing, we argue that teachers and teaching assistants are better equipped to navigate the emotional, intellectual and social complexity that is involved in teaching in primary schools. We do this through a lens of creative learning.

While we come from different professional backgrounds, one education and one therapeutic-psychological, our views and assumptions have synergy in the ways that we have experienced transformations of individuals and school communities through creative learning. We have both worked in schools to support possibility thinking and creative learning to flourish: Jodie as an innovator, arts therapist and business entrepreneur and James as a head teacher, previously advanced skills teacher in music and creativity and academic researcher with expertise in the diversity of creative learning. We both unashamedly and strongly believe that creative learning matters. We are convinced that the future courage of humanity requires generations of people who are creative and who can develop as creative learners. Our argument is that creative learning for educators matters as a vital way for them to support children to navigate creatively the complexities of contemporary globalised life (Sefton-Green, Thomson, Jones, & Bresler, 2011).

The vitality of creative learning for professional learning

In most of the developed world, it is widely accepted that creative learning is an important skill for twenty-first-century learners (Craft, Cremin, Hay, & Clack, 2014): as political aspiration, economic driver, manifesto for school reform, in policy pronouncements and academic research (Sefton-Green et al., 2011, p. 1). Seen in this light, creative learning in education has become part of a global democratic agenda with the following assumptions: all humans are creative by nature; creative learning can be taught and developed; creative learning has purpose across a wide domain; and from a neoliberal position of individualism, the ability to learn with creativity is valuable for a fast-changing knowledge economy. And yet, why is it that so many people say, 'I'm not very creative'? Historically, the dominance of Western thought about creativity (linked with the so called great artists – often white and male) associated it as a mystical phenomenon that arose in the minds of geniuses. This has deep provenance as far as the ancient Greek philosophical tradition of the creative 'muses'. The residue of this 'romantic' view still lives on in the minds of many people: 'I am not creative because I don't play an instrument', 'I cannot paint so I am not creative' or 'I don't sing, dance, act', etc. Both authors have heard such deeply held beliefs in staff rooms and during the workshops we have led in various and diverse educational contexts.

Creative learning is a contested concept. In fact, Professor Pam Burnard has pluralised the concept of creativity (using creativities) to indicate the multiplicity of practices and meanings (Burnard, 2012). So, what could creative learning be? It is a question that has prompted a number of responses from sociocultural, sociological and psychological fields (Glăveanu, Tanggaard, & Wegener, 2016; Owen, 2011; Sefton-Green et al., 2011). Figure 12.1 brings together some of the main findings within the research field.

In many ways, it is related to definitions of creativity, involving playfulness, attributes of possibility thinking and as socially constructed: 'imaginative activity fashioned so as to produce outcomes that are both original and of value' (NACCCE, 1999, p. 29). There is a sense throughout the literature that creative learning is connected with practices that give people access to decision-making, control over some of their activities and acknowledging ideas (Craft et al., 2014). It involves agency, requires change and recognises that we all learn in different ways; that we learn better when there is relevance and that learning can be collaborative and social.

In a professional context, how are teachers and teaching assistants afforded agency and how do they feel the collaborative and social dimensions of learning? Where is the space for educators to think or be or respond creatively? It is a matter of importance that schools create cultures in which such exploration can happen and in doing so, deepen human relationships and create schools that work beyond expectations. Hargreaves and Fullan (2012) argue that improving teaching at an

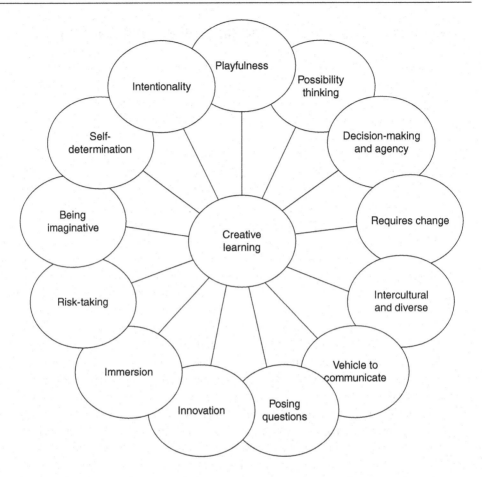

Figure 12.1 Creative learning model

individual level is insufficient. Focusing on the environment – the culture – in which teachers work is as important because teachers are profoundly affected by environments for learning, collaboration and shared endeavour to improve (or environments of competition, individualism and isolation): 'At its best, culture doesn't give you a good teacher here and a weaker teacher there, but many strong and capable teachers working passionately together, under visionary leadership, so all students succeed' (Hargreaves & Fullan, 2012, p. 21). Donald Winnicott (see in Caldwell & Taylor Robinson, 2017) a paediatrician and psychotherapist, whose theories are fundamental to the way we understand child development, suggested that play is the primary form of creativity and acts as a facilitation for mental growth. It helps children to become adults and it helps adults to reach their potential. A useful place for the reader to refer is the Play in Education Development and Learning (PEDAL) research centre at the University of Cambridge, which aims to develop empirical research to make sense of play in children's development and in education. Emphasising the playfulness of creative learning, from a therapeutic perspective, is essentially an externalisation of internal feelings or the manifestation of imagined possibilities. For art therapy, learning through creativities acts as a way of encouraging and allowing individuals to be heard in their world; a vital tool for expression and for understanding complex emotions and ideas and that often acts as a vehicle for communicating deep thoughts and feelings. Essentially, creativity is an important way we find meaning in the world. And therapeutically, when we are able to create we are able to find meaning: 'It has meaning to me because I created it', a teacher told Jodie during a project. Opportunities to release the imagination, which we describe here, build on evidence in other schools and global contexts (Gunzenhauser & Noblit, 2011; McGill, N'Guessan, & Rosen, 2007).

Notes from a therapist ...

Creativity speaks to and from us, most commonly the unconscious parts of ourselves. It can also be in conscious acts, for example what you are wearing, reading, saying, doing, but most often the deep connection we feel to ourselves when being creative is unconscious. By playing creatively whether through dance, art, games, photography, cooking, writing, gardening, cake decorating, sketching, whatever, we are unconsciously allowing ourselves to make sense of the world and of ourselves, which is why it can feel so nourishing.

Why should teachers be creative and reflective?

The *Cambridge Primary Review* (Alexander, 2010, p. 226) suggested the value of creativity (which we extend to creative learning) in primary education, as well as highlighting the problems of the ambiguity of meaning, understanding of practice and the 'loose way' in which language related to it is used. As well as a clear encouragement for a vigorous campaign aimed at advancing public understanding of creativity in education, human development, culture and national life it is also essential for teachers to have time and space to be creative, so that they are able to just 'be', to reflect, connect with their communities of practice and also to be themselves.

Notes from a therapist ...

It is important for educators to have an opportunity to experience creative learning, so that they remain open to learning about themselves and others and from a therapy position, to enhance mental health. This is because when

> we express ourselves, we have a sense of freedom and we feel connected to ourselves: this often feels intrinsically good because feeling lost does not! Feeling lost is also not conducive to mental wellness. In the contemporary world, there is a growing interest by mental health professionals to advocate for the essential use of the arts and creativity as a way to document the journey towards a more peaceful and vibrant life.

The National Alliance for Arts, Health and Wellbeing was launched in 2012 to address such concerns. This overarching body was needed in order to focus the many voices and pieces of evidence that demonstrate how creativity can impact both physical and mental health. Dr Richard Corrigall, a psychiatrist working with adolescents in South London, has written about how creative engagement helps his clients to bring richness and meaning to their lives and focus on more than just eradicating symptoms. Corrigall (2019) places emphasis on the view that there is no right or wrong when it comes to creating something or being creative.

For teachers, this is a profound shift from the pressure of overly prescriptive accountability agenda in which trusting the professional body of teachers is uncommon. To know that there is no right or wrong, in the spaces of creative learning, and that creativity enhances the opportunity for new ideas has the potential to change cultures in school. When creative learning is developed within the whole staff body (including administration teams), the outcomes are different solutions to problems, opening our perspectives, finding new ways to communicate and connect. If teachers are able to do this for themselves they will stand a much better chance of enabling students to do so and to reach their potential.

A model for creative learning in professional development

In order to dispel the strongly held views about creative learning, we frame our professional development using a model devised by Craft, Cremin, Burnard, Dragovic, and Chappell (2013). In their search for creative pedagogies, they developed the notion of *possibility thinking* as a way of conceptualising creative learning. This concept involves:

- posing questions;
- play;
- immersion;
- innovation;
- risk-taking;
- being imaginative;
- self-determination;
- intentionality.

It also involves interactions between learner and teacher, which brings into view the importance of standing back (how and when do teachers do this?), learner agency (where are the opportunities?), enacting within time in space (how much time is possible within a cramped curriculum timetable?): for our purposes in this chapter, giving time within school that encourages standing back, teacher agency and an open enabling space for these attributes of possibility thinking to arise (see Figure 12.2).

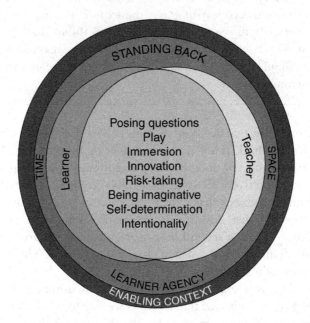

Figure 12.2 Pedagogy that nurtures possibility thinking – initial work

Source: Craft et al. (2013).

A number of questions come to mind: What might constitute *enabling contexts for creative learning/possibility thinking* in professional development contexts? When do in-service training (INSET) days or staff meetings create an enabling space for such possibility thinking features to arise and be developed? When do school leaders stand back and give agency to their teams? If they do, how often? And what is the effect on the learning and response from teachers? How much time is given for immersion and being imaginative? The questions are many. But they direct towards the view that unless teachers have direct and lived experience of these aspects in their own learning, they will not be well equipped to foster such possibility thinking and creative learning in the children they teach. The remainder of this chapter contends with well-received processes that not only created such enabling spaces but also brought about a greater awareness of self, creativities and playfulness.

Step 1: developing consciousness and awareness

Notes from a therapist …

We all have a unique and personal lens on the world. We understand the world as subjective, in terms of relationships, with regard to environments, our sense of learning and the experiences we have. As such, every single person will see, think, hear and feel things differently. An ability to understand ourselves, our resistances, defences, weaknesses, strengths, in all of the complex detail that makes us individual, is also an essential part of understanding others.

As such, reflective practice, which from an arts therapeutic definition is the conscious effort to think about things and develop insights, is fundamental to giving space between the self and the lived experience. By doing this we understand things more objectively. Chris Argyris (2004), who developed the term 'double-loop learning', suggests that reflection allows us to step outside the 'single-loop' normal thinking that flows from experience, reflection, conceptualisation and application, to apply a second loop that encourages us to recognise a new paradigm and reframe ideas in order to change what we do. This is particularly significant in terms of teaching.

Where there is an expectation in a learning environment that young people will learn and progress, it is vital that teachers are able to model this process actively and productively. Reflective practice also allows space for the teacher to apply theory and academic models/learnings to their experiences and those of the children they teach. However, this process is never easy because it is important to remember and understand that some of the most useful reflective practice is not comfortable – it involves risk-taking and posing questions about ourselves, our assumptions and how we behave/act/move in the world – and sometimes we realise this is not in the way that we actually want to be. The biggest growth and change comes from finding out difficult things about ourselves or really understanding that we could have done things differently to get a different outcome.

In the following sections, we share a number of practical strategies that grew from our awareness of the possibility thinking model and the therapeutic literature. The examples are cumulative in that they start with the self, move to notions of the team and then to whole-school possibility thinking/creative learning. As well as instructions to guide the reader to set these up in their own contexts, we include vignettes and signposts to explain how the activities led to the possibility thinking we intended.

Six-piece story-making

A good example of developing awareness of the self is through journaling, as exemplified above. However, there are other tools that help delve beneath surface assumptions. Any activity that helps to support unconscious thoughts and allows feelings to 'speak' is useful for personal and emotional development. It helps shape and articulate things that might be impossible to otherwise acknowledge and then subsequently understand. Activities that can support this for both staff and students are a key part of any progressive learning environment. One of the tools used for this, which is easily implemented in an educational setting, is 'six-piece story-making'. It was conceptualised in Israel in 1980 by Mooli Lahad as a tool to manage stress and anxiety.

Story is a universal language for sharing and encourages growth, choice and connects us to ourselves. The six-piece story tool is a reflective and insightful process, which allows the author and the observer(s) to make sense of complicated and often unsaid but felt aspects of any given situation in life. It is a non-threatening vehicle for observing oneself and others and often a springboard for growth and discussion. It encourages self-reflection, stimulates creativity and encourages us to get connected to our inner worlds. It can take place in pairs, in small groups or even in teacher trainings or with whole staff teams of classes. In these cases, one person needs to lead the activity. If working with children the teacher/adult would lead the activity.

Instructions for the six-piece story activity

1. Take a sheet of A4 paper and fold it into six squares.
2. Number the squares 1–6 in the bottom right corner.
3. Allow 3–6 minutes for each of the six boxes to be completed, depending how long you have for the entire activity.
4. Complete the boxes one at a time, either by drawing, writing words, abstracts or whatever comes to mind.
5. Ask the six questions below one at a time, and after the time allocated for each box move on to the next in number sequence.
6. Do not introduce the whole story concept in one go.

Question 1: Who or what is the main character in your story?
Question 2: Where do they live?
Question 3: What do they want?
Question 4: Who or what is stopping them?
Question 5: Who or what is helping them?
Question 6: What happens in the end? What is the resolution if any?

The questions in point 6 were designed to encourage participants to look within themselves. For example:

- Question 1 is asking who is the most significant person or aspect of your life right now.
- Question 2 gives insight into the symbol of self. What is the environment in which the person is living like? Is it safe, hostile, real, fantastical, busy or quiet, warm or cold? It does in some way give life to the inner world and can give us a sense of what is happening internally for the participant.
- Question 3 gives shape to deepest hopes and desires. What matters to this person? Can they locate anything that does?
- Question 4 shines light on what the deepest fears are. Is it internal or external? What force does it have and how does it impact on the bigger picture?
- Question 5 asks if they can identify any support they have or might have, even in the metaphor. Do I need help to get what I want/need? If so can I ask for it and how? What if I can't locate support or a helper? How does this feel?
- Questions 6 shows that goals can reach a resolution. An openness to what it means if the resolution does not feel satisfactory. What could have been done differently? How might I have changed other boxes to get a different outcome?

Figure 12.3 presents the six-piece story of a teacher. It exemplifies the potential of the activity in deepening understanding of oneself, in one's context, and to see differently the challenges that arise working in the complex social setting of primary schools. Questions arise such as:

- Who represents the evil in the sky (the Office for Standards in Education, Children's Services and Skills (Ofsted), senior leaders, self-perceptions)?
- What was the magic?
- Where can magic be found in this person's work life?
- Who makes the umbrella for the teacher? What is the umbrella in a work context?

The story as told by the teacher (Figure 12.3, top left to right)

There was a magical frog who lived in a pond. Its task was to collect magical water from a reservoir. But there were evil forces from high above that fired burning acid arrows. Tiny invisible flies made an umbrella that would protect the frog. The frog collected all the magical water to fill a pond so that everyone could enjoy the nectar of the magic.

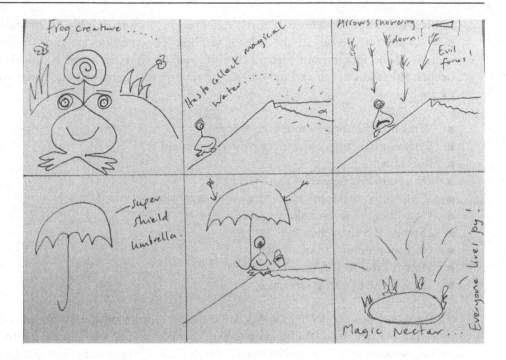

Figure 12.3 A six-piece story

Having understood the purpose and meaning of the six questions, the following continues the activity instructions:

Continuing the six-piece story activity

7. Ask questions and then allow space for the answers to emerge on the page.
8. Give a countdown to what time on each box is left before moving on.
9. Don't talk about what has been created until box 6 is complete.
10. Once the six boxes are complete, allow some time to notice what has been created.
11. Then ask the story to be told with the framework 'once upon a time ...' and then go through each picture 1–6 until the end.
12. Be curious about what you've heard. Think about the following prompts to ask the author.

The activity, used in a coaching context of a one-to-one session, brought up unseen aspects of the teacher's work and attitudes to the challenges with which they were faced. The pressures of external accountability were the fired burning arrows, for example. Through further discussion, it was possible to consider how to protect the self in the role of teacher. The activity does not involve analysis of the images, but through the storytelling, questions can be asked to deepen awareness of self and the differing responses to a particular challenge, for example:

- What do you notice about your story?
- Do you make any connections to your own life?
- If so how?
- Do you recognise any of the characters?
- If you could make any changes to your story what would they be?
- How does the story make you feel?
- How do the characters feel?
- Do they remind you of anyone?
- How do you feel about your story?
- What is the title of your story?

This personal creative technique has demonstrable impact on the quality of self-reflection of individuals. Building on this, in the next section we describe another creative activity, called the 'social atom', which starts with the individual and then brings people together in group reflection.

The social atom

A social atom is a picture, sculpture, or creative construct that represents the nucleus of all individuals or aspects in our lives that we are emotionally connected to and in the way it is created can show the distance and other values between and associated with these aspects. Figure 12.4 is a group social atom that shows a senior leadership team's response to what was happening at the time within the school. This particular social atom encouraged both dialogue and reflection and brought to light aspects of the system that had not before been named, which felt useful to the team and developed dialogue to improve the team dynamic. Each piece placed had purpose and meaning. Through discussion, themes and feelings arose that helped them connect with a moral purpose and the practicalities of working so closely together. The following questions were asked:

- Where are you at as a team?
- How are we doing?
- How do you feel?
- Where are you in the social atom?
- How are you represented here?

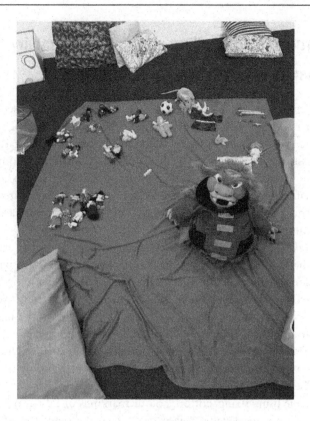

Figure 12.4 Example of a group's social atom representation

Notes from a therapist …

I particularly like the modification of this, which encourages its use within institutions as a team or staff activity. It can be used in this way to explore dynamics within the staff team and institution as a whole and in this way, it can uncover obstacles and challenges that might be felt but not explicitly understood. Using the social atom model allows us the opportunity to also change and move objects around, to make significant alterations that may in reality feel impossible to do. We can map journeys across terms and academic years using this tool, to reflect, celebrate successes and explore challenges.

The exploration of these atoms allows us to explore our connectedness or disconnectedness to people and aspects in our lives. It gives us power to implement changes, to observe things in more detail and to question and to see what might be happening and why. We can observe from a distance aspects that might otherwise remain unconscious or unseen.

Instructions for leading a social atom activity

Social atom creativity

1. *Prepare your resources*: decide which medium is being used. If it is drawing or paint, for example, use a large roll or sheets of paper and if it is with the use of objects or images then make sure these are gathered before the session (all manner of objects can be used – the more quirky the better).

2. *Pose a question or direct the creativity*: the staff group is asked to use the material to create an image of the institution, to represent people and other significant aspects, e.g. parents, governors, learning objectives, building works, music, school exams, finances, etc.

3. *Making observations and asking questions*: the group is asked to consider what images are being used and the space or lack of space lies between each person's contribution. For example, why is the postcard of a tower further away from the centre of flowers and buttons? What metaphorical significance is there? What does this mean for the individual and the group? It is in itself a playful and creative activity.

4. *Observing and reflecting*: once complete the group can be invited to notice what they see, to share anything they had been surprised by or were expecting. They can be encouraged to represent feelings of flow or 'stuckness' on the image using string/cotton, colour markings or Post-it notes.

5. *Making a change to the reality*: once time and space for reflection has been allowed they can then be invited to make changes that they feel would be useful, for example moving aspects, adding or removing things and discussing what they are doing as they go. It is useful to believe and share here what has been changed and it is important to ask participants what it feels like to see what has been made.

6. *Documenting for future reflection*: the creation can be photographed and used in future sessions or perhaps displayed in the school.

In the following section, we focus on one example of the social atom that involved a leadership team of a large primary school. In this example, we share an intimate moment of the team who, over time and with experience of engaging in such creative learning activities and experiences, were able to articulate the 'journey of one term' through which they had experienced many challenging moments. The example shows how from self-consciousness there was a move towards collaboration.

Step 2: from consciousness to collaboration

It is well understood that schools, as with any organisation, develop best when relationships are nurtured, communication is effective and clarity about expectations is shared consistently (Hargreaves & Fullan, 2012). The session was facilitated by a drama therapist and involved all members of the leadership team: business manager, senior teaching assistant, assistant head teacher and head teacher. The leadership team had met once a month for therapist-led sessions. They each lasted one hour. The sessions involved drama and arts practices to engage the team in discussion and self-awareness, to resolve matters and to 'say the unsaid'. There was never a predetermined aim in each session. The group defined the process and outcomes for itself. In the session described, the team was asked to draw the 'journey of the spring term'. They were given art equipment and a roll of paper. Figures 12.5 and 12.6 show the final outcome of the groups' creative expression

Figure 12.5 Example of a leadership team's social atom representation

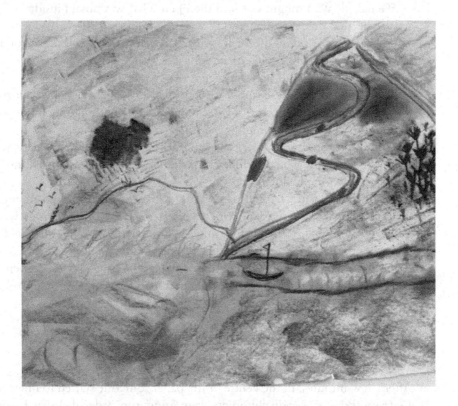

Figure 12.6 Example of a leadership team's social atom representation

(as a therapeutic activity we have gained informed consent from all members of the team). The following documents the reflections of two members of the team, as they responded to what happened during the hour together:

Reflection of the process: voices from the team

From the head teacher ...

We sat in silence for some time.

Then, one by one, each member chose a colour.

Pausing.

Nothing.

(*Who would start? It shouldn't be me ... I am the head teacher ... need to step back. Who will start? Someone start!*)

Someone did ... a mountain formed.

Each member then joined: some drawing a rainbow, a doorless tower with a noose dangling from a darkened window (*pressure from parents, accountability perhaps?*) and a river and a boat, balloons and storms and ladders.

We talked. We brought out into the open what was unsaid inside.

'We needed that mountain didn't we?'

'What does the noose mean? It's dark. Sad that a job should make you feel like that. Do you still feel like that?'

'Ladders are hopeful, stretching up.'

'The rainbow for me is about diversity ... it's a cliché I know, but from the storm and the balance of sun and rain comes something much better ... more important and meaningful.'

'You can't stop the waves ... you can only learn how to surf. That is what it is like in a school. The demands from parents and the world outside are like the storms and the children the sun.'

'I wish people just trusted us more and gave us respect as professionals. They wouldn't tell a surgeon which knife to choose or a barrister which point of law to refer to and yet because they've been to school, they say they know better than we do. That is what the mountain and noose mean for me.'

The drawing and talking continued. Hands weaved as each member shared, crossed paths, changed drawings and mark-making. We stepped back and looked.

From a teaching assistant who is on the leadership team ...

After a few minutes, in the centre of the paper someone started to draw. Still I sat and thought. Gradually others were joining in. I decided that I would start at the beginning, the edge of the page. I drew a ladder structure from the top of the page to the bottom. This would represent the different areas of the journey so far. My colleague had drawn a colourful circle and was beginning to form blue waves next to my ladder. At this stage, an overwhelming sense that we had all been on the same journey together, navigating the same waters struck me. Of course, there are storms along the way, but there are also moments of joy. Just like the weather, children are ever changeable and so are we.

I carried on drawing, layer upon layer, colour upon colour. This in itself is cleansing for the mind. Using a dark crayon to create a storm cloud that represented a difficult but necessary interaction with a parent or colleague. The cloud was small in comparison to my larger picture.

From the ladder, I joined the circle using the school's colours, which for me are representative of the curriculum threads flowing into all that we do. Next a school of fish were entering the sea, they had a long journey ahead of them, over the mountain, past the tree and through the labyrinth – seven years of formal education. I purposely chose a fish to be different from all of the others to represent those children who are different and find school tricky. Protectively the other fish surrounded him, as a tight community.

The activity was satisfyingly beneficial, any stresses that I had entered the room with I was able to leave on the paper. Collectively we had created a joined-up landscape of vision, hope and at times despair. This despair is OK because we had shared it, we laughed and reassured one another.

Step 3: from collaboration to community

From the building of a sense of collaboration there is the possible building of community, rooted in self-reflective and mindful individuals, working in collaboration through creative learning and possibility thinking. One example is from a school that understood the power of working with arts partners (Sefton-Green et al., 2011). In September 2018, the school worked with a West End actor, coach and drama professional. There were two purposes for this particular collaboration: to build a sense of team (because the school had doubled as a staff body with many new members of the team) and to introduce the substantive topic of the upcoming book week. In essence the professional development involved self-development as well as subject-knowledge development for a curriculum area. The following is an overview of the INSET session, led by the head teacher in partnership with the professional actor:

Plan of the creative learning professional development session

Professional development plan: bringing artists into school to inspire creative learning

Part 1: welcome 8.30–9.05
Aims of the session: develop team/develop awareness of process of creative learning/experiences of creative learning.

- Singing games led by head teacher and drama expert.
- Drama warm up games led by drama expert.
- Principles of school led by head teacher.

Part 2: active storytelling 9.10–10.30
Three key sections to focus on:

1. *Oliver in workhouse/orphanage*:
   - I need you to help me tell a story. It is a story from a long way back in the Victorian times, when the grandest of queens, Her Majesty Queen Victoria, was on the throne. But this story is not in a palace … it is not even in a sweet family home … there are no fairy godmothers or princes in shining armour … etc
   - Our story takes place in a workhouse. What is a workhouse?
     - What kind of work?
     - Describe the dark, dank workhouse. Show images.
     - In groups, tear and rip newspaper to make the silhouette of the workhouse.
     - Write words on the paper to describe what it is like.
   - On one cold night (read from the book) a baby was born.
   - Introduce BUMBLE: calls the child = Oliver Twist
   - Describe some of the awful things happening – refer to text.
   - Get group to stand in lines in silence and collect their supper. Go and sit in lines heads down. Pray for the food.
   - Oliver pulling the short straw.
   - I WANT SOME MORE (do this in two lines – one being the adult and one being Oliver).
   - Oliver taken to the board to be punished – act out the scene.
   - Writing from different points of view:
     - from the board;
     - from the children in the room.
   - Being taken by the undertaker – feelings/expressions/physical freeze frames.

- FREEZE frame of the fight scene (what does each character think/feel/say?).
- Oliver escapes. Long journey. What does he need to take with him? Ask group to write a list of things he needs to take. Then invite them to say what they have written and cross off anything that he did not have (to show how poor he was).

2. *Arriving in London*:
   - On the road, an old lady lets him stay in her house and gives him food.
   - Set the London scene.
   - Watch clip from film.
   - Write a London group sound poem in small groups.
   - Artful Dodger meets Oliver.

3. *Being with Fagin*:
   - What does it feel like to be there? What is home (mini-philosophy for children-type circle)?
   - What would he say if he was writing to his friends at the workhouse? Write LETTER.
   - Boys teach Oliver how to steal.
   - Watch film clip of this scene.
   - Conscious alley: should Oliver steal the silk handkerchief?
   - Oliver steals and gets caught.

Principles of our school pedagogy and values – led by head teacher

Reflection on the process.

Break 10.30–10.45.

'Consider yourself at home' led by drama expert. Head teacher on piano. 1 hour 30 mins (10.45–12.15).

- Learn song.
- Get them acting – free shackles of 'being the teacher' and be in new spaces of uncertainty and at edge of comfort zone.
- Laugh. Have fun.
- Improve quality, etc.
- Joyful team building is the main outcome intended.
- Rehearse and improve.
- Perform and film.
- Feedback and new learning.

What became evident in the session is that many of the teachers and teaching assistants were working out of their 'comfort zones'. This was significant. The notion of 'spaces of uncertainty' arose in the doctorate work of Biddulph (2017) as an important aspect of creative learning. He found that in spaces of uncertainty (involving feeling unsure, questioning, insecurity, confusion, frustration), creative responses to challenges were noticed. If we consider that children come to school each day and are asked to learn new things, we realise that as they go through their own spaces of uncertainty every day so do we as educational professionals. The questions for the purpose of this chapter are: when, where and how do teachers experience such spaces of uncertainty in their professional lives (that are healthy and not part of a limiting accountability agenda)? In a healthy and constructive way, where are the spaces of confusion, questioning, frustration that evoke new thinking and different responses to the challenges with which they are faced? As we have argued herein, it is vital that through self-awareness and self-reflection school teams move to being able to be collectively reflective and allow vulnerabilities to exist. This, then, is the starting point of deeper learning, perhaps. The following is a reflection from one teaching assistant who attended the INSET session. She describes the confusions, concerns and nudges towards greater self-awareness. She also identifies the complete confidence from those leading the session in the creative capabilities of the teachers and teaching assistants who participated: *everyone is creative* was the message they conveyed.

Reflecting on the spaces of creativity
The voice from a teaching assistant

Consider yourself one of us!

9 am, Tuesday 4 September 2018. I knew I was in for a treat on the first day of term but I had a feeling that the new members of the team were not prepared for what was in store for them. Some had a rough idea from snippets mentioned at interview or if they had had a guided tour of the school. Our school was slightly different from the norm.

We began in a circle, in the upstairs seminar room, introducing ourselves and stating our role. However, the normal start was soon to be disrupted as our head teacher (in role) shouted us to get in line! Some 13 teachers and 18 learning coaches (teaching assistants) were soon to become inmates of the local workhouse. This is not what I or any of my colleagues had experienced before during a staff INSET. Usually, INSETs would have involved the sharing of data, safeguarding and expectations for the year to come. Never had time or space been made, or allowed, for role play and musical theatre. Our head teacher explained that he wouldn't expect the children to do anything that the team weren't willing to do. Therefore, we were travelling back in time to 1838. We had all fallen on hard times. We were destitute. There was no other place for us but the workhouse.

While Mr Bumble stirred the gruel, I had a few moments to chat with the newbies, especially those who looked like the blood had drained from their faces. One described to me that she had had a dreadful feeling that morning that she might be asked to act or sing. She had explained to her daughter, 'I won't be able to do that'. Another colleague explained that he felt completely out of his comfort zone. I was able to reassure them that they were in a space, a learning environment, which did not judge, criticise or ridicule. Individuals were stepping into the unknown. Stepping outside of their comfort zones, supportively waiting for them, were the founder members who had feasted on a diet of song, dance and joy since we opened the school in 2015.

The bell tolled, we were ordered into lines and the gruel was dished out, workhouse style. We were now in role. For some of the adults, the last time that they had to act was back during their school days. These were new beginnings, just like the children, we were having to use our imaginations. Focusing on our character and their back stories. The nervous feelings soon turned into feelings of joy, warmth and excitement, witnessing colleagues entering the centre of the circle to perform as a main character. One member of staff who appeared the most nervous, stepped forward as Noah Claypole. Where had his new found confidence come from? How in such a short period of time had he found the confidence to offer his vulnerabilities to this space? I was very surprised and felt a sense of pride. This was team building at its best. Little did I know this was just the start.

Our next activity, was not only to learn the song, 'Consider Yourself' (from the 1968 hit musical *Oliver!*) but also the dance moves. We gathered around the piano downstairs in the hall. A visiting West End actor led this session. We were totally immersed: an actual actor who had starred in the West End was guiding us on our musical journey. There was lots of laughter, with some of our new members of staff expressing with complete disbelief that this couldn't be an INSET because it was too much fun, saying 'I've never laughed so much during a training session.'

Our team was beginning to form. Senior leaders, teachers and learning coaches mixed together while using the complete space on offer in the hall. Mistakes were made. Assistance was offered, new learning took place. After several run-throughs, we were ready to film. We gave it our all, singing at the top of our voices. The end product was joyfully mediocre but it was a firm foundation for us to build on for the rest of the year. I realised that it was the art form, dance and drama, together with high expectations, that allowed our team to find new ways of thinking about teaching and learning.

Reflecting on the community-making that arose from the creative learning activity, aspects of possibility thinking were evident, including:

- *Posing questions*: the team were immersed in talking, responding to questions and asking each other to make sense of the creative tasks in which they were engaged.
- *Play*: dancing and acting encouraged playfulness and a 'stepping out' of comfort zones. For example, the team were invited to make up characters and create a workhouse using their bodies.
- *Immersion*: the pace of the session was such that the team were immersed not only in trying to forge new relationships (as a new team) but also aware that they would be planning and delivering a session for children in the coming weeks.
- *Innovation*: the team was asked to create new endings to the story.
- *Risk-taking*: the team were asked to sing, dance and perform.
- *Being imaginative*: the team was asked to think imaginatively about how they would apply what they had experienced to the children whom they teach.
- *Self-determination*: there was a determination to improve the quality of their individual performances (especially with awareness that they would all be filmed)
- *Intentionality*: there was a shared understanding that this creative learning session aimed to develop a sense of team spirit.

Step 4: from community to creative communities

In this chapter, we have explored how, from different professional perspectives, professional learning that is focused on creative learning has the potential to unlock opportunities for educators to lead courageously, with resilience, awareness and *joie de vivre*: to release their imaginations and celebrate the art of the possible. Not only is our argument that creativities and creative learning matter as a vital way for educators to creatively navigate the complexities of contemporary globalised life, we have seen the value for all when it is fostered, inspired and principled (Craft, 2008). And so, we have asked and tried to suggest answers to the following:

- How can primary school educators become more creative?
- What does this involve?
- What type of professional learning is needed?
- And how can schools foster risk-taking, innovation, boldness and an insatiable curiosity to ask 'why?' and 'why not?' in their staff rooms?

We suggest it starts with building self-aware individuals. From this, individuals who are then able to 'be' in spaces of uncertainty. In these spaces, creative learning and possibility thinking arise in collaborative teams, as a social activity. This reflexivity in collaboration then builds a sense of community. What we have shared moves from the individual level to the community level. If a community can engage creatively, who knows what possibility thinking will arise? Who knows what our futures might hold?

References

Alexander, R. (2010). *Children, their world, their education: Final report and recommendations of the Cambridge Primary Review.* Abingdon, UK: Routledge.

Argyris, C. (2004). Double-loop learning and implementable validity. In H. Tsoukas & N. Mylonopoulos (Eds.), *Organizations as knowledge systems* (pp. 29–45). London: Palgrave Macmillan.

Biddulph, J. (2017). *The diverse diversities of creative learning at home: Three case studies of ethnic minority immigrant children* (PhD thesis), Cambridge University Library, Cambridge, UK.

Burnard, P. (2012). *Musical creativities in practice.* Oxford: Oxford University Press.

Caldwell, L., & Taylor Robinson, H. (2017). *The collected works of D. W. Winnicott.* New York, NY: Oxford University Press.

Corrigall, R. (2019). Mental health and creativity: Dr Richard Corrigal's perspective. Retrieved from https://createarts.org.uk/2019/10/mental-health-and-creativity.

Craft, A. (2008). Tensions in creativity and education: Enter wisdom and trusteeship. In A. Craft, H. Gardner, & G. Claxton (Eds.), *Creativity, wisdom and trusteeship: Exploring the role of education* (pp. 16–34). New York, NY: Corwin Press.

Craft, A., Cremin, T., Burnard, P., Dragovic, T., & Chappell, K. (2013). Possibility thinking: Cumulative studies of an evidence-based concept driving creativity? *Education 3–13: International Journal of Primary, Elementary and Early Years Education, 41*(5), 538–556.

Craft, A., Cremin, T., Hay P., & Clack, J. (2014). Creative primary schools: Developing and maintaining pedagogy for creativity. *Ethnography and Education, 9*(1), 16–34.

Glăveanu, V., Tanggaard, L., & Wegener, C. (2016). *Creativity: A new vocabulary.* Basingstoke, UK: Palgrave Macmillan.

Gunzenhauser, M. G., & Noblit, G. W. (2011). What the arts can teach school reform. In J. Sefton-Green, P. Thomson, K. Jones, & L. Bresler (Eds.), *The Routledge handbook of creative learning* (pp. 428–437). Abingdon, UK: Routledge.

Hargreaves, A., & Fullan, M. (2012). *Professional capital: Transforming teaching in every school.* New York, NY: Routledge.

McGill, C., N'Guessan, T., & Rosen, M. (Eds.) (2007). *Exploring creative learning.* Stoke-on-Trent, UK: Trentham Books.

National Advisory Committee on Creative and Cultural Education (NACCCE) (1999). *All our futures: Creativity, culture & education.* London: DfE.

Owen, N. (2011). *Placing students at the heart of creative learning.* London: David Fulton.

Sefton-Green, J., Thomson, P., Jones, K., & Bresler, L. (Eds.) (2011). *The Routledge handbook of creative learning.* Abingdon, UK: Routledge.

13

Becoming our best practice: professional learning to develop singing and musicianship

Doreen Rao and Jane Wheeler

Introduction: choral music education professional development – a way of becoming

In her recent book, former first lady Michelle Obama (2018, p. 419) writes about *becoming* as, 'a process, steps along a path'. She tells us that the notion of *becoming*, 'requires equal parts, patience and rigor. Becoming is never giving up on the idea that there's more growing to be done'. This chapter focuses on the subject of professional development in singing as an interconnected space between theory and practice, as a means of motivating and empowering teachers to motivate and empower their students. As such, the processes we describe point towards the key characteristics of enacting a facilitative leadership and participative learning approach in which, 'a greater focus on becoming than being ... and the quality of the journey as more educationally significant than the speed at which the destination is reached' (Eisner, 2005, p. 10).

The world is essentially 'storied' (Atkinson, 2015): we each have a story, a response to our social contexts, a desire to take further steps on our own journeys through life. Through sharing stories of professional learning and through the intertwining of research-informed practices, we hope to showcase in this chapter what is possible when professionals approach their own development as a process of 'becoming' and a process of 'becoming our best practice'. Teachers' stories weave throughout our chapter, to bring to life the steps of professional development to consider how they enact their musicianship.

Jane's story
The voice of a musician, songwriter, teacher

I came to teaching in a very unplanned way. I was a piano bar entertainer, singing and playing a canon of jazz standards and popular songs in hotels and piano bars in Europe, Dubai and London. I supported myself as a singer song-writer, published by Chrysalis Music and with a small, short recording deal in Munich for three years. I also ran my own rock band and was daydreaming of fame and fortune; talented, but naive and foolish! I had few academic qualifications, and had been raised to believe my musical skills were an 'accomplishment' (very middle-class perspective of a girl's attributes), rather than a hard-earned skill and talent worthy of developing.

In 1982, I became a parent and quickly realised I needed a 'day job'. So, in 1985, I went to university as a 'mature' student and did a modular degree in women's studies and third world development. I went on to take a post-graduate certificate in music education with a university, happy to take my experience as a professional musician, including using music software and composing songs ... as a music degree (combined with the first-class degree I had – yes me, the person who did not enjoy formal learning!). I later did a master's in music, to be sure I was legally qualified to teach the subject! Steps on my own pathway ...

In Jane's reflection, she highlights the difference between formal learning and prac-titioner learning, as if they are distinct things. The career of her co-author, Doreen Rao, has been different: as an academic and music practitioner who spent much of her career promoting the vital and essential relationship between theory and prac-tice. Doreen's work in leading professional development courses and workshops for conductors and teachers was different to the often academic and rigid forms of choral learning: it required an action-oriented, practice-based curriculum supported by a wide range of contemporary research and learning theories.

The Choral Music Experience approach to professional learning

The Choral Music Experience (CME) Institute for Choral Teacher Education curriculum, which Doreen created, exemplifies the intersections between theory and practice – the space between university degree programmes and the highest standards of professional expertise. Established in 1986, the CME Institute links the highest standards of educational practice with the human values of diversity, inclusion and social responsibility. Offered in the United States, Canada, Ireland and UK, the annual, ongoing postgraduate professional development courses seek to build a community of practice, motivate and empower teachers to realise their full potential and renew and enhance the skills of working professionals. Courses designed to encourage teachers and students to return to the very root of their practice with the key question: What is it about music and teaching that makes me feel alive?

Directed by a course leader and supported by a team of coaches and mentors, the annual course intensives offer a supportive space for developing professionals to return to the source of their inspiration, explore new theories and practices and connect with new and unknown materials and pedagogies. The course leader introduces musical concepts and educational theories as these relate to and enhance the practice segments of the course curriculum. Courses move from lived experiences to relevant research, not the other way around. Teacher participants enjoy lectures, participatory discussions and study sessions on every element of the practice in preparation for a daily choral teaching laboratory. These content-rich and rigorously interactive sessions take teachers deep into the heart of the practice, deconstructing subject matter, introducing new materials, plus analysing, demonstrating and practising related pedagogies. As suggested above, the practice-based sessions are largely participatory with related theories introduced as needed in support of practice.

Each day culminates in the form of a public masterclass (a teaching laboratory). Teachers register to conduct in the masterclass and to demonstrate their newly acquired teaching skills during the interactive 20-minute choral lab. During the masterclass, instructor feedback is respectfully generated by both the course leader and the participating choristers. Each teacher receives multiple layers of feedback and reflections from course mentors and peer participants with the added benefit of self-assessment taken from video feedback.

The CME approach is significantly different to other forms of professional learning for music and singing. For example, instead of focusing learning *about* music, the focus is on *being* the music (by this we mean, listening, using the body to experience and respond to music, breathing musically and doing music). It always *builds on* the practice and experiences of the individuals in attendance, *deepening awareness* and layering theory and relevant research on the practice. It is *empowering* in that it models the highest expectations of adult and children learners; *agency* is afforded in relevant places so that it is fully participatory.

The pedagogies used involve *non-verbal teaching*: rather than talking about music and singing, the teacher is taught how to model and be the music. Rather than purely intellectualising the process of music-making, the CME approach becomes an embodied one, where the use of the body helps the adult appreciate the complexity of singing and music-making. What follows is description of the ways this was translated into the context of UK primary education.

Learning as a process of becoming

The space between theory and practice often feels enormous. Academic research often lacks immediate classroom applicability. The gap between scholarly research and educational trends finds academics mostly collaborating with academics. Research collaborations between academics and practitioners are few and far between. For these reasons alone, professional development courses and ongoing teacher training workshops may be the ideal environments to accommodate the dynamic intersections and fertile relationships embodied in the space between theory and practice. As viewed through the lens of what we may call a 'feminine way of knowing and doing' (Greene, 1988, 1998), the authors review an established professional development model for music educators. It is the bridging of theory and practice. And essentially it is about doing and through doing, becoming a better professional because of improved practices.

The following examples of Emmanuel, a generalist primary teacher, evidence the approach and describe his practice both before and after attending the CME institute. What is evident is a different culture, a musically led (rather than verbally led) teaching technique and more awareness of the dynamics, expertise and knowledge of the group.

Emmanuel's reflections on learning with his choir

Before CME residential

The children assembled in the room. It was hot and the tables had not been stacked properly. The children sat on the carpet chatting while I moved the tables to give more space. The children were fidgeting and chatting a lot, the noise levels rising. I stood behind the piano and counted back from three, indicating discontent with their behaviour. I told them what we were going to sing: 'Ain't No Mountain High Enough'. I played and we sang. I stopped a few times and explained that they needed to be louder and build to the chorus. We started again. We sang. I stopped again and spoke about the text and that the words were important and that we need to sing clearly. I told them that the music needed to be expressive and hopeful and that the audience wanted to hear this. They looked frustrated.

After CME residential: learning and becoming

I cringe reading the 'before CME' reflection. I had not prepared the space before the children came – of course they would be distracted. Unconsciously I had told them the session was not that important because I had not even bothered to set the room properly. Why should they take it seriously if I didn't?

This time I thought differently. They came in. They were chatting and lively. I greeted them at the door smiling and silent. I stood silently, making eye contact with as many children as I could and smiled. We moved into a circle. I exaggeratedly breathed in … out … deeply … smiling. The children, all of them, eventually (after less than a minute) were mirroring me. I invited them to stand without talking. I used a signal. They responded silently. We then did a body and breath warm-up and I modelled making different sounds with my voice: mmmmm … ahh … eeeeeee … ooooooooo … breathing in deeply, out smiling. They laughed a little. I made no comment but waited until they had stilled again. I said we would be singing 'Ain't No Mountain High Enough'. No pause. I played and did not sing along with them. They sang. I listened attentively to their voices. I noticed that the rhythm was not accurate in one line. I stopped at the next line of music and sang the rhythm and they copied it. I then clapped it and they copied. I sang it in a 'witch's voice' and they copied. Each iteration their sense of the rhythm improved. They sang the line in full. It had improved. I listened.

With Emmanuel's reflections, he points to some of the key principles of the CME approach to developing singing and singing leadership. The learning for Emmanuel and indeed the intention of CME teachers is to teach singing through *doing* and *being* rather than talking and purely intellectualising. In the second vignette, Emmanuel describes shift in his practice: being present, setting up a positive space and a culture of connection, of modelling expectations, of maintaining positivity. The examples from Emmanuel point to how the professional learning advocated by CME involves lived experiences (starting where the children are at), modelling excellence and being musical.

Jane's reflections on learning with CME

Discovering a way for me to become …

My first job as a secondary music teacher in the inner city of London, taught me that there was so much more to teaching than just loving the subject and wanting to share the love. Not only did I lack basic pedagogic skills, but I lacked musical skills to empower the children in what I knew and what they wanted to know, even though I had learned so much from the experiences in my life: listening to my parents' music around the house, the opportunities in school, listening to music on the streets in Libya where I grew up initially.

That was when I discovered CME, Canterbury. I was clueless when I first attended a course. But I knew very quickly the model held keys for me to open so many more doors for the children and young people I worked with, and subsequently to the teachers I now help to educate.

One of the principles of the professional learning pedagogy is acknowledging that at points in our learning we will feel 'clueless'. It is vital as the starting position for rich learning. Stopping 'being the teacher' and starting to 'become a learner' is a mind shift necessary to take full advantage of the CME approach to professional learning. It is a mindset we suggest brings about profound changes in practice because not only does it change what we do, it also changes how we do it. With an approach based on mastery, rooted in both academic theory and practical application, questions about why we do what we do are all explored, understood, critiqued and answered. Jane's reflection articulates a significant shift in her thinking and way of being, as a singing teacher and conductor, which led to changes in her practice.

Jane's reflections on one masterclass

I found the piece very difficult to conduct. It was a Bernstein piece in mixed metre. I had a great choir in front of me – world class. I tried. I had studied the score. I was trying my very best to make them sound good. The pressure of being in front of peers (all of whom were world-class conductors in their own right) and with the master teacher ready to give feedback. The children sang. I pulsed the music. I was stopped. And the feedback came. Boy, it came!

'Get yourself out of the way of the music, Jane', was the comment.

Silence as the children in the choir and my colleagues looked on. Harsh, perhaps, but because of the space of care and consideration that was always part of the CME approach, I understood what was meant. In my efforts to be accepted as a conductor with skill, I was trying to be an accomplished conductor rather than opening up a musical space for the young singers to sing, to release their voices. The focus was on me not on the children and not on the music. I breathed in the profound sense of becoming – which was almost therapeutic in its impact on me. I relaxed. The tough love recognised by all. And as I lifted my arms in regular pulse again, the children sang beautifully because I trusted them and I gave space for them to be the music. Trust the children. Open spaces of possibility. Be the music. It was a vital moment and has stuck with me: golden professional learning.

The significance of Jane's learning resulted from the distinctive building blocks of this professional development curriculum. This feedback could only be given because of the professional space that was created by Doreen and her team. Creating space, therefore, and a culture of care and highest expectations seemed the unique trade mark of the professional learning experiences offered by CME.

All about culture

Hargreaves and Fullan (2012) say that highly effective schools not only focus on individuals and their teaching but also, most importantly, on the culture and environment in which teaching and learning takes place. With CME, effort is made to construct teaching and learning spaces with a contemplative oriented environment that supports all forms of inquiry, external and internal. CME Institute courses take place in an environment of compassion and kindness. A growing body of contemporary research on mindfulness practice in education suggests its impact on student learning, including the ability to focus and concentrate (Rao & Perison, 2005). Within this space, experiential teaching methods developed within the framework of contemplative practice offer a rich set of tools for exploring the mind, the heart and the world (Rao & Perison, 2005). When contemplative methods are combined with conventional practices, we found that an enriched educational environment improves communication, deepens concentration and enlarges perspectives. Through the use of contemplative-based instruction, teacher participants learn to practice deep listening and to be fully present. For example, Doreen's innovative practice brought Eastern philosophy and martial arts to the practice of singing (Rao & Perison, 2005).

The space is also infused with the sense of community and collaboration. To this, we emphasise the importance of the master–student relationship and the space of the masterclass as space for deep learning. Again, this is not dissimilar to the master–disciple relationship in a Tai Chi class. As a model of reflective practice and an example of cognitive apprenticeship, the choral lab of children and teachers working together as a supportive *family of practice* represents true collaboration. Sessions generally host a young 'laboratory choir' made up of local children and young people who participate each afternoon for the masterclass. Similarly, teacher participants and faculty together comprise what we call a 'conductor's choir' to support choral lab conductors. In this way, teachers and students learn in symbiotic ways: teachers are students and students become teachers. It is a uniquely powerful approach that develops kindness, honesty and a reframing of knowledge and its acquisition. Our choral lab formation is an example of 'contextualised practice' related to the *cognitive apprenticeship* model of education. The learners (teacher apprentices) are immersed in situations of practice to provide an authentic context in which to develop expertise. The learner is supported by their a 'faculty of peers' – fellow course participants of varying experience levels, some of whom have mastered certain skills. This 'layers of apprenticeship' approach to professional development enhances the learning dynamic overall and supports individual mastery at each level of learning.

As we have indicated and to emphasise the significance, in this dynamic environment, the children are often viewed as the *teachers of teachers*. They respond to the work of each teacher participant with honest enthusiasm and they are often eager to encourage teachers with their thoughtful, sensitive and insightful feedback. With feedback from both the master teacher and the lab choir, teacher participants gain the advantage of learning simultaneously from the top down and the bottom up. For all of us, this is the best time of the day and a truly valuable part of the course.

Building blocks for professional learning in musical spaces

Where do we start? How do we 'get ourselves out of the way' of learning? How do we step out of 'being the teacher' to 'becoming the learner'? Through this process, how do we raise the quality of singing to the excellence standards that we believe is inherent in every singing group or choir?

Building opportunities to assure transformative experience requires a deep and long-term commitment to performance excellence. It requires the kind of professional development programme that extends beyond a one-off workshop or one-day immersion. Ongoing, annual courses that encourage long-term participation spanning years of deeper and deeper study constitute the kind of *best practice professionalism* that keeps the brightest and best teachers in the classroom. There are key themes that seem to make a difference to the learning for professionals, both in the United States and also in the context of generalist primary teachers in the UK.

To build a professional development curriculum in which learning is a creative process whereby individuals construct meaning, ideas or concepts based on lived experience, certain beliefs and assumptions are required to guide instruction:

- Developing and refining teacher expertise is fundamental. The definition of expertise in the context of developing singing includes the teacher's ability to transcend technical mastery and view the educational experience broadly as an opportunity to empower and transform the lives of children, young people and their communities.
- We believe that there is an *artist* in every child, that all children can sing and that singing in a choir is a dynamic educational experience that is simultaneously artistic, socialising and therapeutic (Biddulph & Wheeler, 2017).
- Learning should be scholarly, socialising and empowering. Relative to the generalist primary school teacher, we suppose similarly that there is a *scholar* in every child and that all children can master subjects like mathematics (the *mathematician* in every child), science (the *scientist* in every child), history (the

historian in every child) – all dynamic educational experiences that are simultaneously scholarly, socialising and empowering.

■ Mastering concepts and techniques takes time. One-off courses do not transform practice.

The way in which CME and the model of professional learning adapted in the UK context has adaptability at its core. Courses and 'training days' are dynamic, flexible and adapt to the needs of the community they serve. The structure of the sessions is determined by a 'faculty' of experts – or master teachers – whose role it is to model, coach and mentor the course participants seeking the next level of expertise. It is not dissimilar to the notion of communities of practice, or a Vygotskian model of learning in which the learner moves closer to the community knowledge and practices through various iterations and experiences. Some of the sessions are enriched with a guest artist, distinguished visitor or subject-related specialist. Bringing musicians from diverse musical traditions is key in helping teacher and student in learning across and through cultural diversities. For example, often the courses feature a local or nationally regarded composer to introduce her new composition as *composer-in-residence*. The composer-in-residence sometimes builds commissioning partnerships with the course participants, followed by a new work written especially for that teacher and her students. The artist-in-residence may also work with the lab choir (a lab choir is a group who are 'practised' on by teachers who are themselves learning, guided by the master teacher).

A model with excellence and community at its core

In this section, we explain each aspect before bringing together practical applications through a conversation between both authors. Figure 13.1 brings together the key characteristics and building blocks of the CME approach, although they do not represent the 'pure' systematic course, which can be found online.[1] It was necessary to make adaptations and evolve ideas because each context required both being rooted in the principles of CME as well as being open to make changes to meet the needs of the singers in their different contexts.

Knowledge of the repertoire

Related to the importance of authenticity and the essential use of authentic context in the cognitive apprenticeship theory of education, the musical repertoire selected for course study includes a *balanced curriculum* of classical, contemporary, popular and world music. These materials serve as the authentic context for all theoretical and practical study included in the course.

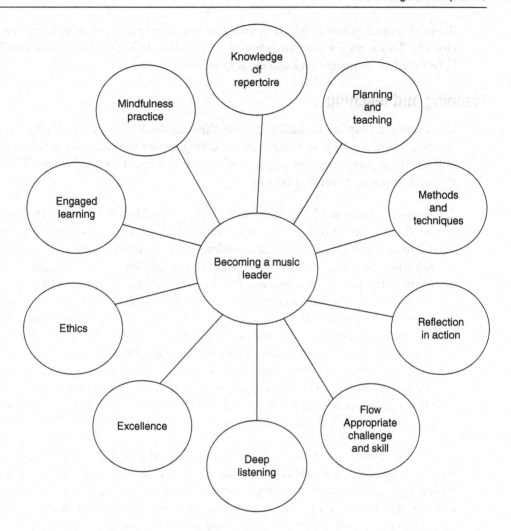

Figure 13.1 Music leader competencies model

The culturally diverse and historically distinguished repertoire is included for its artistic, educational and social values. There is always a special emphasis on the music of living composers and specialist tradition bearers from diverse cultural contexts. These composers, tradition bearers and multicultural specialists visit the teacher training course to talk about their work and their lives. They teach the teachers and the lab choir children, engaging them in new music and world music traditions. Each day of the course, these materials are studied, analysed and practised by the teacher participants as a pathway to deep understanding.

Related to the artistic, educational and social value of song repertoire, we emphasise Harvard University's cross-disciplinary research, concluding that artistic excellence alone is an insufficient objective without a conscious commitment to the social concerns that influence learning at any given place and time, locally and globally. This meta research known as the *GoodWork Project*,[2] defines work that is both excellent in quality and socially responsible.

Planning and teaching

Once teachers have internalised the music through detailed study and practice, the teachers introduce them to a sequenced teaching approach that takes the form of a holistic, three-part process to engage children in singing. This is called the Three P model: produce, practise, perform.

1. *Produce*: musical teaching starts with singing – children first *produce* the song (or short segment of a song) with their singing voices. Non-verbal teaching continues with the use of vocal modelling, or call-and-response-style singing, engaging the children in producing the song regardless of early outcomes.
2. *Practise*: after the children produce the song through group singing as described above, they are engaged in different ways to practise the song. Using a variety of song-related pedagogies and creative problem-solving methods of instruction, the children learn to sing the song more skilfully, and with musical understanding.
3. *Perform*: in the third and final segment of this instructional sequence, the children demonstrate their learning – they perform the song with greater skill and understanding. This rendition compares very favourably to their original efforts to produce (sing) the song at the start of the instructional sequence and they are excited by their accomplishments.

The teaching sequence outlined above emphasises what we know theoretically as *procedural knowledge*, non-verbal knowledge, or 'knowing-in-action'. Distinguished from propositional knowledge, or verbal knowing, the use of non-verbal teaching is about demonstrating by showing, or modelling an idea. Related to theories of reflective practice, the ability to *sing* (or *produce*) a song, *practise* a song and *perform* a song engages the learner in a cyclic pattern of musical experience and conscious decision-making that deeply impacts the quality of engagement. A reflective practitioner is described by social scientist Donald Schön (1991) as one who thinks-in-action – a teacher who relies less on formulas and more on improvisation.

Achieving flow: methods and teaching techniques

While the CME Institute course curriculum described here emphasises what we call a *performance approach* to music teaching and learning, this educational paradigm is more comprehensive than a course curriculum or teaching method alone. Based in its entirety on the principals of diversity, inclusion and social responsibility, the professional development approach is informed by the *psychology of optimal experience*, popularly known as 'flow' (Csikszentmihalyi, 1997).

From decades of research at the University of Chicago, education is only one discipline that has benefitted from Mihalyi Csikszentmihalyi's (1997) profound contributions. Flow may be described as the mental state in which a person performing an activity is completely immersed, with energised focus, full involvement and enjoyment in the process of the activity. Being in flow occurs when two conditions are in place: there must be something to do, known as a 'challenge', and there must be the capability to do it, known as 'know-how'. When the challenge and the know-how are equally matched, the learner experiences flow – defined as *self-growth and enjoyment* (see Figure 13.2).

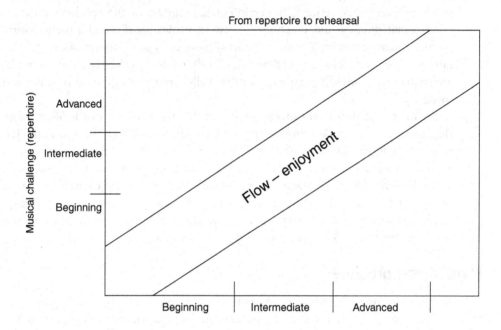

Figure 13.2 Music learning flow model

If, however, the level of challenge is too great in relation to the level of know-how, frustration may result. For example, if we teach a technically demanding, advanced-level song to a beginning-level singer with no musical training, the student may feel anxious or frustrated. Moreover, if the level of challenge is too little in relation to the level of know-how, boredom may result. For example, if we teach a very simple, beginning-level song to an advanced-level singer with musical training, the student may feel bored and uninterested. The implications of this psychological theory are important for all subjects and all levels of learning, including professional development curriculum and instructional methods. The author has adapted this paradigm for music education to show how song repertoire serves as the *musical challenge* and how musicianship serves as musical know-how. The challenges of the song repertoire and instructional goals to develop musical know-how are organised by levels – beginning, intermediate and advanced levels. When the level of know-how matches the level of challenge, the learners experience flow – growth and enjoyment.

Excellence, ethics and engaged learning

In the CME professional development course context, we view the definition of educational excellence as a form of wisdom, known also as 'expertise-in-action'. The concept of *excellence* is taken from the ancient Greek origin, *phronesis* – a form of practical wisdom, good judgement and good character. This kind of wisdom, or *wise action*, might be described as a form of *ethical discernment*: the ability to do *the right thing at the right time with the right intent*. In relation to teaching excellence, ethical discernment is manifest in the teacher's character, educational fluency and teaching agility. In professional development courses, we teach teachers with a sense of mutuality, openness, cooperation, respect and fairness. We see teaching excellence as closely related to the ethics of caring, the ability to invest oneself personally in the well-being of students and professional integrity.

As artists and music educators, we accept that there are standards of excellence that require us to make choices, preferences and actions in the moment. Each moment may be different from the next, but teacher expertise, the fluency to respond quickly, intuitively and contextually in any given moment or circumstance is, we believe, a form of teaching excellence. What we do as teachers exemplifies our character and embodies our personality. Teaching then is always contingent upon, and never separate from, the invisible, internal skills of adaptability, cooperation, receptivity and respect such as those described next.

Mindfulness practice

Because so much of what we *do* as teachers is grounded in practice as a form of musical *doing*, the external, observable actions of our work can deplete us intellectually and emotionally. The energy and continuous activities that surround us in the classroom may occasionally distract us from what could be most important in the moment. For this reason, teachers need to develop the internal, invisible skills that invite quiet, calm, concentration and deep understanding from within.

Using mindfulness breathing as a therapeutic corrective, the CME Institute takes a contemplative approach to teacher education courses. At the beginning of each day, teacher participants practise a carefully sequenced contemplative approach to singing that includes *conscious breathing, intentional movement* and *informed vocalisation*. As participants complete this sequenced series of exercises, they begin to feel quiet, calm and with focused attention. Through this repeated series of exercises, awareness grows to include knowing *where* we are, *what* we are doing and *whom* we are doing it with. Mindfulness practice brings us into the present moment, teaching us *how to listen deeply* and teach thoughtfully. We learn to *feel* the focus and *hear* the quiet. We learn to move from mind*less* to mind*ful*, thought*less* to thought*ful*. Table 13.1 gives practical examples of implementing the principles upon which the CME approach has been developed.

Table 13.1 Principles and practice tools for developing expertise

Principle of practice ...	Practical steps of becoming ...
Knowledge and repertoire	Choose music wisely. Popular music can often be pitched too low for primary voices. Use well-regarded sources of repertoire like SingUp.org.uk or the CME series published by Boosey & Hawkes. Know the music inside out. Listen to it and sing it until you know it really well. Write notes against the text and if you can read music, highlight areas that might be challenging. Share repertoire. Other teachers will know what has worked well in their context.
Planning and instruction ■ Produce ■ Practise ■ Perform	Always start with children singing, without comment and long instructions from teacher. Don't sing along with the children. You cannot listen if you are singing. Listen deeply. Really focus on listening to their individual and collective voices. Can you hear the boy at the back? What is he contributing to the whole? Listen! Identify the aspect that needs work and model how it could be. Don't talk about it. Model the excellence you want (and you need to know what you are wanting to model this. Know the music inside out!) Perform small sections to show that they are heading to excellence. Don't talk about the music too much. Live it! Be the music through your body and voice and breath.
Achieving flow	How have I assessed the experience and quality of the group of children in front of me? Is the music too easy or too difficult? What will I see when they are in flow?
Excellence, ethics and engaged learning	How do I show my own good wisdom and good character to the children? Model how to be at all times: if you want mindful responses, act and speak consciously and mindfully. Am I modelling mutuality, openness, cooperation, respect and fairness?
Mindfulness practice	Take time before a session to breathe deeply and connect with your body. Don't rush in! Do I have the energy to do this session right now? How will I gain the energy, enthusiasm and joy? Ask yourself these mindful questions: ■ Where am I? ■ What am I doing? ■ With whom am I doing it? What is the purpose and intention of your work with the children in front of you? Am I there to control or to open spaces of possibility?

Developing a living song: CME principles in practice in the UK

The following segment takes the form of a conversation between the authors to further exemplify the practical application and transferability of the theories and principles of the CME approach in the UK context. While Doreen's work focuses almost exclusively on conducting choirs, teaching graduate and postgraduate conductors, Jane's pioneering work includes teaching song leaders around the world, working with refugee choirs, conducting her local choirs in East London and leading singing workshops for primary school teachers.

As we struggled to unify a descriptive language for this chapter, we laughed at the American and British differences that distinguish educational terminology and academic programmes in our respective countries. The challenge also acknowledges the bridges needed between different forms of knowledge, from academia and practice, and the intercultural diversities that exist from classroom to classroom, school to school, country to country and the countless other diversities that exist (Biddulph, 2017). We worried about the lack of consistent terminology to describe these professional development models. But then we realised what was most important: at the heart of this entire endeavour is our mutual love of the transformative power of singing and our devotion to teach singing as peace-making in the world today. What has already been described throughout this chapter is elaborated here as an informal conversation between the authors.

Doreen: Jane, as a consultant and teacher trainer in the UK, how do you adapt the CME Institute course model and song repertoire selections for use in a primary classroom workshop context?

Jane: I do the same thing in my course preparation that I hope the teachers will learn to do in the course that I'm teaching. First, I identify a diverse range of song repertoire and song-related pedagogies that I think may be relevant to the primary school curriculum context. I study and prepare this song repertoire and related pedagogies to assure my own in-depth understanding. Knowledge of these materials affords me fluency and frees me to focus on and facilitate a variety of creative course processes and possibilities to engage the teachers. As the teachers gain confidence in singing these songs, they are motivated to replicate the process in their classrooms. It's time well spent.

Doreen: Jane, how do you teach teachers how to use singing or song repertoire in their overall primary school curriculum?

Jane: As we look at the overall primary classroom curriculum, we identify places where songs and song-related pedagogies might enhance learning. For example, how is the song text related to the topic being studied? Alternatively, how can we use rhythmic chanting or improvisatory vocalisation to refocus attention? How can the choice of song change the classroom energy to a more meditative, joyful or invigorating state of mind?

Doreen: In the general primary school context, is there any use for song or song-related pedagogies for deepening the musical experience itself?

Jane: Absolutely. There are multidimensional applications for singing in primary school education. Even the short segments of singing used to enhance energy, refocus attention or enhance subject learning can emphasise the quality of singing experience. My teacher training courses emphasise the child's singing voice and how to develop resonant vocal tone; how to sing in tune and how to sing expressively and stylistically. Even short singing interludes can include an emphasis on the song's cultural, geographical or historical context.

Doreen: Jane, how do you use experientially oriented instructional methods and teaching techniques, particularly non-verbal instruction to motivate and empower primary classroom teachers in your workshops?

Jane: Teachers can often talk so much more than they mean to, or need to, in the classroom. Yet, for the majority of learners, it is the 'musical doing', the non-verbal act of musicking that engages them fully with the subject, versus being verbally told *how to do it*, *when to do it* and so on. Non-verbal teaching is a powerful technique. It saves time and energy and it enables learners to grasp and internalise the experience more immediately.

For example, rather than describe how you want the music to be, we sing it, giving options for children to make decisions. In the teacher education courses, my aim is to do as little talking as possible. I *demonstrate* the way I hope teachers will teach using the holistic, three-part instructional sequence: produce, practise and perform (PPP). The example that follows illustrates the type of song repertoire and song-related pedagogy perfectly suited for primary classroom teaching. The song is a traditional Namibian song (see Figure 13.3).

Non-verbal teaching sequence

Produce

1. The leader *models* the song 'O Kana Kameme'. She sings stylistically with the use of breath, movement and body percussion.
2. The leader *gestures* teachers to join her *chanting* the words, 'E umbo' from the B section, repeating the chant until the teachers demonstrate confidence.
3. The leader again models the song singing the B Section, 'E umbo' gesturing the teachers to breath and then *sing* with her. She repeats this segment again and teachers are invited to sing until they demonstrate confidence.

Figure 13.3 'O Kana Kame Me' traditional song

Note: Song translation: My mother's child, there is a house / I'm going away now so take care of everything / The house, the house, there is a house / I'm going away now so take care of everything.

Practise

1. As the teachers *listen*, the leader invites the group to identify and discuss the song origin and text translation.
2. The leader invites the teachers to sing independently while she *listens* and diagnoses any uncertainties. She then demonstrates how to improve the song through *singing*, *chanting* or *gesture* to *perform* a more musical version, where the text is clear and intonation secure. The leader now introduces the entire song from the beginning, repeating her modelling, chanting, moving and body percussion.
3. Through conducting gesture, the leader invites teachers to chant, move and sing with her.

Perform

1. When the teachers are confident and secure, the leader *gestures* the group to *perform* together with simple *body percussion* as she leads by *drumming*.

Jane: Sometimes I begin by inviting the teachers to move or to dance while they listen to a recording of the song or to me singing the song for the first time. If I am working with a lyric sheet, I might invite teachers to read a section of the text as a way for them to experience the meaning of the words. Following any discussion, we always sing.

Doreen: Jane, in your teacher training courses, how do you encourage classroom teachers to trust themselves – to rely on their intuitive choices and preferences and take the new course ideas and techniques into their classrooms?

Jane: One of the most challenging aspects of teacher education is the need to build a sense of trust with the delegates. It is important that teachers experience success from the start – that they sing, and through practise sing more skilfully. Feeling successful builds trust and confidence. When teachers make improvements in tone quality, pitch and intonation, they feel the joy of success and they are more likely to carry on teaching their classroom students how to do the same. I think it is safe to say that the majority of teachers care deeply for the children in their classrooms. Most teachers learn to adapt their teaching to the needs of the children they teach. I teach course participants with great respect and admiration for their specific knowledge, experience and developing expertise.

Doreen: Jane, what is your view on the use of contemplative practice for class-room teaching and how do you use meditation techniques in your teacher training courses?

Jane: I think mindfulness practice is important in two ways: when I first began practising mindfulness meditation, it helped me to find calm and focus. I became present wherever I was, whatever I was doing and with whom-ever I was teaching. My awareness increased over time. Second, my personal experience with mindfulness breathing helped me bring this practice into my own choir work and into the teacher education courses I teach. I was able to maintain a calm learning environment that enabled me to listen much more deeply. Bringing mindfulness practice into the choirs and teacher training courses I lead gives everyone the opportunity to become present in each moment – leaving their troubles or distractions at the door, and entering the teaching and learning space with calm and concentration.

Taken from Doreen Rao's *Circle of Sound Voice Education* (2005), the following exercise shows the sequenced core practice. Repeat each section three times.

> ## Core practice breathing exercise
>
> Breathing – in
> Breathing – out
> Key words: in, out
>
> Breathing – in deeply
> Breathing – out slowly
> Key words: deep, slow
>
> Breathing – in calmly
> Breathing – out with ease
> Key words: calm, ease
>
> Breathing – in smiling
> Breathing – out release
> Key words: smile, release

Doreen: Jane, how do you adapt this exercise for a primary classroom setting?
Jane: I may add phrases like 'breathing-in listening (to the sounds in the room)', 'breathing-out listening (to the sounds beyond the room)'. If there are particular challenges with focus or behaviour in the groups, I might add 'breathing-in stillness, breathing-out kindness (to yourself and others)'. I close the exercises with the last segment of the core practice, 'breathing-in smiling and breathing-out release'. There is absolutely no doubt in my mind that this practice transforms the connection between participants and their sense of calm and focus, enabling a really positive and joyful learning environment. With my youth choir, I have learned *not* to omit this exercise, even when we are pressed for time with a concert the same day!

Becoming our best practice: never-ending steps …

Finding the space between theory and practice is no easy matter, and crossing the divide between academic research and classroom practice in order to *professionalise the profession* is like crossing the Rio Grande. But crossing over against the stream to become our best practice is a twenty-first-century imperative.

Universities and colleges do not always prepare teachers for the challenges they face or the realities of their school classrooms or choir rehearsals. In university contexts, generalist teachers rarely delve deeply into subject matter. Similarly, specialists may focus more on competitive performance results than on student growth and enjoyment (flow).

Professional development programmes like the CME Institute courses aim to create an inclusive space for novice teachers, dedicated professionals and support personnel at all levels of experience. In this space, teachers build community, continue developing their expertise and connect with what brought them to the education of children in the first place. Connecting at the soul level, in the context of rigorous course expectations, high-quality materials, expert and empathetic course leaders is the space between theory and practice.

Professionalising the profession, inspiring practice and supporting expertise is building a bridge that links the past and present with future. Teachers come from past experiences, educational backgrounds and diverse cultural contexts to get better at what they do. The Vietnamese Zen teacher, Thich Nhat Hanh, tells us that *the truth we seek is already in us*. We think professional development programmes like the models we have described mirror what the First Nations people of the Americas call a 'rite of passage'.

Jane's learning and evolution of her practice: a reflection

Taking a principled approach has become my practice because of the ongoing professional learning with the CME Institute and with Doreen in particular. I take those principles with me into every situation I work in. They can by synthesised as follows:

- Prepare and know the music thoroughly.
- Listen deeply and develop a toolkit to know how to help progress the learning.
- Doing and being is the valuable learning; listening to the teacher explaining is not sufficient.
- Empower the students to own the musical learning through collaborative techniques – ask their opinion, seek their voices about musical decisions.
- Being in one's own body and breath can be a visible model for learners and in life.
- Developing one's own calm ability to be present in the moment enables greater collaboration with what singers bring to the table.
- Connect one's own body and breath with tone in order to support others to do the same.
- Exploring the beautiful repertoire of all styles and origins in a mutual equal respect models a new world order into the twenty-first century.
- Build relationships with living composers of diverse styles for musical, social and even political awareness building.

Like the space between theory and practice, fear and non-fear, fixed and transformative experience, postgraduate or post-practical experience, professional development is where the real journey begins. In a 'rite of passage' journey, we leave the 'old ways' (familiar ways, like the ways we were taught in formative times and places), we make the steps that Michelle Obama inspires us to make. We enter a new *community of practice* in the form of a teacher education course or series of workshops designed to teach us 'new ways'. We delve deeper (sometimes reluctantly or tearfully) and learn 'new ways'. We then pass the threshold of deeper understanding. As Michelle Obama (2018, p. 419) concludes in *Becoming*, 'journeys do not end'. Becoming our best practice means, 'never giving up on the idea that there's more growing to be done'. Sharing stories of our journeying can deepen our practice and resolve with others who, like us, believe that singing has the power to transform, connect and inspire more peaceful and wholesome communities.

Notes

1   See www.choralmusicexperience.com/courses.
2   See https://pz.harvard.edu/projects/the-good-project.

References

Atkinson, P. (2015). *For ethnography*. Dorchester, UK: Sage.

Biddulph, J. (2017). *The diverse diversities of creative learning at home: Three case studies of ethnic minority immigrant children* (PhD thesis), Cambridge University Library, Cambridge, UK.

Biddulph, J., & Wheeler, J. (2017). Singing the primary curriculum. In P. Burnard & and R. Murphey (Eds.), *Teaching music creatively* (pp. 69–84). Oxford: Routledge.

Csikszentmihalyi, M. (1997). *Creativity: Flow and the psychology of discovery and invention*. New York, NY: Harper Perennial.

Eisner, E. (2005). *Reimagining schools: The selected works of Elliot W. Eisner*. Abingdon, UK: Routledge.

Greene, M. (1988). *The dialectic of freedom*. New York, NY: Teachers College Press.

Greene, M. (1998). *Releasing the imagination: Essays on education, the arts and social change*. San Francisco, CA: Jossey-Bass.

Hargreaves, A., & Fullan, M. (2012). *Professional capital: Transforming teaching in every school*. New York, NY: Routledge.

Obama, M. (2018). *Becoming*. New York, NY: Penguin.

Rao, D., & Perison, W. (2005). *Circle of sound voice education: A contemplative approach to singing through meditation, movement and vocalization*. New York, NY: Boosey & Hawkes.

Schön, D. A. (Ed.) (1991). *The reflective turn: Case studies in and on educational practice*. New York, NY: Teachers College Press.

Support and teacher well-being

Jonathan Glazzard, Jane Stokoe and Samuel Stones

'Just living isn't enough,' said the butterfly, 'one must have sunshine, freedom and a little flower'.

(Hans Christian Anderson, 'The Butterfly', 1861)

Introduction

Evidence suggests that teacher stress is a significant concern across the world. We argue that the reasons for this are complex and high workload is only one contributing factor. Recent policy initiatives in England have focused on reducing teacher workload but this alone will not address all the issues. Teachers in leadership positions and those new to teaching experience significantly higher rates of stress than other teachers (ESP, 2018), suggesting that there are 'pinch points' within a teacher's career. Evidence indicates that teacher burnout and retention are significant issues, not just in England, but also globally. Teachers who are mentally healthy are more likely to remain in teaching, teach well and have a positive impact on the progress of their pupils (Glazzard & Rose, 2019). The external policy climate, including rigorous inspection regimes, increased accountability of schools and teachers and the climate of competition between schools can result in a toxic culture that impacts negatively on teacher well-being. However, school leaders have the power to shape school cultures, positively or negatively, within their own schools and despite the external drivers the best leaders empower teachers, trust them and allow them agency. Positive school cultures enable teachers to thrive, while negative cultures can break even the most dedicated teachers. This chapter addresses these key issues and provides some recommendations for best practice.

Research findings

The World Health Organisation (2014, p. 13) defines mental health as:

> A state of well-being in which every individual realizes his or her own potential, can cope with the normal stresses of life, can work productively and fruitfully, and is able to make a contribution to her or his community. Health is a state of complete physical, mental and social well-being and not merely the absence of disease or infirmity.

We adopt a multidimensional perspective on well-being that acknowledges the different dimensions of health – physical, social, emotional and psychological. These dimensions overlap and interrelate (Danby & Hamilton, 2016). Seligman's (2011) model of well-being also demonstrates the factors that result in well-being. These are outlined in Figure 14.1.

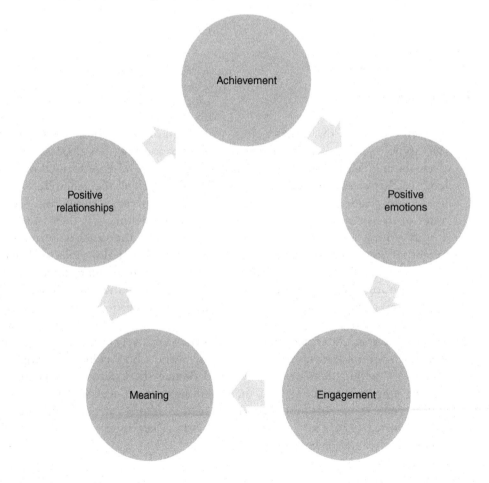

Figure 14.1 Seligman's model of well-being

The model demonstrates how positive well-being is established through:

- achieving goals;
- showing positive emotions;
- actively participating in meaningful tasks;
- having a sense of purpose (meaning);
- forming positive relationships with others.

Well-being is an outcome of mental health that affects people's participation in daily life. Definitions of stress tend to focus on the adverse reactions that people have to excessive pressure or other types of demands placed on them (HSE, 2017). Not all stressors are detrimental to health, some act as motivators. However, when stress starts to affect people's participation in daily life it can then result in poor mental health. Anxiety is used as a general term for several disorders that cause nervousness, turmoil, fear, apprehension, panic and worrying (Bouras & Holt, 2007). Children and young people can experience general anxiety or specific phobias that may result from individual, family, community or school-related factors.

The problem of teacher stress is pervasive. It is evident across all sectors of education and across countries (Gray, Wilcox, & Nordstokke, 2017) and results in burnout and lower job satisfaction. Teachers are consistently reported to experience an increased risk of developing mental ill health (Kidger et al., 2016; Stansfeld, Rasul, Head, & Singleton, 2011). Teacher well-being appears to be mediated by factors such as life satisfaction and personal happiness (hedonic perspective) and positive psychological functioning (Harding et al., 2019). Teachers are able to demonstrate positive psychological functioning when they are able to form good interpersonal relationships with others, have a sense of autonomy and competence and when they have opportunities for personal growth (Harding et al., 2019).

School climate makes a difference to teacher and student well-being (Gray et al., 2017). A negative climate is associated with reduced teacher agency (Beck et al., 2011), absenteeism and staff turnover (Grayson & Alvarez, 2008). These factors have the potential to impact negatively on pupils' experiences and achievement (MacNeil, Prater, & Busch, 2009). Conversely, research suggests that a positive school climate can mitigate the negative effects of socio-economic context on students' academic success (Thapa, Cohen, Guffey, & Higgins-D'Alessandro, 2013).

Positive teacher–student relationships support children and young people to be mentally healthy (Kidger, Araya, Donovan, & Gunnell, 2012; Plenty, Östberg, Almquist, Augustine, & Modin, 2014). These relationships help students to feel more connected to their school (Harding et al., 2019) and improve student well-being (Aldridge & McChesney, 2018) through fostering a sense of belonging. Research demonstrates that teachers with poor mental health may find it more difficult to develop and model positive relationships with their students (Jennings & Greenberg, 2009; Kidger, Gunnell, Biddle, Campbell, & Donovan, 2010). In addition, higher rates of teacher absence can impact on the quality of teacher–student

209

relationships (Jamal et al., 2013). This is because relationships are fostered through human connection.

Research demonstrates that teachers with poor mental health may have less belief that they can support the well-being and mental health of their students (Sisask et al., 2014), particularly if they are struggling with their own well-being and mental health. Poor teacher well-being could therefore be problematic for student well-being (Harding et al., 2019). In addition, research demonstrates that teachers who demonstrate 'presenteeism' find it more difficult to manage their classrooms effectively (Jennings & Greenberg, 2009) and are less likely to develop positive classroom and behaviour management strategies (Harding et al., 2019). Presenteeism is evident when teachers with poor well-being and mental health continue to work. The quality of their work is reduced and this affects the quality of their relationships with their students (Jennings & Greenberg, 2009), student well-being (Harding et al., 2019) and overall teacher performance (Beck et al., 2011; Jain et al., 2013).

There is an association between better teacher well-being and lower student psychological difficulties (Harding et al., 2019). There is also an association between lower teacher depression and better student well-being (Harding et al., 2019). In addition, there is an association between teacher presenteeism, student well-being and psychological difficulties (Harding et al., 2019). Thus, there appears to be an association between teacher and student mental health (Harding et al., 2019).

There is a consensus in the literature that positive well-being in teachers is influenced by school climate and that school climate also impacts on student well-being and attainment. There is also consensus that positive teacher well-being enhances the quality of teacher–student relationships, student well-being and teacher performance (Glazzard & Rose, 2019). However, there is limited direct evidence of a causal relationship between teacher well-being and student attainment; possibly an area for further research. There also exists a paucity of literature examining student perspectives on how the mental health of their teachers impacts on their learning and progress. This small-scale study therefore extends the existing research on teacher well-being by examining the perspectives of pupils on how they are affected by the mental health of their teachers.

The context in England

The Teacher Wellbeing Index (ESP, 2018) demonstrates that staff who work in education face significant amounts of stress, which is disproportionate compared to other professions. Key findings from this research are as follows:

- 67 per cent of education professionals describe themselves as stressed.
- 80 per cent of senior leaders describe themselves as stressed.
- 31 per cent of education professionals have experienced a mental health issue in the past year.

- 76 per cent of education professionals have experienced negative behavioural, psychological or physical symptoms due to their work compared to 60 per cent of UK employees.

The context paints a bleak picture of education and teacher burnout and speaks to the high attrition rates that are the cause of significant challenges in the education system. The UK government has recognised these issues and taken some steps to reduce workload for teachers in schools and for trainee teachers. However, the existence of policies does not guarantee that these will be translated into practice in all institutions, and teachers in some schools continue to experience unreasonably high workloads and work-related stress.

Triggers of poor teacher well-being

Multiple factors can influence teacher well-being. Glazzard and Rose (2019) found that work and non-work-related stress triggers include:

- 'pinch points' during the year, including assessment periods when marking loads can be high, parents' evenings or report writing;
- unexpected and/or unplanned tasks that are assigned to teachers;
- keeping up with the pace of change within schools;
- changes in school leadership teams that result in the introduction of new policies, practices and changes in school culture;
- personal relationship breakdowns;
- family illness or bereavement, particularly in the case of elderly parents or young children;
- childcare responsibilities.

They found that teachers can generally cope with the demands of their jobs but when there is a change in their personal circumstances this can trigger the onset of mental ill health. This is particularly the case when family members become ill and they feel torn between their personal responsibilities and their professional commitments (Glazzard & Rose, 2019).

Case study (Emma)

I had been in the teaching profession for 35 years and felt fortunate to have chosen a career that continued to motivate and excite me. Throughout my career, I had enjoyed significant success and was always highly motivated to meet the diverse learning needs of my pupils. I had always enjoyed working with children from more deprived social backgrounds as well as children with additional learning needs. I was delighted to be offered a teaching role in a school in an area of social deprivation that also hosted provision for 12 pupils with autistic spectrum conditions. Never had I been more challenged but never had I been so motivated. The 12 years passed so quickly, and I relished every minute of every day. Initially my area of responsibility was the early years foundation stage and Key Stage 1.

Children entered full time education in the school with attainment well below that expected of children nationally of the same age. Year in and year out, I was able to significantly build on the progress made by these young children. School monitoring processes suggested to all that I was a consistently good teacher and all inspections by the Office for Standards in Education, Children's Services and Skills (Ofsted) highlighted that progress was at least 'good' for all pupils that I taught.

Over the next couple of years there was a dramatic change in parental attitudes towards the school. The health of the head teacher was clearly in rapid decline and her determination to continually advance the school came to a sudden stand-still. Many parents voted with their feet and children left the school. At the same time many new families moved into the area, frequently on a temporary basis, and their children were registered at the school. Many families had significant social needs and an ever-increasing percentage of the school population was identified as having special educational needs/disabilities.

Two years later the head teacher left the school and the local authority finally came to the rescue. Support came from the head teacher from another local school until the end of the academic year. At this point a new head teacher was appointed and a new leadership team began to unpick and address the issues. I became a member of the senior leadership team as assistant head teacher and special educational needs coordinator (SENCO) alongside my full-time teaching responsibilities. In a small school there were many additional duties to complete and alongside the head teacher I also took responsibility for assessment and behaviour management as well as phonics lead. It quickly became clear that progress and attainment throughout the school were significantly below expected national attainment levels. Additional support was provided by the local authority and local head teachers also worked alongside the school to raise standards. They came and went, each offering their own unique 'formula' for success before moving on and being replaced. For both myself and the new head teacher, it was a roller coaster ride that involved extremely long hours as progress and attainment were scrutinised and the threats of poor outcomes in future Ofsted inspections rang in our ears. Inevitably Ofsted arrived and the hard work, dedication and clear vision of all staff was acknowledged. The outcome at the time was that the school was judged to be 'satisfactory' but had clear capacity to improve before the next inspection, which was scheduled for 18 months later.

We now faced intense pressure to improve further. There was another change in support and a head teacher from a school judged as 'outstanding' by Ofsted was engaged to work with the school in making further rapid progress. He had a very disciplined approach and his reputation came before him, resulting in three staff members resigning before he had even begun to work with the school. Unfortunately, two of the staff, who had resigned voluntarily, decided that they were not going quietly and incited a small group of parents to target the school and the senior leadership team. Throughout the ordeal there was little visible support for the new head teacher. I was appointed as a non-teaching deputy head teacher and the work continued. A new and very rigid structure for teaching was imposed on all teachers by the supporting head teacher and the school environment was overhauled. Teachers were monitored rigidly and frequently. Reports were written and endless meetings seemed to continually communicate the negative aspects of the school. No one could ever deny that the school team worked with dedication and everyone was determined to succeed. Amid the hard work, the school was faced with one parent who made several complaints to Ofsted. The local authority investigated and the complaints were deemed to be unfounded. The parent continued to make further allegations and this triggered an early Ofsted inspection. In retrospect this was a 'tipping point' for the school.

There was a Section 8 inspection but within 48 hours the school was placed in special measures. It was the end of the summer term and legal time constraints meant that parents could not be informed until the start of the next academic year. We carried the burden throughout the summer break, during which time the battle to improve continued. Within the first half-term of the following academic year the head teacher left. She was totally and completely exhausted and broken, despite always communicating a positive attitude and a belief that the school would overcome its problems and win through.

The supporting head and his team moved in permanently and a well-considered but extremely prescriptive approach to teaching followed. We were now working every waking hour and every aspect of the school was under scrutiny. There were clear and rigid expectations and staff were there to conform. There was no room for professional debate and opinion. It was not uncommon for the teaching staff to start drifting into the building before 6.30 a.m. and many did not leave until 7.00 p.m. There were termly monitoring visits from Ofsted and we were buoyed by positive outcomes and a recognition that success lay just around the corner. Shortly before the end of the academic year, the caretaker head teacher announced his intention to take up a new post. The school waited with bated breath until a local academy agreed to work with the school.

During the summer break I was faced by several personal difficulties that involved me needing to care for three family members who suffered unexpected but significant ill health. I returned to school and new leadership in September totally exhausted. My demise was swift. The new leadership team had very differing views on how to address the failings of the school and it was time to begin yet again with a new and very different formula to fix the problems. Within six weeks I faced the reality of mental illness. Confused, exhausted and destroyed, I left the school to begin my long journey of recovery from mental ill health. Two years later, the school enjoyed its rewards for a long battle fought. I continue to fight my own battle for good mental health, away from the profession I loved.

Question

■ What factors contributed to the poor teacher mental health of Emma in this case study?

Impact of poor teacher well-being on the quality of teaching

While there is a lack of research to directly attribute an association between poor teacher mental health, teaching quality and pupil progress, our own research illustrates that teachers perceive that their poor mental health has a detrimental impact on the quality of their lesson planning, teaching delivery, relationships with children and colleagues, behaviour management and pupils' progress (Glazzard, 2018). In this research, teachers commented that when they had poor mental health, they lacked the energy needed to plan creative lessons for their pupils and they were less patient and more irritable with their pupils. They perceived that these factors impacted detrimentally on their teaching and on pupils' progress (Glazzard, 2018). More research is needed in this area to justify a direct link between teacher mental health and the progress of pupils.

Coping strategies

Teachers use a range of coping strategies to stay resilient. These might include:

■ being organised;
■ limiting the amount of work they do at home;
■ putting time aside for hobbies;
■ talking to family and friends.

According to Glazzard and Rose (2019, p. 26),

Prioritisation and organisation appear to be key skills that those prone to poor mental health often reported learning after they had had a crisis; a sign that beforehand they were seeking perfection and thought they could (and should) do everything all of the time. They came to realise that this is not always possible and sometimes there have to be compromises.

Creating positive school cultures

The school leadership team is responsible for shaping the school culture that teachers experience. Positive school cultures enable teachers to thrive and stay mentally healthy. Teachers tend to have positive well-being in schools if they are valued, trusted to do their jobs and provided with some ownership of their roles. Mentally healthy schools have a positive culture in which staff work collegiately and talk openly about the challenges they are experiencing in their roles without fear of judgement. Leaders should take steps to reduce unnecessary planning, assessment and data management tasks so that teachers can concentrate on their core responsibility of teaching. In addition, the management of change in schools should be carefully considered. Introducing too many changes at the same time can be overwhelming for staff, unnecessary and create additional workload. Staff should be consulted about planned changes and their contributions should be sought. This will provide staff with ownership and foster a sense of collegiality. Leaders who take steps to reduce bureaucracy, accountability and promote a good work–life balance enable their staff to stay mentally healthy. Workload is only one contributor to poor teacher well-being. The way staff are treated by other colleagues in school plays a critical role in creating mentally healthy cultures in schools.

Questions

- Why do you think there is a high level of teacher attrition among early career teachers?
- Why do you think senior leaders are vulnerable to developing mental ill health?
- Do you think that providing relaxation sessions for staff is the solution to the problem of mental ill health in teachers?

Case study (Jane Stokoe)

It has been an absolute privilege to have contributed to the education of hundreds of children throughout my career in teaching. When my career began over 40 years ago, I was responsible for the education of 30 young people for 12 months before I sent them on their way to the next stage in their education. This responsibility continued throughout my teaching life, but alongside it many additional responsibilities became part of my role as a teacher and life became increasingly pressurised. In retrospect I now realise that I was in a very enviable position when my career began. I had qualified as a teacher and, much like someone who has just passed a driving test, it was at this point that my learning really began. I was encouraged and allowed to take risks, I was allowed to make mistakes and to consider approaches to rectifying them. It was such an exciting journey and through it I developed my own values and beliefs as a teacher.

For those who have entered the profession in more recent years the reality is in stark contrast. They are launched into a world of accountability and a pace of working life that must be experienced to be believed. It saddens me to read in the media that so many teachers are leaving the profession after only a few years. Teachers are burning out in huge numbers and many are experiencing poor mental health. However, those that remain frequently do so not only because they are resilient, but because they have a disciplined approach to their role that benefits the needs of their learners while also benefiting their own very important professional and personal needs.

First and foremost, it is important to accept that teachers will never have a completed 'to do' list. I have written so many lists, worked a full day and finished the day with a list twice as long as the list I started with. That's teaching! I tried so hard to complete that list and doing so made me consistently feel that I was failing. It was many months before I accepted that I was striving for the impossible. My 'to do' list became a work in progress and once I accepted this it felt more manageable. I recall comparing my role to that of a doctor or nurse working in an accident and emergency (A & E) department. The day may begin with a few patients needing stitches to small wounds. These patients cannot receive treatment according to the order in which they presented at A & E. When more needy patients/emergencies arrive, they must be treated first. Teaching is no different. When a day begins, we cannot foresee the challenges ahead, but we must respond to them and prioritise them accordingly.

A teacher's work is never done. This does not mean that a teacher should work every waking hour of every working day. Again, prioritising tasks is the key. Taking control when you can is essential. You will never work from 9 a.m. to 3.30 p.m. However, it is important that you set yourself work-related guidelines. The role is unpredictable and there are certainly periods when there will be greater demands on your time and you will want and be expected to meet professional expectations. At other times you will have greater ownership of how you manage your time. There are no hard and fast rules. Some people will prefer to work a few hours each evening while others may prefer to work fewer evenings in longer blocks of time. The choice is yours but by planning ahead you will also be identifying periods of time for you to recharge your batteries and to spend time with friends, family or in solitude pursuing your own interests. We are more than a teacher. We are also partners, mothers, fathers, brothers, sisters, friends. These roles also need to be cherished and valued.

There are of course aspects to the job that are unpredictable and cannot be avoided while also causing stress. Behaviour management is addressed frequently during teacher training and in the years beyond. Negative behaviours can be stressful, not only because of their unpredictability but because each occurrence is unique. Two children may exhibit the same negative behaviours and will respond in totally different ways. A child who has simply strayed from the task in hand may respond to a simple 'look' from the teacher while another child will continue to push the boundaries and further intervention will be needed. All schools have a behaviour policy and it is essential to familiarise yourself with this document and to follow it to ensure consistency in terms of expectations. There is no doubt that many teachers try to cope with challenging behaviours for fear of feeling they will be perceived as weak teachers. Trying to carry on simply adds to your own stress and anxiety. Behaviour management will be a designated area of responsibility for a member of staff in your school. Turn to that person for support and guidance. This may be a short conversation in which you share ideas. It may be asking for the behaviour support lead to engage with a specific child. It's always good to talk.

An often overlooked stressor can be parents and carers. Overall, they are very supportive of the work we do. Engaging with them is a very important and essential part of our role. They are a child's first teacher. It is essential that we are approachable. Being available for parents' evenings is an expectation but good communication with parents at other times is invaluable. Working as a team with parents is of great benefit to everyone. Parents' evenings should never be a nasty surprise for parents and carers. Addressing concerns with parents as they occur is vital. A few minutes of your time, either sharing concerns or indeed celebrating a child's success, pays dividends and is time well spent. When parents or carers contact you needing to talk, it is important that you arrange to do so as quickly as possible. Keep meetings focused. Listen to what is said and consider your responses. If you need time to further consider a situation then say so. A hasty but poorly considered response can frequently come back to haunt you. In situations that you anticipate may be challenging, approach a member of the leadership team to accompany you. In situations that become unexpectedly aggressive, do not hesitate to calmly halt the meeting and explain that it would be better to reconvene when the discussion can be continued in a more positive manner. In such situations it is vital that you remain professional but terminate the meeting until you can access additional support after speaking to a member of the leadership team. Remember that you are there to be supportive to parents but never to be abused by them.

Teaching is a rich tapestry of experiences and expectations. There is never a dull moment. There will be so much fun, so much laughter, there will be tears and there will be times of stress. You will engage with others to share the fun and the laughter, but it is equally important to engage with others on the occasions when the tears flow and those feelings of stress become overwhelming. Share the many good times but do not be afraid to share the difficulties. There is much wisdom indeed in the proverb, 'a problem shared is a problem halved'.

Recommendations

The following recommendations appear to support the well-being of staff who work in education:

- All school leaders should be proactive in reducing unnecessary workload for teachers.

- All school leaders should develop a positive school climate to enable staff and pupils to thrive.
- The well-being of staff should be a focus of the school improvement plan and should be a standing item for discussion at governors' meetings.
- Senior leaders need to know their staff and be aware of the pressures they are feeling; not just from a work perspective, but also in their personal life.
- Professional development for senior leaders should include approaches to enhancing staff well-being.
- School leaders should improve signposting of external support services. For example, the charity Education Support Partnership run a free and confidential 24/7 helpline staffed by accredited counsellors, which is available to the entire education workforce.
- Teachers should be provided with professional development to support them in managing their own mental health.
- Professional supervision, not linked to performance management, should be offered to staff who work in challenging roles (including school leaders, SENCOs and designated safeguarding leads).

Summary

This chapter has outlined some of the causes of poor teacher mental health and well-being and its effects on teaching, relationships and pupils' learning. It has presented case studies that illuminate the factors that can result in mental ill health and made recommendations that might help to address the issues.

References

Aldridge, J. M., & McChesney, K. (2018). The relationships between school climate and adolescent mental health and wellbeing: A systematic literature review. *International Journal of Educational Research, 88*, 121–145.

Beck, A., Crain, A. L., Solberg, L. I., Unützer, J., Glasgow, R. E., Maciosek, M. V., & Whitebird, R. (2011). Severity of depression and magnitude of productivity loss. *Annals of Family Medicine, 9*(4), 305–311.

Bouras, N., & Holt, G. (2007). *Psychiatric and behavioural disorders in intellectual and developmental disabilities* (2nd ed.). Cambridge, UK: Cambridge University Press.

Danby, G., & Hamilton, P. (2016). Addressing the 'elephant in the room': The role of the primary school practitioner in supporting children's mental well-being. *Pastoral Care in Education, 34*(2), 90–103.

Education Support Partnership (ESP) (2018). *Teacher wellbeing index 2018*. Retrieved from www.educationsupportpartnership.org.uk/resources/research-reports/teacher-wellbeing-index-2018.

Glazzard, J. (2018, 23 January). Pupil progress held back by teachers' poor mental health. Leeds Beckett University. Retrieved from www.leedsbeckett.ac.uk/news/0118-mental-health-survey.

Glazzard, J., & Rose, A. (2019). *The impact of teacher wellbeing and mental health on pupil progress in primary schools*. Leeds Beckett University. Retrieved from www.leedsbeckett. ac.uk/-/media/files/schools/school-of-education/teacher-wellbeing--pupil-progress-research.pdf?la=en.

Gray, C., Wilcox, G., & Nordstokke, D. (2017). Teacher mental health, school climate, inclusive education and student learning: A review. *Canadian Psychology, 58*(3), 203–210.

Grayson, J. L., & Alvarez, H. K. (2008). School climate factors relating to teacher burnout: A mediator model. *Teaching and Teacher Education, 24*, 1349–1363.

Harding, S., Morris, R., Gunnella, D., Ford, T., Hollingworth, W., Tilling, K., … Kidger, J. (2019). Is teachers' mental health and wellbeing associated with students' mental health and wellbeing? *Journal of Affective Disorders, 242*, 180–187.

Health and Safety Executive (HSE) (2017). Health and safety at work: Summary statistics for Great Britain 2017. Retrieved from www.hse.gov.uk/statistics/overall/hssh1617.pdf.

Jain, G., Roy, A., Harikrishnan, V., Yu, S., Dabbous, O., & Lawrence, C. (2013). Patient-reported depression severity measured by the PHQ-9 and impact on work productivity: Results from a survey of full-time employees in the United States. *Journal of Occupational and Environmental Medicine, 55*(3), 252–258.

Jamal, F., Fletcher, A., Harden, A., Wells, H., Thomas, J., & Bonell, C. (2013). The school environment and student health: A systematic review and meta-ethnography of qualitative research. *BMC Public Health, 13*(1), 798.

Jennings, P.A., & Greenberg, M.T. (2009). The prosocial classroom: Teacher social and emotional competence in relation to student and classroom outcomes. *Review of Educational Research, 79*(1), 491–525.

Kidger, J., Araya, R., Donovan, J., & Gunnell, D. (2012). The effect of the school environment on the emotional health of adolescents: A systematic review. *Pediatrics, 129*(5), 2011–2248.

Kidger, J., Brockman, R., Tilling, K., Campbell, R., Ford, T., Araya, R., … Gunnell, D. (2016). Teachers' wellbeing and depressive symptoms, and associated risk factors: A large cross-sectional study in English secondary schools. *Journal of Affective Disorders, 192*, 76–82.

Kidger, J., Gunnell, D., Biddle, L., Campbell, R., & Donovan, J. (2010). Part and parcel of teaching? Secondary school staff's views on supporting student emotional health and well-being. *British Educational Research Journal, 36*(6), 919–935.

MacNeil, A. J., Prater, D. L., & Busch, S. (2009). The effects of school culture and climate on student achievement. *International Journal of Leadership in Education, 12*, 73–84.

Plenty, S., Östberg, V., Almquist, Y. B., Augustine, L., & Modin, B. (2014). Psychosocial working conditions: An analysis of emotional symptoms and conduct problems amongst adolescent students. *Journal of Adolescence, 37*(4), 407–417.

Seligman, M. E. P. (2011). *Flourish*. Sydney: Random House Australia.

Sisask, M., Värnik, P., Värnik, A., Apter, A., Balazs, J., Balint, M., … Wasserman, D. (2014). Teacher satisfaction with school and psychological well-being affects their readiness to help children with mental health problems. *Health Education Journal, 73*(4), 382–393.

Stansfeld, S.A., Rasul, F., Head, J., & Singleton, N. (2011). Occupation and mental health in a national UK survey. *Social Psychiatry and Psychiatric Epidemiology, 46*(2), 101–110.

Thapa, A., Cohen, D., Guffey, S., & Higgins-D'Alessandro, A. (2013). A review of school climate research. *Review of Educational Research, 83*, 357–385.

World Health Organization (WHO) (2004). *Promoting mental health: concepts, emerging evidence, practice (summary report)*. Geneva: World Health Organization.

Afterword: 'teaching is not a profession' – discuss

James Biddulph

> Teaching is a craft and it is best learnt as an apprentice observing a master craftsman or woman. Watching others, and being rigorously observed yourself as you develop, is the best route to acquiring mastery in the classroom.
>
> *(Michael Gove, 2010)*

Teaching is not a profession and teachers are not professionals. In a neoliberal-dominated political UK context, both statements are affirmed by the way language is used to describe what teachers do. Teaching as a craft, a vocation, a highly skilled form of work, as facilitation, as coaching, as guidance, as delivery of preconceived knowledge have all played out in the literature and discourse. Michael Gove settled on the word 'craft' and in doing so he problematises the notion of what teachers are, what they do and how they learn and continue to learn. In making such statements, he, without knowing, unleashed the professionalism of teachers who, discontent with the metaphors applied to them, now want to define for themselves who they are and what they do (Biesta, 2007).

As Smyth (2011, p. 14) argues, 'teachers have been universally and systematically dealt with harshly by neoliberal reform ... systematically excluded from and denied a voice in the nature of reforms'. In recent times, in what is now described as post-truth world, teachers are viewed with scepticism, because of their perceived (by those in charge, like politicians) left-leaning politics, unionised behaviours and the suggested inability to close the gaps for disadvantaged children, despite government efforts to enforce this. Her Majesty's Inspectorate for Education (Office for Standards in Education, Children's Services and Skills (Ofsted)), itself seen as a de-professionalising system of control, has adapted its framework for inspection on so many occasions, always in search of the Holy Grail, to define good quality teaching, what good learning is and how school leaders make 'it' happen. Moreover, neoliberal forms of governance have introduced market logic, supported by technocratic systems and structures that aim to normalise, structure and predetermine outcomes. Children are commodities. Teachers are factory workers. And herein lies the problem about teacher professionalism and the challenge of professional learning and development.

The issue of performativity questions the notion of professionalism. If teachers are to be professional, they need the autonomy to define their own terms of reference and qualities of control, professional behaviour and accountability. In the UK, we have neither (yet). There is such a degree of hyper-accountability and surveillance in education: of teachers, teaching, schools and learning. Teachers and school leaders do not have the sufficient professional freedoms to enact the changes and develop the agency to improve the quality of their work. The role of the state is prominent and yet, 'frontline practitioners such as teachers have a key role in making effective decisions about complex human situations; in other words, their professional agency is vital' (Priestley, Biesta, & Robinson, 2019, p. 109). When Michael Gove says that the best way we learn to teach is as an apprentice learns, this denies the social complexity of teaching and renegades it to purely skill (interestingly he also fails to understand the complexity of apprenticeship learning and the time needed to develop to mastery level).

In a neoliberal context, teachers are not professionals but are, instead, performers. However, the nature of the performance is not determined by the community of professionals who define the standards of the profession. Rather, there is a, 'pressure to perform in particular ways, most notably in terms defined and measured by external actors' (Priestley et al., 2019, p. 107; Shore & Wright, 2000). For example, the anxiety and confusion that one could argue has arisen because of the new Ofsted requirement to define the curriculum in UK schools, reveals the underlying acceptance of our community to be deliverers and producers of performance statistics. How can we become the designers, creators, imaginers and producers of teaching resources and educational experiences and opportunities? For example, the current accountability system stands in tension with professional discourses in education. The time spent on 'maintaining and achieving a public image of a good school [means that] less time and energy is spent on pedagogic and curricular substance' (Apple, 2001, p. 416). Professional learning can become narrowed to focus purely on subject knowledge acquisition, which I do not deny is important but do suggest is but one aspect of the professional learning needed.

We know that teachers' beliefs are instrumental in shaping teachers' practice (Priestley et al., 2019). In a similar way to Priestley et al. (2019), our current book and indeed the series of Unlocking Research books, raises questions about teachers' beliefs and how these are enacted in classrooms and schools and how, in this book, they contribute to the concepts of professional learning. But beliefs are only one aspect. Teachers' discourses and the relational structures within schools and wider systems also help conceptualise what it is that we do and how we ought to do it (Hargreaves & Fullan, 2012). For example, as Priestley et al. (2019, p. 108) point out:

> The issue of professional agency has been injected with renewed significance in recent years by the widespread development of new rhetorics of professionalism

in public policy, which have increasingly emphasised the central position of professional practitioners in the enactment of policy, for example as agents of change in curriculum making.

What happens when agentic teachers meet a culture of performativity, when teachers are meant to make decisions and yet are still held to account by externally defined decisions? Some of the possibilities to answer this question are shared in the book *Unlocking Research: Inspiring Primary Curriculum Design* (Biddulph & Flutter, 2020).

This current book is about professional development. But what is the learning needed in our profession? What constitutes *professional* learning? Is it skill learning? Or knowledge acquisition? Or pedagogy learning? What is the learning in our profession? For example, when do we learn to develop the qualities that we expect of the profession? How do we nurture the sense of vocation that is inherent in many teachers' beliefs about the moral imperative of their chosen career? For example, for Biddulph and Cariss (Chapter 12, this volume), the learning is not about a particular subject or skill; rather it is learning to become more self-aware and in doing so to develop the capacity for reflexivity that aims to influence how a teacher approaches a challenging situation or responds to something that goes wrong. Theirs is not professional learning about grammar or times tables with the intention to improve chances for the school to pass the latest external performance measure for government. Obviously professional development should not be restricted to the prescription of standards documents and yet because of the accountability agenda, how much time is given for teachers to explore who they are, what they do, why they do it and how they do it?

Someone who questions authority and who acts on judgement and experience is, in my view, someone who is enacting their professionalism. Developing a sense of critical pedagogy in professional learning is one of liberation to ask questions of oneself and one's institutions. As Smyth (2011, p. 21) suggests, 'being critical, or engaging in critique, involves analysis, enquiry and critique into the transformative possibilities implicit in the social context of classrooms and schooling itself'– which are complex professional practices beyond complying with externally monitored systems of control. How do we develop the capacity to *explore*, *understand* and *transform* our own thinking? How could this lead us to becoming autonomous professionals who are not afraid of challenge or of raising standards or of improving our schools but who embrace the professional standards that are required of us?

The leitmotif in this book, and evident in each chapter, is the central aim of professional learning as one that fosters communities of practice. From the notion of teaching as an art form and the invocation of the Chartered College of Teaching (the professional body for teaching), the importance of learning that nurtures the well-being of teachers and the children whom they teach and the value of partnership with those beyond the walls of our schools all point towards communities of practice. It is argued that lesson study, coaching and mentoring, and the use of research-informed models of professional development that create professional discourse are key ways to develop such communities.

What professionalism is, how it can be defined and by whom, are still sites of struggle within the education sector. A profession is a community in which individuals come together to consider how that community ought to function. Professional learning arises when, having defined how the community of practitioners ought to be and what they ought to know, opportunities to develop, to be a better version of a previous professional self can be nurtured. And importantly, opportunities in which professional discourse invites challenge to the structures, assumptions and un-critiqued forms of knowledge that can too often exist. It is a process and a mindset of always being 'on the way', in the words attributed to Maxine Greene, who claimed, 'I am forever on the way' (Greene, 1995, p. 1).

Being 'on the way' means also that as lead learners in our schools, we are always on the journey, always looking forward, to consider the transformations in ourselves, our communities and most importantly in our children.

I am a fellow of the Chartered College of Teaching. This means I subscribe to the notion that we are professionals because our work as educators, as teachers, as teaching assistants, as school leaders, is complex social practice, that it involves profoundly complex forms of knowledge, skills and diverse human qualities. Aligned to the vision of the Chartered College, I advocate the view that our work involves intellectual enquiry that stretches beyond metaphors of craftsmanship or highly skilled labour. I also build my professional knowledge on theoretical foundations that indeed challenge my own thinking and require me to persistently ask questions: what is happening here? Who says this is the way things ought to happen? How is so-called 'school knowledge' transmitted?

Teaching *is* a profession and teachers are professional *if* they are prepared to mould a future that is bold, in which they are vocal in challenging the 'external' voices (e.g. politicians and technocrats) and if they inculcate a spirit of optimism, enthusiasm, possibility thinking and utter belief in the capacity of every human, child and teacher, to cause surprise and to be surprised. Teaching is, after all not only *a* profession … but is *the most powerful* profession in which to engage in changing the future. This is one view of our profession: it is now for the reader and their own community of professionals to develop their own discourse and in doing so to contribute to the wider discourse of our professional authority and professional capital. We are forever on the way; we need to be forever learning.

References

Apple, M. W. (2001). Comparing neo-liberal projects and inequality in education. *Comparative Education, 37*, 409–423.

Biddulph, J., & Flutter, J. (2020). *Unlocking research: Inspiring primary curriculum design.* London: Routledge.

Biesta, G. (2007). *Beyond learning: Democratic education for a human future.* London: Paradigm.

Gove, M. (2010). Speech: Michael Gove to the National College Annual Conference. Retrieved from www.gov.uk/government/speeches/michael-gove-to-the-national-college-annual-conference-birmingham.

Greene, M. (1995). *Releasing the imagination: Essays on education, the arts, and social change.* San Francisco, CA: Jossey-Bass.

Hargreaves, A., & Fullan, M. (2012). *Professional capital: Transforming teaching in every school.* New York, NY: Routledge.

Priestley, M., Biesta, G., & Robinson, S. (2019). *Teacher agency: An ecological approach.* London: Bloomsbury.

Shore, C., & Wright, S. (2000). Coercive accountability: The rise of audit culture in Higher Education. In M. Strathern (Ed.), *Audit culture: Anthropological studies in accountability, ethics and the academy* (pp. 57–89). London: Routledge.

Smyth, J. (2011). *Critical pedagogy for social justice.* New York, NY: Continuum.

Index

Note: Page locators in *italic* refer to figures and in **bold** refer to tables.

—